# Spiritual Hypnotherapy Scripts for Body, Mind, and Spirit

### Holly Holmes-Meredith
Doctor of Ministry
Licensed Marriage Family Therapist

TO PAUL MICHAEL MEREDITH

My partner in the greatest sense of the word, my loving husband, and the giver

of the greatest gift of my life: the experience of Love manifest.

SPIRITUAL HYPNOTHERAPY SCRIPTS for BODY, MIND, and SPIRIT

Copyright © 2014, Published by HCH Publishing

All rights reserved.

ISBN-13: 978-1497593442
ISBN-10: 1497593441

Excerpts from # 10(12), 37(3), 27(11), 23(3), 61(8), 74(4), 28(5), 32(3), 20(2 twice) from TAO TE CHING BY LAO TZU, A NEW ENGLISH VERSION, WITH FORWARD AND NOTES BY STEPHEN MITCHELL. Translation Copyright © 1987 by Stephen Mitchell. Reprinted by permission of HarperCollins Publishers.

# HYPNOTHERAPIST REVIEWS

"A wonderful book for the hypnotherapy practitioner or indeed any person on the journey of life. Holly Holmes-Meredith's experience and wisdom entrance the reader in this beautiful analogy between hypnotherapy and the principles of Tao."

— Virginia Holmes, CCHT

"The Charkra Balancing script takes us deep inside our core, following the radiant path of our internal energy centers, the seven chakras. Each chakra is gently opened up and explored, healed where needed, balanced, and set in motion with the other chakras until our whole body is humming with energy and vitality. This script offers us a profound tool kit using color, sound, vision, scent, touch, and taste to connect us with our inner healing world. It brings us back to the center where are body, mind and spirit function in complete harmony."

— Susa Black, CCHT

"By immersing myself in Holly Holmes-Meredith's scripts as a new Hypnotherapist, my hypnotic language began to flow freely and naturally when I was in sessions. The scripts also served as templates that I could draw on as needed to be more effective with clients. Holly's use of open-ended questions serve to draw out the client's own inner wisdom and empower them with their innate healing ability. Holly takes the best of what is available for healing (EFT, inner-child work, past-life therapy, etc.) and creates these wonderful scripts that can really change lives."

— Susan Nayak, Ph.D., CCHT

"Dr. Holly Holmes-Meredith reveals the highest form of hypnotherapy: helping people heal themselves by using their own inner wisdom and connection to spirit. This is the book to show you how to do that—there is no wiser teacher of hypnotherapy than Holly."

— Michael Linenberger, CCHT

*Spiritual Hypnotherapy Scripts for Body, Mind, and Spirit*

# TABLE OF CONTENTS

Acknowledgments . . . . . . . . . . . . . . . . . . . . . . . . . . . . . . . . . . . . . . . . . . . . . . . . . . . . . . . xiii

Part One: The Tao of Spiritual Hypnotherapy . . . . . . . . . . . . . . . . . . . . . . . . . . . . . . . . . . .1

Introduction to Part One . . . . . . . . . . . . . . . . . . . . . . . . . . . . . . . . . . . . . . . . . . . . . . . . 3

1. What is Hypnotherapy? . . . . . . . . . . . . . . . . . . . . . . . . . . . . . . . . . . . . . . . . . . . . 5
  Hypnotherapy as a Spiritual Practice . . . . . . . . . . . . . . . . . . . . . . . . . . . . . . 6
  The Higher Self . . . . . . . . . . . . . . . . . . . . . . . . . . . . . . . . . . . . . . . . . . . . . . 6
  Accessing the Higher Self in Hypnotherapy . . . . . . . . . . . . . . . . . . . . . . . . . 7
  The Real Voice of Spirit . . . . . . . . . . . . . . . . . . . . . . . . . . . . . . . . . . . . . . . . 8

2. Taoism and Hypnotherapy . . . . . . . . . . . . . . . . . . . . . . . . . . . . . . . . . . . . . . . . . 9
  Taoist Principles in Hypnotherapy . . . . . . . . . . . . . . . . . . . . . . . . . . . . . . . . 9
  Taoist Principle: Wu-wei (non-action) . . . . . . . . . . . . . . . . . . . . . . . . . . . . . 9
  Taoist Principle: Trust in Nature as an organic pattern and our unity with it. . . . . . . . . .12
  Taoist Principle: Accessing Chi and the energy work of Hypnotherapy . . . . . . . . . . . . .13
  Taoist Principle: Yin/Yang: the balancing and integrating of opposites and the
  idea that all phenomena contain seeds of their counterparts. . . . . . . . . . . . . . . . . . . .13
  Taoist Principle: Go with the flow. Be like water. Spontaneity and "right response"
  come from listening to the way things are. . . . . . . . . . . . . . . . . . . . . . . . . . . . . . .15
  Taoist principle: Everything is cyclical, transient, and changing. The only constant is change. . . . . . . . . . . . . .16
  Taoist principle: Return to the state of "uncarved wood" or the natural state. . . . . . . . . . .17
  Taoist principle: Interdependence: all things are a part of a unified field. . . . . . . . . . . . . .18
  Taoist principle: The Law of Reversed Effect: to change anything, you must first accept it the way it is. . . . . . . .18
  Taoist principle: Emptiness, non-doing. . . . . . . . . . . . . . . . . . . . . . . . . . . . . . . .20

3. Hypnotherapists: Transforming Consciousness as a Spiritual Practice . . . . . . . . . . . . . . . . .21
  Reflections and Learnings . . . . . . . . . . . . . . . . . . . . . . . . . . . . . . . . . . . . . . . 22
  Rick R., CCHT . . . . . . . . . . . . . . . . . . . . . . . . . . . . . . . . . . . . . . . . . . . . . . 22
  Julie L., MFT, CHT . . . . . . . . . . . . . . . . . . . . . . . . . . . . . . . . . . . . . . . . . . 24
  Tammy H., CCHT . . . . . . . . . . . . . . . . . . . . . . . . . . . . . . . . . . . . . . . . . . . 25
  Julie S., CCHT . . . . . . . . . . . . . . . . . . . . . . . . . . . . . . . . . . . . . . . . . . . . . 26
  Rosetta B., CCHT . . . . . . . . . . . . . . . . . . . . . . . . . . . . . . . . . . . . . . . . . . . 27

*Spiritual Hypnotherapy Scripts for Body, Mind, and Spirit*

Jane H., CCHT . . . . . . . . . . . . . . . . . . . . . . . . . . . . . . . . . . . . . . . . . . . . . . . . . . 28
Summary of Interviews . . . . . . . . . . . . . . . . . . . . . . . . . . . . . . . . . . . . . . . . . . . . 29

Part Two: Spiritual Hypnotherapy Scripts . . . . . . . . . . . . . . . . . . . . . . . . . . . . . . . . . 33

Introduction to Using these Scripts . . . . . . . . . . . . . . . . . . . . . . . . . . . . . . . . . . . . . 35
About the Hypnotic Inductions used in these Scripts . . . . . . . . . . . . . . . . . . . . . . . 37
Using EFT (Emotional Freedom Technique) along with Hypnotherapy . . . . . . . . . . . . 37

4. Hypnotherapy for the Body . . . . . . . . . . . . . . . . . . . . . . . . . . . . . . . . . . . . . . . . . 39

Self-Hypnosis . . . . . . . . . . . . . . . . . . . . . . . . . . . . . . . . . . . . . . . . . . . . . . . . . . 39
Introduction to Self-Hypnosis . . . . . . . . . . . . . . . . . . . . . . . . . . . . . . . . . . . . . . . 39
Self-Hypnosis Script . . . . . . . . . . . . . . . . . . . . . . . . . . . . . . . . . . . . . . . . . . . . . 41

HYPNOSIS for STRESS MANAGEMENT . . . . . . . . . . . . . . . . . . . . . . . . . . . . . . . 42
Introduction to A Hypnotic Vacation . . . . . . . . . . . . . . . . . . . . . . . . . . . . . . . . . . 42
A Hypnotic Vacation . . . . . . . . . . . . . . . . . . . . . . . . . . . . . . . . . . . . . . . . . . . . . 42
Hypnotic Anchoring for Being Calm and Relaxed . . . . . . . . . . . . . . . . . . . . . . . . . 44

Hypnosis for Stopping Smoking . . . . . . . . . . . . . . . . . . . . . . . . . . . . . . . . . . . . . 45
Pre-session Interview for Stopping Smoking . . . . . . . . . . . . . . . . . . . . . . . . . . . . . 45
Education and Pre-talk for Reframing for Stop Smoking . . . . . . . . . . . . . . . . . . . . . 45
Reframing Hypnotherapy for Stopping Smoking . . . . . . . . . . . . . . . . . . . . . . . . . . 46
Hypnotic Skill Rehearsal: Becoming an Air Breather . . . . . . . . . . . . . . . . . . . . . . . 48

HYPNOTHERAPY for PAIN MANAGEMENT . . . . . . . . . . . . . . . . . . . . . . . . . . . . 50
Introduction to Pain Management . . . . . . . . . . . . . . . . . . . . . . . . . . . . . . . . . . . . 50
Lowering the Pain . . . . . . . . . . . . . . . . . . . . . . . . . . . . . . . . . . . . . . . . . . . . . . . 51
Healing Journey . . . . . . . . . . . . . . . . . . . . . . . . . . . . . . . . . . . . . . . . . . . . . . . . 52
Hypnotic Analgesia . . . . . . . . . . . . . . . . . . . . . . . . . . . . . . . . . . . . . . . . . . . . . 54
Sleep Hypnosis for Pain Management . . . . . . . . . . . . . . . . . . . . . . . . . . . . . . . . . 55

HYPNOSIS for WEIGHT MANAGEMENT . . . . . . . . . . . . . . . . . . . . . . . . . . . . . . 57
Reframing for Weight Loss . . . . . . . . . . . . . . . . . . . . . . . . . . . . . . . . . . . . . . . . 57
Reframing Hypnosis for Exercising . . . . . . . . . . . . . . . . . . . . . . . . . . . . . . . . . . . 59
Introduction to Hypnosis and NLP for Healthy Eating and Exercising . . . . . . . . . . . . 60
Hypnosis and NLP for Healthy Eating and Exercising . . . . . . . . . . . . . . . . . . . . . . 61
Introduction to Hypnosis for Boosting Metabolism . . . . . . . . . . . . . . . . . . . . . . . . 62
Hypnosis for Boosting your Metabolism . . . . . . . . . . . . . . . . . . . . . . . . . . . . . . . 62
Sleep Hypnosis for Reinforcing Healthy Living . . . . . . . . . . . . . . . . . . . . . . . . . . . 64

HYPNOSIS for SURGERY . . . . . . . . . . . . . . . . . . . . . . . . . . . . . . . . . . . . . . . . . 65

5. Hypnotherapy for the Mind . . . . . . . . . . . . . . . . . . . . . . . . . . . . . . . . . . . . . . . . . 67

    Hypnotherapy for Insomnia . . . . . . . . . . . . . . . . . . . . . . . . . . . . . . . . . . . . . . . . . 67

    Important Pointers for Sleep Hygiene . . . . . . . . . . . . . . . . . . . . . . . . . . . . . . . . . 68

    Systematic Relaxation for Enhancing Sleep . . . . . . . . . . . . . . . . . . . . . . . . . . . . 68

    HYPNOTHERAPY for ANXIETY . . . . . . . . . . . . . . . . . . . . . . . . . . . . . . . . . . . . 72

    Space Induction Hypnosis for Anxiety and Fears . . . . . . . . . . . . . . . . . . . . . . . 72

    Sleep Hypnosis for Anxiety with Tree Metaphor . . . . . . . . . . . . . . . . . . . . . . . 74

    INNER FAMILY . . . . . . . . . . . . . . . . . . . . . . . . . . . . . . . . . . . . . . . . . . . . . . . . . . 75

    Introduction to Creating the Inner Family and Healing the Inner Child . . . . . . 75

    Hypnosis to Create the Inner Father . . . . . . . . . . . . . . . . . . . . . . . . . . . . . . . . . 75

    Hypnosis to Create an Inner Mother . . . . . . . . . . . . . . . . . . . . . . . . . . . . . . . . . 76

    Introduction to Hypnosis for Healing Your Inner Child . . . . . . . . . . . . . . . . . . 77

    Hypnosis for Healing the Inner Child . . . . . . . . . . . . . . . . . . . . . . . . . . . . . . . . 78

    DREAM WORK IN HYPNOTHERAPY . . . . . . . . . . . . . . . . . . . . . . . . . . . . . 80

    Introduction to Dream Work . . . . . . . . . . . . . . . . . . . . . . . . . . . . . . . . . . . . . . . 80

    Types of Dreams . . . . . . . . . . . . . . . . . . . . . . . . . . . . . . . . . . . . . . . . . . . . . . . . . 80

    Guidelines for Working with Dreams . . . . . . . . . . . . . . . . . . . . . . . . . . . . . . . . 81

    Introduction to Hypnosis for Remembering your Dreams . . . . . . . . . . . . . . . . 81

    Hypnosis for Remembering your Dreams . . . . . . . . . . . . . . . . . . . . . . . . . . . . . 82

    Introduction to Hypnotic Dream Work . . . . . . . . . . . . . . . . . . . . . . . . . . . . . . 83

    Hypnosis for Working with your Dreams . . . . . . . . . . . . . . . . . . . . . . . . . . . . . 84

    Introduction to Advanced Dream Work . . . . . . . . . . . . . . . . . . . . . . . . . . . . . . 86

    Introduction to Hypnosis to Seed or Manifest a Dream . . . . . . . . . . . . . . . . . . 86

    Hypnosis to Seed a Healing or a Teaching Dream . . . . . . . . . . . . . . . . . . . . . . 87

    Introduction to Lucid Dreaming . . . . . . . . . . . . . . . . . . . . . . . . . . . . . . . . . . . . 88

    Hypnotic Skill Rehearsal for Lucid Dreaming . . . . . . . . . . . . . . . . . . . . . . . . . 89

    Sleep Hypnosis for Lucid Dreaming . . . . . . . . . . . . . . . . . . . . . . . . . . . . . . . . . 90

6. Hypnotherapy for the Spirit . . . . . . . . . . . . . . . . . . . . . . . . . . . . . . . . . . . . . . . . 91

    HIGHER SELF HYPNOTHERAPY . . . . . . . . . . . . . . . . . . . . . . . . . . . . . . . . . 91

    Introduction to Higher Self Hypnotherapy . . . . . . . . . . . . . . . . . . . . . . . . . . . 91

    Higher Self Hypnotherapy . . . . . . . . . . . . . . . . . . . . . . . . . . . . . . . . . . . . . . . . 91

    Introduction to the Inner Healer . . . . . . . . . . . . . . . . . . . . . . . . . . . . . . . . . . . . 93

    Inner Healer Hypnosis . . . . . . . . . . . . . . . . . . . . . . . . . . . . . . . . . . . . . . . . . . . . 93

    HYPNOTIC ENERGY BALANCING . . . . . . . . . . . . . . . . . . . . . . . . . . . . . . . 95

    Introduction to Chakra Balancing . . . . . . . . . . . . . . . . . . . . . . . . . . . . . . . . . . 95

    Chakra Balancing . . . . . . . . . . . . . . . . . . . . . . . . . . . . . . . . . . . . . . . . . . . . . . . 96

    Introduction to Grounding and Protection . . . . . . . . . . . . . . . . . . . . . . . . . . . 98

    Grounding and Protection: How to Be in your Body Right Here, Right Now . . . . . . 98

Triangles of Light: Clearing your Auric Field . . . . . . . . . . . . . . . . . . . . . . . . . . . . . . . . . . . . . . . . . 99

Environmental Clearing . . . . . . . . . . . . . . . . . . . . . . . . . . . . . . . . . . . . . . . . . . . . . . . . . . . . . . . . 100

On the Go Psychic Protection . . . . . . . . . . . . . . . . . . . . . . . . . . . . . . . . . . . . . . . . . . . . . . . . . . . 101

## HYPNOTIC REGRESSION THERAPY . . . . . . . . . . . . . . . . . . . . . . . . . . . . . . . . . . . . . . . 102

Introduction to Experiencing Past-Life Regressions . . . . . . . . . . . . . . . . . . . . . . . . . . . . . . . . . 102

Past-Life Regression for a Current-Life Question, Concern, or Issue . . . . . . . . . . . . . . . . . . . . 102

Exploring a Past-Life Relationship . . . . . . . . . . . . . . . . . . . . . . . . . . . . . . . . . . . . . . . . . . . . . . . 105

## EXPLORING the INTERLIFE . . . . . . . . . . . . . . . . . . . . . . . . . . . . . . . . . . . . . . . . . . . . . . . 108

Introduction to Exploring the Interlife . . . . . . . . . . . . . . . . . . . . . . . . . . . . . . . . . . . . . . . . . . . 108

Introduction to Interlife After Death Hypnosis . . . . . . . . . . . . . . . . . . . . . . . . . . . . . . . . . . . . 108

Exploring the Interlife after Death . . . . . . . . . . . . . . . . . . . . . . . . . . . . . . . . . . . . . . . . . . . . . . 108

Introduction to Exploring the Interlife Before Birth . . . . . . . . . . . . . . . . . . . . . . . . . . . . . . . . 110

Exploring the Interlife Before Birth . . . . . . . . . . . . . . . . . . . . . . . . . . . . . . . . . . . . . . . . . . . . . 110

## EXPLORING FUTURE-LIFE HYPNOSIS . . . . . . . . . . . . . . . . . . . . . . . . . . . . . . . . . . . . . 113

Introduction to Future-Life Hypnosis . . . . . . . . . . . . . . . . . . . . . . . . . . . . . . . . . . . . . . . . . . . 113

Introduction to the Future-Life Progression in your Current Life . . . . . . . . . . . . . . . . . . . . . . 113

Present-Life Progression . . . . . . . . . . . . . . . . . . . . . . . . . . . . . . . . . . . . . . . . . . . . . . . . . . . . . 114

Introduction to Future-Incarnation Progression . . . . . . . . . . . . . . . . . . . . . . . . . . . . . . . . . . . 115

Future-Incarnation Progression . . . . . . . . . . . . . . . . . . . . . . . . . . . . . . . . . . . . . . . . . . . . . . . . 116

## SPIRIT RELEASEMENT . . . . . . . . . . . . . . . . . . . . . . . . . . . . . . . . . . . . . . . . . . . . . . . . . . 119

Introduction to Hypnosis for Spirit Releasement . . . . . . . . . . . . . . . . . . . . . . . . . . . . . . . . . . 119

Body and Energy Scan . . . . . . . . . . . . . . . . . . . . . . . . . . . . . . . . . . . . . . . . . . . . . . . . . . . . . . 120

Spirit-Releasement Hypnosis . . . . . . . . . . . . . . . . . . . . . . . . . . . . . . . . . . . . . . . . . . . . . . . . . 120

Important Guidelines for Post-Releasement . . . . . . . . . . . . . . . . . . . . . . . . . . . . . . . . . . . . . . 123

## TALKING with the DEAD . . . . . . . . . . . . . . . . . . . . . . . . . . . . . . . . . . . . . . . . . . . . . . . . 124

Introduction to Talking with the Dead . . . . . . . . . . . . . . . . . . . . . . . . . . . . . . . . . . . . . . . . . . 124

Hypnosis for Talking with the Dead . . . . . . . . . . . . . . . . . . . . . . . . . . . . . . . . . . . . . . . . . . . . 125

## 7. Hypnosis for Children . . . . . . . . . . . . . . . . . . . . . . . . . . . . . . . . . . . . . . . . . . . . . . . . . . 127

### HYPNOSIS for SLEEP . . . . . . . . . . . . . . . . . . . . . . . . . . . . . . . . . . . . . . . . . . . . . . . . . . 127

Introduction to Hypnosis for Restful Sleep and Sweet Dreams . . . . . . . . . . . . . . . . . . . . . . . . 127

Sweet Dreams Sleep Hypnosis . . . . . . . . . . . . . . . . . . . . . . . . . . . . . . . . . . . . . . . . . . . . . . . . 127

Hypnosis for Self Esteem, Communications, and Healing Trauma . . . . . . . . . . . . . . . . . . . . . 129

Izzie the Cricket . . . . . . . . . . . . . . . . . . . . . . . . . . . . . . . . . . . . . . . . . . . . . . . . . . . . . . . . . . . 129

### HYPNOSIS for CONTROLLING BODILY FUNCTIONS . . . . . . . . . . . . . . . . . . . . . . . . 131

Hypnosis for Bed Wetting and Potty Training . . . . . . . . . . . . . . . . . . . . . . . . . . . . . . . . . . . . 131

8. EMOTIONAL FREEDOM TECHNIQUE . . . . . . . . . . . . . . . . . . . . . . . . . . . . . . . . . . 133

    Diagram of EFT Tapping Points . . . . . . . . . . . . . . . . . . . . . . . . . . . . . . . . 134

    Learning EFT . . . . . . . . . . . . . . . . . . . . . . . . . . . . . . . . . . . . . . . . . . . 135

    Sample EFT Set-up Phrases . . . . . . . . . . . . . . . . . . . . . . . . . . . . . . . . . . 137

9. Becoming the Ultimate Hypnotherapist . . . . . . . . . . . . . . . . . . . . . . . . . . . . . . . 143

    Hypnosis for Success in your Hypnotherapy Practice . . . . . . . . . . . . . . . . . . . 143

    Guidelines for Manifesting . . . . . . . . . . . . . . . . . . . . . . . . . . . . . . . . . . . 143

    Hypnosis for Intentional Manifesting . . . . . . . . . . . . . . . . . . . . . . . . . . . . . 144

    Manifesting Prayer . . . . . . . . . . . . . . . . . . . . . . . . . . . . . . . . . . . . . . . 146

    Cosmic Marketing for a Successful Hypnotherapy Practice . . . . . . . . . . . . . . . 146

    LEARNING ENHANCEMENTS for HYPNOTHERAPISTS . . . . . . . . . . . . . . . . 148

    Crystal Cave Learning Enhancement . . . . . . . . . . . . . . . . . . . . . . . . . . . . 148

    Ultimate Hypnotherapist Skill Rehearsal . . . . . . . . . . . . . . . . . . . . . . . . . . 150

About the Author . . . . . . . . . . . . . . . . . . . . . . . . . . . . . . . . . . . . . . . . . . . . . . 151

REFERENCE LIST . . . . . . . . . . . . . . . . . . . . . . . . . . . . . . . . . . . . . . . . . . . . . 152

RESOURCES . . . . . . . . . . . . . . . . . . . . . . . . . . . . . . . . . . . . . . . . . . . . . . . . 153

# ACKNOWLEDGMENTS

*I*am grateful to all of my clients and students for teaching me about presence and transformation. It has been an honor to share in the grace of your healing and growth.

Thank you, Paul, for your belief in me, for your daily acts of love, for the beauty and magic of your music, and for the joy of sharing our spiritual work at HCH. Thank you to all the teachers at HCH who share their constant wisdom and expertise as they inspire and accompany the students at HCH through the hypnotherapy training: John Thatcher, Ph.D.; Greg Harper, Ph.D., Carolyn Rigiero, CCHT, and David Leong, MA. Thank you Freda Morris Hedges, Ph.D, now in spirit, for her mentoring in hypnotherapy and for passing HCH on to me. And special thanks to Dr. Ronald W. Jue for permission to use his Inner Family hypnosis processes and to P.M.H. Atwater for her permission to use her Real Voice of Spirit chart. Your work has guided and supported me and my students and clients throughout the years. I also wish to thank Cynthia Moore for her editing, friendship, and collegial support and Chris Bronsten, MBA, for the final editing expertise and her hard work in helping this book come into final form. The EFT model is an original drawing by Rosetta Bonavita, CCHT, my colleague and friend for whom I am grateful. And finally, thank you to HarperCollins Publishing for permission to use excerpts of Stephen Mitchell's translation of the *Tao Te Ching*.

# Part One

# The Tao of Spiritual Hypnotherapy

# Introduction to Part One

Hypnotherapy is a spiritual practice and, in my experience, it reflects many respected spiritual principles. These principles are known through many different sacred traditions; however, I specifically focus on Taoism because I believe Taoism to be the most pure in form and the closest to nature. I also have a personal affinity for Taoism and the Tao Te Ching and I relished revisiting the text for this writing.

Hypnotherapy has become a spiritual practice for me over the years. It teaches and reinforces all that I have studied and learned about spirituality and consciousness. Through the process of being in a non-ordinary state of consciousness called hypnosis, I directly experience the realm of which many mystics have written. I know that I am more than my body and I know that I am eternal. I know it because I have experienced it. In addition, I have been guide and witness to thousands of people who independently experience and know the same for themselves. After experiencing that we are eternal and embodying being present and in the flow, people's consciousness expands. This writing includes personal stories of those whose consciousness shifted through being hypnotees and/or hypnotherapist guides for others.

This book has been sixty-two years in the making. It is the culmination of my journey so far this lifetime into the nature of the psyche, spirit, and the exploration of human consciousness. As a child while lying in bed at night I had experiences of feeling that I was as large as the universe; that I was not limited to my physical body. I now know that my child awareness was not limited to my few years of life experience. I know that I was naturally remembering what I have repeatedly learned through many lifetimes and through being a transpersonal psychotherapist as a guide for thousands of hypnotherapy sessions: we are not our body. We are an energetic expression and creation of the Divine. Chapter ten of the *Tao Te Ching* encapsulates this writing and alludes to most every point I wish to make as to how hypnotherapy is a spiritual practice. A transpersonal approach to hypnotherapy allows a direct experience of what is outlined in the quote on the following page.

*Spiritual Hypnotherapy Scripts for Body, Mind, and Spirit*

Can you coax your mind from its wandering
and keep to the original oneness?

Can you let your body become
supple as a newborn child's?

Can you cleanse your inner vision
until you see nothing but the light?

Can you love people and lead them
without imposing your will?

Can you deal with the most vital matters
by letting events take their course?

Can you step back from your own mind
and thus understand all things?

(Mitchell, 10)

# 1. WHAT is HYPNOTHERAPY?

Hypnosis is a process, which creates a non-ordinary state of consciousness. This non-ordinary state of consciousness, which is a different state from normal waking consciousness, allows clients to respond to suggestions with higher than normal receptivity. Hypnotic consciousness is a state that can spontaneously occur or it is a state that can be self-induced or induced with the help of a facilitator or hypnotherapist. All hypnosis is self-hypnosis because the hypnotic state of consciousness is generated within the hypnotee. The hypnotee allows herself to actively engage in the process. In some situations, the hypnotee may choose to not respond. Experiencing the hypnotic state is a skill that can be learned and cultivated.

Hypnotherapy is the practice of therapy that takes place in the non-ordinary state of hypnotic consciousness. Hypnotherapy directly engages the client's conscious and subconscious mind in the therapy process. Hypnotherapy is usually interactive and involves verbal and non-verbal communications between the client and hypnotherapist while the client is in the non-ordinary state of consciousness. Most therapeutic work is greatly enhanced while clients are in a hypnotic state because they are able to access information, healing, creativity, memories, and insight that is not normally available when in the waking conscious state. Change is facilitated from within the clients in hypnotherapy; it is inwardly generated and intrinsic to the clients, themselves. The hypnotherapist is responsible for having the tools and skills to assist the clients in helping themselves, which minimizes the often incorrectly perceived "power" the therapist has over the client.

By engaging a transpersonal or spiritual focus in hypnotherapy, the client's personal transformation can be supported even further. By invoking and accessing the client's higher Self or the wisest transcendent aspect of consciousness, clients are also able to access expanded states of consciousness similar to those experienced in meditation or in profound states of presence: states when the egoic or self-involved consciousness is transcended or simply out of the way. Through these transpersonal states of consciousness, healing and profound change can take place, often fairly effortlessly.

Clients report that these expanded states of consciousness change them in lasting positive ways. Clients realize that, for instance, although they have pain, they are not the pain, that is, they can dis-identify from the pain. They can potentially experience themselves as spiritual in essence: as a spiritual being having a human experience of pain. From these hypnotically accessed transcendent states, clients begin to have a new sense of self and a new way of relating to the challenges of their lives. They become dis-identified from their stories and the previously perceived roles they have played in their lives. Their consciousness is expanded along with an expanded sense of Self.

Spiritual Hypnotherapy Scripts for Body, Mind, and Spirit

## Hypnotherapy as a Spiritual Practice

I became a transpersonal psychotherapist because of my passion for work that engages people's consciousness to promote change, healing, and transformation. As a client of hypnotherapy, a long-time practitioner of self-hypnosis, and as a hypnotherapist who has facilitated thousands of hypnotic sessions, I have many experiences of knowing the profound and lasting effects of hypnotherapeutic work. Over and over, I have discovered that facilitating a transpersonal form of hypnotherapy is a mystical and spiritual practice for both the client and the hypnotherapist. In hypnotherapy we can learn to access and utilize expanded states of consciousness directly, at will, and for a variety of personal goals and purposes. The process of being in an expanded state is just as healing and significant in supporting change as is directing the state of consciousness towards a therapeutic personal goal or outcome.

For the client in the hypnotic state, accessing awareness of the higher Self becomes a profound teacher of how our consciousness works to create our realities. These hypnotic states also become vehicles through which we can re-create our realities. Additionally, the hypnotherapist is often in an expanded state of profound presence entrained and aligned with the client's state of consciousness. The art of guiding a client's process involves being so present that the hypnotherapist is out of her own way and accessing her own higher Self as the hypnotic guide. The practice of hypnotherapy, both as a client and as a hypnotherapist, then, becomes another form of spiritual practice that puts us directly in touch with our spiritual nature and how our consciousness creates the forms and structures of our lives.

Spiritual awareness and presence can be cultivated as a spiritual practice by working with many of the energetic principles that are intrinsic to hypnotherapy. These principles and precepts, naturally mirrored in Taoist philosophy, are intrinsic to working with hypnotherapy as a spiritual practice.

## The Higher Self

Throughout the history of hypnosis and since the first psychological theories of Sigmund Freud, we have understood that there are two aspects of consciousness that come into play in the hypnotic process: the conscious and the subconscious (or unconscious mind, as Jung referred to it ). However, with the work of Roberto Assagioli and the birth of transpersonal psychology, there emerged an acknowledgement of a third aspect of consciousness: the higher Self, or the transcendent aspect of consciousness.

The higher Self, a spiritual, wise, and infinite aspect of our consciousness, can be directly accessed and engaged as the inner therapist/healer in the hypnotherapy process. It is an aspect of human consciousness that goes beyond our waking, ordinary ego consciousness that embodies, presents, or can access certain wisdom not experienced in normal consciousness (Alexander, 11).

Arthur Hastings, a professor of transpersonal psychology states,"… the higher Self is said to be a distinct part or function of the individual. It is an entity in itself, with consciousness or awareness like the ego, and it is assumed to be a part of everyone. It witnesses the person's experiences. It is non-punitive, objective, and non-judgmental. Its orientation is towards higher values, life purpose, healthy emotional and mental development, and spiritual qualities" (Hastings, 180).

Willis Harman believes that in all major religious and mystical traditions there is a parallel wisdom that is a necessary component of being human and is an impetus for the inner search of higher Self: In studies of comparative religion it appears that, besides the many exoteric forms, there is within any of the major traditions an esoteric or "inner circle" form, which is essentially the same for all traditions. This "perennial wisdom" seems to recommend an inner search involving some sort of meditative or yogic discipline, and discovery and identification with, a "higher" or "true" Self (Harman, 34).

The perennial wisdom of the *Tao Te Ching* is tremendously supportive of the practice of hypnotherapy and the evolution of consciousness that comes from doing hypnotic work.

Tao remains quiescent, and yet leaves nothing undone.
If a wise person could hold it, all things would of their own accord transform.
If in the process of transformation desire should arise,
I would check it by the simplicity of the nameless.
The ineffable simplicity would bring about an absence of desire,
And rest would come back again.
Desireless and at rest, all things are at peace (Medhurst and Gorn-Old adaptation, 37).

**Accessing the Higher Self in Hypnotherapy**

Now that we understand the concept of the higher Self, how do we access it and utilize its resources in the hypnotherapy process? By directly invoking the higher Self and by facilitating a technique of voice dialogue, the higher Self can become a resource for inner guidance and self-healing in the hypnotherapy process. Learning to distinguish the higher Self from the egoic self is crucial when in hypnosis. How does a client know which "voices" to listen to and which ones to trust? Many years ago a friend gave me a simple diagram, which follows, that categorizes the differences between the higher Self and the egoic consciousness. This chart was developed by PMH Atwater and is featured in her book, *Goddess Runes*. The diagram follows:

# THE REAL VOICE OF SPIRIT

If voices or thoughts, other than your own, seek your attention or attempt to come through you, use the following charts, which compare energies from different levels, as a guide before you decide to accept or reject what is happening.

| LESSER MIND | GREATER MIND |
|---|---|
| **THE VOICE OF EGO**<br><br>PERSONALITY LEVEL<br>• flatters<br>• commands<br>• demands<br>• tests<br>• chooses for you<br>• imprisons<br>• promotes dependency<br>• intrudes<br>• pushes<br>• excludes<br>• is status oriented<br>• insists on obedience<br>• often claims ultimate authority<br>• offers short cuts<br>• seeks personal gratification | **THE VOICE OF SPIRIT**<br><br>SOUL LEVEL<br>• informs<br>• suggests<br>• guides<br>• nudges<br>• leaves choices to you<br>• empowers<br>• promotes independence<br>• respects<br>• supports<br>• includes<br>• is free and open<br>• encourages growth and development<br>• recognizes a greater power or God<br>• offers integration<br>• affirms divine order along with the good of the whole |

Atwater, P.M.H. adapted with permission

By studying this diagram and by becoming familiar with the different tones and qualities of the ego's voice and the voice of Spirit, one has a valuable tool with which to access the source of inner and outer guidance or teaching. With practice, we can know from which state the information or guidance is coming, and which guidance is empowering and supportive of our own highest good. Clarity and empowerment come from the practice of choosing the wisdom and guidance of the higher Self, as does a growing experience of knowing and accessing our intuition, our deepest inner wisdom. When we access the higher Self we are naturally in the flow of the Tao. "If powerful men and women could center themselves in it, the whole world would be transformed" (Mitchell, 37).

In the hypnotherapy session, the facilitator or hypnotherapist can ask the client's higher Self or voice of Spirit to be the inner guide and director for the client. The hypnotherapist aligns with this part of the client through direct dialogue and verbal exchange. In self-hypnosis processes, the higher Self becomes the inner hypnotist.

# 2. TAOISM and HYPNOTHERAPY

*A*s a student of many spiritual traditions and as a practitioner who combines spiritual practices while working with clients, I have observed that many of the tenets of Taoism are at play in the process of working with the higher Self in hypnotherapy. The proverbial Taoist concept of "going with the flow" lies at the heart of the hypnotherapy process I use with clients and teach to hypnotherapists. As I discuss specific Taoist concepts and show how they support, and at times determine, the structure and evolution of hypnotherapy sessions, I weave in quotes from the Tao Te Ching that illuminate the concepts.

It must also be stated that writing about Taoism is difficult and paradoxical because, as stated in the first line of book One in the *Tao Te Ching,* "The Tao that can be told, is not the eternal Tao" (Feng and English, line 1). Words are too limiting to capture the essence of the Tao; rather the Tao is to be lived and experienced. As a hypnotherapist, I have learned about living the Tao through the practice of presence in the non-ordinary and mystical states accessed in hypnotherapy. The practice of hypnotherapy brings to life the philosophy and spiritual practice of Taoism's "going with the flow." In addition, accessing the higher Self brings wisdom, healing, and expansion of consciousness to both the client and the practitioner.

## Taoist Principles in Hypnotherapy

In this chapter I weave in quotes from the *Tao Te Ching* as I discuss ten different Taoist tenets and exemplify their principles in the context of practicing spiritual hypnotherapy. Most of these tenets are introduced in some form in the book *The Complete Idiot's Guide to Taoism* by Brandon Toropov and Chad Hansen.

## Taoist Principle: Wu-wei (non-action)

A good traveler has no fixed plans
and is not intent upon arriving.
A good artist lets his intuition
lead him wherever it wants.
A good scientist has freed himself of concepts
and keeps his mind open to what is.

Thus the Master is available to all people
and doesn't reject anyone.
He is ready to use all situations
and doesn't waste anything.
This is called embodying the light (Mitchell, 27).

To be sparing of words is natural.
A violent wind cannot last a whole morning;
Pelting rain cannot last a whole day.
Who have made these things but heaven and earth?
Inasmuch as heaven and earth cannot last forever, how can man?

He who engages himself in Tao is identified with Tao.
He who engages himself in virtue is identified with virtue.
He who engages himself in abandonment is identified with abandonment.
Identified by Tao, he will be well received by Tao.
Identified with virtue, he will be well received by virtue.
Identified with abandonment, he will be well received by abandonment (Ta-Kao, 27).

In a Taoist-influenced form of spiritual hypnotherapy, the hypnotherapist works with *wu-wei* and is like the good traveler written about in chapter 27 of the *Tao Te Ching*. He has no fixed plans and allows his intuition to lead.

In hypnotherapy, *wu-wei* is working with the energy, not against it, and allowing the process to unfold. *Wu-wei* is the experience of non-doing or doing without trying. The goal of *wu-wei* is to achieve a state of alignment with the Tao and a state of perfect equilibrium. In a practical sense, *wu-wei* means knowing when to act and knowing when not to act. This is an experience of being "out of our own way". For example, in *wu-wei,* the dance dances the dancer. Further examples of wu-wei are experiencing life living through us or our body breathing us. Wu-wei is an effortless effort.

In an empowering and transpersonal form of hypnotherapy, the practice of *wu-wei* or non-doing is crucial. The non-doing comes into play by allowing the client space and time to access resources from "within". The hypnotherapist supports and allows what is. Timing is of the essence. By asking interactive, open-ended questions and giving the client the opportunity to access and respond, even if the client's response is to not respond, *wu-wei* is honored. The hypnotherapist and hypnotee are both sensitive to what is happening or not happening in the moment, and are both flowing with the unfolding process. The expanded state of consciousness accessed in hypnosis leads to an open-minded and open-hearted state. Out of this state of being present and open to the flow of what is, insights, creativity, and knowingness emerge. Out of this openness one can also access the voice of Spirit which is very much like the "voice" or message of *wu-wei*. Pamela Ball in *The Essence of Tao* writes that:

> … the solution to any problem is to stop trying to control events. If the will is resigned to the Tao – the greater scheme of things – the individual becomes an instrument of its eternal Way. This does not mean becoming passive and fatalistic but actually means becoming more involved in the wider issues of the physical plane. The ideal person (or Perfected Man) in operating in *wu-wei* can act in three different ways; sometimes in only one; but more often in all three. These are:

1. Effortlessness
2. Responsiveness
3. Unobtrusiveness (Ball, 179).

A skilled hypnotherapist is constantly dancing with these three ways of responding to the client's emerging process. The hypnotherapeutic process emerges from the verbal and energetic dance that is co-created in the session, rather than the hypnotherapist superimposing a specific technique, his own style, or projected experience onto the client.

By doing without doing, the hypnotherapist allows the Tao to flow and with it comes healing, insight, and empowerment. For both the client and the hypnotherapist, by doing less one can accomplish more. This approach to hypnotherapy is similar to engaging in a verbal and energetic form of Tai Chi.

Effortlessness:

The spiritual approach to hypnotherapy utilizes what already is by working with the client's language. The hypnotherapist will incorporate the client's phrasing, metaphors, and life perspective in the hypnotherapeutic process by joining the client wherever he is.

Clients report that they feel met, heard, and understood when the hypnotherapist utilizes the reality and the language of the client as a starting point. As the therapeutic process and hypnotherapy journey evolves, the client's structure of reality is honored and then expanded as he is led to the therapeutic goal or desired state of being.

Responsiveness:

For the hypnotherapist, being present to the hypnotee's energetic, physical, and emotional shifts is imperative. The changes and movement the client makes while in trance are clues that subtly guide the hypnotherapist into the flow of the client's process.

Tears, deep breaths, subtle movements, quizzical expressions need to be acknowledged by the hypnotherapist. Inviting the client to share what is happening when these changes occur supports the hypnotherapist in guiding the hypnotherapy process. It is an act of following the client so the client can be led to where he wants to be. The hypnotherapist must pay attention in an open and receptive way by watching, listening, and feeling what is going on with the client in trance. Appropriate responses will naturally come with pacing and leading as *wu-wei* is embodied in the hypnotherapy relationship and hypnosis process.

> The reason rivers and seas are called the kings of the valley is because they keep below them. Therefore the wise man desiring to be above his people must in his demeanor keep below them; wishing to benefit his people, he must ever keep himself out of sight.

> The wise man dwells above, yet the people do not feel the burden; he is the leader and the people suffer no harm. Therefore the world rejoices to exalt him and never wearies of him.

> Because he will not quarrel with anyone, no one can quarrel with him (Goodard, 66).

Unobtrusiveness:

By joining the client, resistance is avoided. By using the client's language, rapport and ease are created since the hypnotherapist's skills are unobtrusive and subtle. The hypnotherapist helps the client to help herself. Because the hypnotherapy process seems effortless and easy, there is nothing that can't be met, and nothing to resist.

One example of responding to the client with unobtrusiveness comes up periodically in the context of a client feeling blocked or stuck and unable to respond or go further in the hypnotic process. Rather than colluding with the client by stopping the session, or giving up, the skilled facilitator has the client go into the block or stuckness. Thus, the facilitator unobtrusively joins with what is already there: resistance. In the unobtrusiveness of going with the client's resistance, the block is often loosened and the client's process begins to flow.

> The world is ruled by letting things take their course. It cannot be ruled by interfering (Feng and English, 48).

**Taoist Principle: Trust in Nature as an organic pattern and our unity with it.**

> The ancient wise men were skillful and subtle.
> They were fathomless in their depths; so profound, that it is difficult to describe them.
> They were cautious, like one who crosses a swollen river.
> They were reserved, like one who doubts his fellows.
> They were watchful, like one who travels abroad.
> They were retiring, like snow beneath the sun.
> They were simple, like newly felled timber.
> They were lowly, like the valley. They were obscure, like muddy water.
> May not a man take muddy water and make it clear by keeping still?
> May not a man take a dead thing and make it alive by continuous motion?
> Those who follow the Tao have no need of replenishing,
> And being devoid of all properties,
> They grow old without need of being filled (Gorn-Old adaptation, 15).

Natural settings, nature metaphors and the elements are all used in the hypnotherapeutic process. Nature teaches, supports, and sustains us, and empowers the hypnotherapy process by bringing to awareness what the client already knows and uses in her daily life.

Commonly, in a hypnotherapy induction, the client will be invited to go to a healing and safe place in nature. As the client chooses and inwardly accesses the place, either from memory or from her imagination, she describes the surroundings. While invoking all of the inner senses: seeing with the inner eyes, feeling the emotions and physical sensations in the body, hearing with the inner ears and simply by knowing, she focuses on the supporting effects of the natural surroundings. The hypnotherapist asks open-ended questions about the preferred place as a way to draw out and embellish the hypnotee's experience. Taoism relies on nature as a teacher and guide for being in the now. Nature is a pure expression of the Tao. We cannot name the Tao, but we can observe it all around us in nature.

When in the natural setting in trance, working with the elements can be very supportive in many ways. Breathing in fresh air may support ongoing relaxation. Being in or by water may cleanse, soothe, and balance the body or the energy system. Feeling the sunlight on the skin may calm and relax the body tensions. Because the unconscious does not know the difference between the imagination through inner perceptions and the external physical experience of outer physical reality, the body responds to the nature images as if it is actually in nature. The body and mind respond to the inner images and experience of nature and benefits from this mental hypnotic natural retreat.

Therapeutic metaphors that focus on the natural elements and the patterns and seasons in nature and life can remind the client about her role in life as a part of the natural world. Birth, death, change of the seasons, all familiar to the client in her daily life, can be natural reminders to support a client going through her own losses or changes and remind her that she is a part of a greater whole. Change is the only constant and embracing change by accepting what is, supports the client in being in the Tao.

A hypnotic metaphor that I created incorporates the story of a middle-aged woman who is adjusting to her son's leaving home for college. Her planting of a garden is a turning point for her in her healing and acceptance. Her experience of loss and grief is transformed by her relationship with the earth and her aligning with Mother Nature as she plants and tends the garden. The story reminds people facing change that there is always rebirth out of death, and that nature is a resource to support our understanding and acceptance of what is. The Tao surrounds us all in the form of nature. Reflect on nature to find enlightenment and healing.

## Taoist Principle: Accessing Chi and the energy work of Hypnotherapy

Open yourself to the Tao,
then trust your natural responses;
and everything will fall into place (Mitchell, 23).

The process of engaging in hypnotherapy is similar to a martial art. Both the hypnotherapist and the hypnotee are engaging in an energetic "battle" over resistance, blocks, misperceptions, and limiting beliefs that create the hypnotee's distorted perceptions of reality and limited expressions of Self. As with much of the Taoist paradoxical philosophy, the therapeutic "battle" is one of calling a truce. By working with the blocks and joining the energy of the client's resistance, the blocks melt away. The life force or chi is liberated for the client's transformation in various ways. One of the most common methods is through abreaction: the emotional and physical release of blocked energy. When a client moves through a block, healing occurs.

It is common in regression therapy that by contacting the source of a dis-ease in one's life, that the dis-ease releases. For example, a man with severe arthritis in his wrists hypnotically regresses to the source of the pain. He discovers that in a past life he is held by the head and wrists in the stocks at the town square for being a "witch" and healing people. She (in his past life) is humiliated and taunted by the townspeople for four days with no food or bathroom privileges. From this trauma, she decides that it is unsafe to allow herself to use her knowledge and skills as a healer and she vows to never heal others again. In his present life, the man is a novelist and body worker who is healing others through his hands and his stories. As he becomes more visible to the public through his published novels and his flourishing massage business, the past-life decision reactivates: it is unsafe to be visible as a healer and the energy is once again blocked in his wrists. This blocked energy in his wrists, which manifests as arthritis, is an echo of the trauma of his past life as a healer being held in the stocks. By accessing the memory and trauma, and by choosing to allow the healing to flow through him this current lifetime, his block is released and his arthritis is healed.

While the hypnotherapist is engaging in the therapeutic Tai Chi with the client, the client is also doing Tai Chi with different parts of herself that have been at odds with each other, which created the inner "battle" or block. When the Tao is accessed, the chi flows, and order is restored.

When Tao is manifest in the world, evil actions have no power.
When evil has no power, man cannot be hurt (Mears adaptation, 60).
Give evil nothing to oppose and it will disappear by itself (Mitchell, 60).

## Taoist Principle: Yin/Yang: the balancing and integrating of opposites and the idea that all phenomena contain seeds of their counterparts.

Reason begets unity;
Unity begets duality;
Duality begets trinity;
And trinity begets the ten thousand things.

The ten thousand things are sustained by Yin [the negative principle].
They are encompassed by Yang [the positive principle].
And the immaterial breath, renders them harmonious (Suzuki and Carus, 42).

All of life, as it manifests on the physical plane, is a dance of opposites: male/female; birth/death; light/dark. When a client comes for hypnotherapy, the presenting issue almost always involves some imbalance of opposites in his or her life. The focus of the work is to collapse any polarization, or identification with one side of the problem over the other. For some people the focus will be to bring in the Light by accessing resources, shifting or reframing perspectives, working towards empowerment or forgiveness, and accessing the Self and the voice of Spirit. For others, the work is to address and heal the shadow, the darkness that is most often projected outwards onto others. This healing involves work with the victim part of the self, co-dependence, addictions, as well as all of the projected pain, unconscious behaviors, and motivations. Until the battle of opposites is addressed, the inner battle continues. When a client moves towards balance of the yin and yang, peace and equanimity emerge and the client no longer magnetizes situations that keep the imbalances activated.

> A great nation is like a great man:
> When he makes a mistake, he realizes it.
> Having realized it, he admits it.
> Having admitted it, he corrects it.
> He considers those who point out his faults
> are his most benevolent teachers.
> He thinks of his enemy
> as the shadow he himself casts (Mitchell, 61).

The balancing of opposites is addressed most effectively through hypnotic regression therapy. For example, a client may present the issue of abuse as a long-time theme in her life. Through childhood regressions, the client is able to access a chain of present life events where the pattern is established and repeated. Unknowingly, the client perpetuates the abuse through her own unconscious mental, emotional, and physical energetic fields that attracts more and more abuse. The law of attraction is in place when an abused person radiates the unconscious message, "I am abused," to the world. When a client is ready to acknowledge the pattern and to look deeply into what the pattern is teaching her on a soul level, there is an opportunity to collapse the dynamic and to stop the pattern.

The collapsing, in my experience, comes when the client is willing to look at the shadow expression of the abuse: the role of being an abuser. In such cases, past-life regression therapy is an effective approach.

I will share a personal experience that is a part of my own healing journey. I grew up with an alcoholic, physically abusive mother. Of her four daughters, I was the one she physically abused. I was angry and indignant when she was drunk and abusive. I was confrontational with her about her drinking and I often refused to do what she asked. I didn't want to be controlled by a drunk, abusive mother whom I did not respect. My responses activated an abuse cycle, and she would get even more angry and abusive with me. Until my mother went into recovery for her alcoholism, I truly felt disdain towards her.

In my early thirties, a few years before she died from liver cancer, I had an amazingly healing experience in which I understood my mother's focus on me as the outlet for the abuse. I spontaneously regressed into a past life during a hypnotherapy session. I experienced myself as a stepmother of a girl child whom I was physically abusing. I felt resentment and hatred towards this child and I was cruel and very abusive towards her. I experienced that I was beating her in a corner of a room so she could not escape my wrath. She cowered in fear and pain. When I looked into the child's eyes I recognized her as the soul of my mother. No wonder my mother was abusive towards me in my present life! She and I were in a karmic dance of balancing the abuser/abused role in this lifetime. During this regression, I realized that I had the opportunity to forgive both myself and my mother for being abusive. It was my unconscious guilt and remorse for what I had done to my stepchild in the past life that attracted the karmic payback and balancing of the abuse from my present life mother. After the regression, my disdain for my mother, which was in part my projected hatred towards my own abusive self, collapsed. I saw my mother with understanding and compassion. I felt forgiveness for us both. I experienced that the abusive cycle ended between us and I was able to feel love. This was a true blessing for us both. In the last few years of her life we were able to heal many aspects of our relationship.

From my own personal experience and my years of work with past-life therapy, I have seen many times that when we are polarized with specific dysfunctional dynamics, we have often had past-life experiences in which we were living out the opposite role. Everything contains its own opposite. When we can see and own our own shadow aspects, we are no longer victimizing ourselves or magnetizing the opportunities to learn and balance the lessons over and over again. When the lessons are learned and the opposites are balanced, the dynamic is healed. In Taoism and in the human conditions which express polarized opposites, there is a fundamental and pervasive unity.

**Taoist Principle: Go with the flow. Be like water. Spontaneity and "right response" come from listening to the way things are.**

> True goodness is like water,
> in that it benefits everything and harms nothing.
> Like water it ever seeks the lowest place,
> the place that all others avoid.
> It is closely kin to the Tao.
> For a dwelling it chooses the quiet meadow;
> For a heart the circling eddy.
> In generosity it is kind;
> In speech it is sincere;
> In authority it is order;
> In affairs it is ability;
> In movement it is rhythm.
> Inasmuch as it is always peaceful, it has no enemies (Goodard adaptation, 8).

When in hypnosis, a person can flow into her own deepest nature, into her true Self. Like water, the hypnotic process supports and allows one to sink to the depths of Self and nourish all things of the psyche. Consciousness expands as does access to the inner resources of creativity, memory, insight, and healing. The proverbial phrase "go with the flow" comes from this Taoist wisdom suggesting that we be like the pattern of water's natural action … that we flow with, rather than against, the natural expression of energy.

Like water, when we meet resistance, we conform to the obstacle and slowly and patiently go around it or incorporate it into our path.

> In all the world, there is nothing more submissive and weak than water. Yet, for attacking that which is hard and strong, nothing can surpass it (Toropov, Hansen, p. 133).

The most therapeutic and helpful guidance a hypnotherapist can provide a hypnotee is authentic, spontaneous, and without an agenda. This support results from being present in the moment, and following the flow of the client's process. The appropriate response is always waiting to rise to the surface. As the guide, we wait, listen, watch, and feel in order to be moved in the moment to know when to guide, when to be silent, and as to what to say and do. When we respond or move, it is from a place of stillness.

The principle of flowing like water is crucial to someone learning to respond as a hypnotee. Where and when do we learn to allow, and to flow with what is? Unless one is a meditator or a student of martial arts, it is unlikely that "going with the flow" is a known experience to a person in Western culture. Learning self-hypnosis, or engaging in a hypnotherapeutic process, will teach the participant to allow what is, and how to flow like water. The hypnotherapist must understand and embody going with the flow in order to facilitate it with her clients.

In my experience of studying hypnosis, I know that most traditionally-trained directive hypnotists do not practice the Taoist principle of flowing like water, which is why there are so many reports that not everyone can be hypnotized. The client is expected to match the style and approach of the hypnotist. And if she can't respond, it is assumed that she can't be hypnotized! However, when a "flowing-with-what-is" Taoist approach to hypnosis is facilitated, there is no resistance to overcome. The watery process goes around obstacles and any blocks in the way.

> This is called the small dark light:
> The soft, the weak prevail
> Over the hard, the strong. (Le Guin, 36).

One of my favorite teachings that I share with my hypnotherapy students is that "nothing is something". When a hypnotee reports that nothing is happening in the hypnotic process, the client is supported and encouraged to go into the nothingness. By going with the flow of the nothingness, something always arises. Usually the client's state will deepen by allowing the nothingness to be okay and to be what it is. Certainly, having many experiences with the act of allowing trains the client to know the state and experience of flow. Eventually, the hypnotic experience carries over into one's daily experiences and she can flow with her own life.

**Taoist principle: Everything is cyclical, transient, and changing. The only constant is change.**

> Not-being and being arise the one from the other.
> So also do the difficult and the easy;
> The long and the short;
> The high and the low;
> Sounds and voices;
> The preceding and the following.
>
> Therefore the Wise Man abides by non-attachment is his affairs
> And practices a doctrine which cannot be imparted by speech.
> He attends to everything in its turn and declines nothing;
> Produces without claiming;
> Acts without dwelling thereon;
> Completes his purposes without resting in them.
> Inasmuch as he does this, he loses nothing (Medhurst, 2).

Many clients are dealing with the difficulties that come with change: changes that are forced on them because life circumstances change, and changes they choose. Stress increases when there is change, especially if we do not know how to trust and stay present. If we grieve for what was or could have been, or we constantly fantasize about what will come or could happen, we are out of the now. If we can stay present to what is in the moment, we alleviate fear and stress. Everything we need in the moment exists, even if we are taking our last breath.

Hypnotherapy is a phenomenal tool for helping people to become more present and cope with change. Grief work is profoundly supportive in helping clients move hypnotically through the grieving process. Clients may need to communicate soul to soul with loved ones who have passed, or they may need to work on acceptance of their own losses whether they involve a job, youth, money, health, or the impending loss of one's own life. By accessing the voice of Spirit and expanding their consciousness to be more in the flow of the now or Tao, the egoic mind that wants to know and control takes a big step aside.

> If you realize that all things change,
> there is nothing you will try to hold on to.

If you aren't afraid of dying,
there is nothing you can't achieve (Mitchell, 74).

To let go of control is, paradoxically, to gain control. The ego lets go and the higher Self takes over, allowing one to be fully in alignment with what is. When we begin to have a direct and personal experience of allowing and letting go, we realize the futility of trying to control. Who do we think we are to argue with the Tao?

Tao produces all things.
Virtue feeds them.
All appear in different forms;
Each is perfect by being given power.
Therefore the numerous things honour Tao and esteem virtue.
The honouring of Tao and the esteem of virtue are done,
Not by command, but always of their own accord.
Tao produces them, makes them grow, nourishes them,
Shelters them, brings them up and protects them.
When all things come into being, Tao does not reject them.
It produces them without holding possession of them.
It acts without depending upon them,
And raises them without lording over them.
When merits are accomplished, it does not lay claim to them.
Because it does not lay claim to them, it does not lose them (Ta-Kao, 51).

**Taoist principle: Return to the state of "uncarved wood" or the natural state.**

The world is formed from the void,
like utensils from a block of wood.
The Master knows the utensils,
yet keeps to the block:
thus she can use all things (Mitchell, 28).

Empty yourself of everything.
Let the mind rest at peace.
The ten thousand things rise and fall while the Self watches their return.
They grow and flourish and then return to their source.
Returning to the source is stillness, which is the way of nature (Feng and English, 16).

Becoming empty and being present in the now is the most important of all Taoist principles. It is through presence that one accesses the Tao, or the flow of what is. In hypnotherapy, presence is crucial for both the hypnotherapist and the hypnotee. It is from being present that the healing and transformation takes place. Hypnosis is a practice and pathway to presence. In presence our consciousness expands.

Hypnotic consciousness allows a person to dis-identify with egoic perceptions and to move away from a limited experience of self. I worked with a man who later became my student. He sought hypnotherapy for debilitating chronic physical pain. This man was badly injured at work and had multiple surgeries as an attempt to repair structural damage to his upper body. His life was a daily living hell of pain and limitations. He couldn't work or drive, and needed help dressing himself because of his upper body damage. He was barely able to walk into my office. On a scale of 0 to 10, he lived at a constant pain level of 10.

In the first session of hypnotherapy he had, what was, for him, an amazing experience. By following a pain management process, he realized that he was not the pain. He experienced himself as the observer of the pain, the witness to what the body and emotions were expressing. He returned to the "uncarved wood" of his Self and his awareness. This experience was a turning point for him. He learned self-hypnosis and energy therapy techniques that he used for himself and his healing began. The anxiety, physical tightening up against the pain, and hopelessness he carried began to soften. As he softened, the energy began to flow and the pain subsided. Hypnotherapy helped him dis-identify from the pain.

**Taoist principle: Interdependence: all things are a part of a unified field.**

> The Tao can't be perceived.
> Smaller than an electron,
> It contains uncountable galaxies (Mitchell, 32).

Commonly people who alter their consciousness through hypnosis expand their psychic abilities. It is not unusual for a person to have clairvoyance, precognition or telepathy when in a hypnotic state. Often, clients want to use hypnosis to develop their psychic abilities. As a hypnotherapist, I know from my own experience that my intuitive and psychic abilities have developed through being in the expanded state I experience when guiding a client in hypnosis. I often have what is called "psychic rapport" with a client. I can, at times, experience telepathy. Sometimes I know where the client is in her experience, or what the client is experiencing before she verbalizes her experience. I also often feel what the client feels during a session. And conversely, at times clients will report the same experience.

For instance, commonly, a client will say that she knew what I was going to say to her before I said it. While it is important to have healthy boundaries so that the hypnotherapist is not bombarded by the emotional and psychic turmoil or debris released by the client, it is also an advantage to "know" what is going on with the client so the process can be skillfully guided in support of the client's needs. Part of the art of being a grounded and compassionate hypnotherapist requires an ability to psychically merge and then to detach and observe at appropriate times. Psychological and psychic codependence is disempowering for both the client and the hypnotherapist; however, experiencing the unified field of connectedness and interdependence is very useful. When consciously accessing the unified field, the hypnotherapist can facilitate the session more easily and the client will feel understood, seen, and mirrored on all levels in the work. This interdependence creates phenomenal rapport and emotional closeness. Compassion flows more freely. For the client, a feeling of not being alone is generated. Knowing that on a quantum level we are all one can dramatically alter one's experience of being a part of a greater whole.

At HCH Institute, I facilitate an exercise to practice psychokinesis (PK) to bend spoons. Psychokinesis is the experience of affecting matter with something other than physical force, or mind over matter. I learned years ago how to have "PK Parties" and at the graduation for the hypnotherapy trainings, I facilitate an experience of PK through a group induction to bend spoons. As evidence for future PK benders, I have a box of unusable spoons and forks which my past students bent using PK. If a person can bend metal with her mind, just imagine what she can do in the area of self-healing or in generating world peace. By accessing the unified field, she can truly expand to know that she is a part of the bigger whole.

**Taoist principle: The Law of Reversed Effect: to change anything, you must first accept it the way it is.**

Paradox is paramount to Taoism and to healing as well. Through embracing opposites and moving into what is most feared and resisted, tension, pain, and fear soften and dissolve. A spiritual approach to working with physical and emotional pain and addictions in hypnotherapy exemplifies this paradox of the law of reversed effect.

Our Western scientific culture has high regard for the medical model. Typically, when someone is in pain, the symptoms are treated with pain medications. The pain symptoms are masked to diminish suffering. In the work of hypnotherapy; however, when working with a client experiencing pain, the focus is to go into the pain, into what is usually avoided and resisted. I have assisted hundreds of chronic pain sufferers to melt the pain and move into a state of liberation from chronic pain simply by teaching them to go with it, and to experience it fully through new expanded perceptions. The muscular constriction is released and the blocking of the body's life force energy is freed up to flow again. Through working with these pain management approaches, often the client becomes pain free.

For Western minds, going into the pain is counter-intuitive. We have been socially hypnotized to block and avoid pain, and to fear it. To witness a chronic pain sufferer move into what has been avoided for a long time is miraculous and liberating. Clients become one with the pain, transform it, and let it go from the inside out, without medications, side effects, or a need to continue medication. Chronic pain sufferers discover that they are not the pain. They access a witness consciousness and let go of the identification with the pain.

> To know one's ignorance is the best part of knowledge.
> To be ignorant of such knowledge is a disease.
> If one only regards it as a disease, he will soon be cured of it.
> The wise man is exempt from this disease.
> He knows it for what it is, and so is free from it (Gorn-Old, 71).

> In order to contract a thing, one should surely expand it first.
> In order to weaken, one will surely strengthen first.
> In order to overthrow, one will surely exalt first.
> In order to take, one will surely give first.
> This is called subtle wisdom.
> The soft and the weak can overcome the hard and the strong (Kao, 36).

Hypnotherapy, then, supports the shrinking of the pain by first allowing it to expand.

> Give evil nothing to oppose,
> and it will disappear by itself (Mitchell, 60).

> Act non-action; undertake no undertaking; taste the tasteless.
> The Sage desires the desireless, and prizes no articles that are difficult to get.
> He learns no learning, but reviews what others have taught.
> Thus he lets all things develop in their own natural way, and does not venture to act.
> Regard the small as the great; regard the few as many.
> Manage the difficult while they are easy;
> Manage the great while they are small.
> All difficult things in the world start from the easy.
> All the great things in the world start from the small.
> The tree that fills a man's arms arises from a tender shoot.
> The nine-storied tower is raised from a heap of earth;
> A thousand miles' journey begins from the spot under one's feet.
> Therefore the Sage never attempts great things, and thus he can achieve what is great.
> He who makes easy promises will seldom keep his word;
> He who regards many things as easy will find many difficulties.
> Therefore the Sage regards things as difficult, and consequently never has difficulties (Kao adaptation, 63).

This law of reverse effect is also at play when working with addictions. Before a person can work with his addictions, he must first of all accept that he is addicted and has no control over the addictive substance or behavior. The way to change anything is to initially accept it the way it is.

A hypnotherapeutic approach to addictions is to support the client in accessing the feelings, needs, and compulsions underneath the addictions, which, in most cases, is triggered by anxiety. By going into the anxiety, the anxiety begins to change. The anxiety that the addiction has been covering or managing is addressed head on. As one knows firsthand what has been avoided, it transforms. The client begins to have a tool to manage the anxiety and a chance to have a choice about behaviors. The driving need behind the addiction or compulsion is addressed directly and transformed.

I work with people who are ready to quit smoking. The hypnotherapeutic approach I use addresses what motivates the smoker part of the person to breathe smoke. I help the client to know consciously what the smoking part has unconsciously been trying to do for the client by smoking. The needs become conscious and then the client's higher Self is engaged to find other life-affirming ways to meet the needs. Once the needs are truly met, and met well and lovingly, the client is able to let go of the addiction, and practice healthier behaviors instead. The client becomes an air breather.

**Taoist principle: Emptiness, non-doing.**

> Although the wheel has thirty spokes its utility lies in the emptiness of the hub.
> The jar is made by kneading clay, but its usefulness consists in its capacity.
> A room is made by cutting out windows and doors through the walls,
> But the space the walls contain measures the room's value.
>
> In the same way matter is necessary to form,
> But the value of reality lies in its immateriality (Goddard, 11).

Sometimes the core of a client's issue is how to be a "human-being", rather than a "human-doing". Hypnotherapy can have many of the same effects as meditation. Hypnotic consciousness may be utilized, for instance, simply to know the state of Being, to directly experience that the source of all thought and action is the pregnant "nothing" from which "doing" is born. When a highly stressed "human-doing" comes in for help with symptoms of anxiety, sleeplessness, or compulsive behaviors, hypnotherapy collapses the compulsive patterns of having to constantly "do". A person can finally have a skill that allows the experience of being and nothingness, a skill that is not a part of our Western culture's conditioning.

The principles of Taoism join the heart of our being hypnotherapists. reminding us of how to do without doing, to be present with the client in ways that empower, to promote wisdom and healing through going with the resistance, and to honor that the client has the capacity to heal herself.

# 3. HYPNOTHERAPISTS: TRANSFORMING CONSCIOUSNESS as a SPIRITUAL PRACTICE

The practice of hypnotherapy is also a spiritual practice that promotes the expansion of consciousness of the practitioner as well as that of the client. A study conducted in the field of past-life therapy in 1989, using a device developed by Maxwell C. Cade called a Mind Mirror (Cade and Coxhead, 1979), exemplifies the matching of therapist and client brainwaves in a non-ordinary state induced through hypnosis while accessing past-life information. This study done by Winafred Lucas, Ph.D., and her colleagues at the Brentwood Psychological Center, used two Mind Mirror devices simultaneously, one connected to the client and one to the regression therapist. The Mind Mirror measures the brain waves of both the right and left brains of the subject simultaneously, between 1.5 and 40 hertz, and responds rapidly to changes in brain-wave frequency.

In Lucas' experiment, the three therapists who guided the regression sessions and the individually hypnotized non-meditator subjects, who had little training in non-ordinary states, showed a distinctive brain wave pattern of primarily beta and delta. These patterns are different from the patterns typical in the waking, dreaming, or meditation states. The subjects' GSRs (Galvanic Skin Response, which measures sweating and levels of anxiety,) fluctuated appropriately according to the events they related in their past lives. Lucas reported that the two subjects who meditated exhibited brain waves that were different from the other nine subjects, and that they were typical of other meditators even while in hypnosis. Also, their reports of past lives, even during traumatic events, tended to be less emotional. The GSR of these long time meditating subjects fell to a low level throughout the regression and remained there. The brain waves of the meditators remained stationary and didn't fluctuate (Freedman, p. 28, 2000).

A most interesting fact is that the brainwaves of the hypnotherapists facilitating the regression and the nine clients undergoing dramatic past-life experiences were the same beta and delta. In other words, the therapists and the clients have brain wave rapport as they enter and work in the non-ordinary state simultaneously. When in the state of hypnotic consciousness, there is a psychic and energetic rapport between the hypnotherapist and client that can be measured through brain waves.

Many hypnotherapy graduates of HCH Institute have had life-changing experiences and major shifts of perceptions and consciousness simply by guiding others in hypnotherapeutic work. Hypnotherapists working with the empowering and client-centered Taoist principles discussed in the previous chapter agree that their consciousness, in some way, joins the consciousness of their client; that their consciousnesses are united with the client's in a quantum field of thought, being, and energy. Even though these hypnotherapists and hypnotees use many of the Taoist precepts outlined in this book, they don't necessarily work overtly with the Taoist language or concepts. These Taoist principles are universal principles that can be understood from many different systems or spiritual paradigms. The Taoist concepts are intrinsically a part of the empowerment and transpersonal style of hypnotherapy.

In my experience, that same type of psychic rapport measured by Lucas in the Mind Mirror experiment commonly takes place between the client and hypnotherapist. The following condensed interviews of HCH graduates, who now practice hypnotherapy, show examples of this psychic rapport and mutual transformation.

## Reflections and Learnings

I made some wonderful, unsuspected discoveries through the process of writing and interviewing for this book. Conducting the interviews with my hypnotherapy graduates and colleagues gave me an intimate experience of knowing some of their deepest and most transformative experiences with hypnotherapy. For as much time as I have spent with these people as colleagues, there were parts of their experiences of doing this work that they had never previously shared with me. I was profoundly affected to realize just how *consistently* life-changing this work is for both the hypnotherapists and their clients. Over time, the practice of doing this work results in shifts of perceptions of reality, shifts in levels of consciousness, and more joy and ease in life.

By focusing on Taoist principles, there is a backbone of wisdom that gives us the language and conceptual framework to understand and embody, as practitioners, the spiritual aspects of hypnotherapy in a more grounded way.

We transpersonal hypnotherapists are doing spiritual work in the world with a commitment to help others transform and heal. In the future, spiritual hypnotherapy may also become known as a spiritual practice for expanding consciousness and moving its practitioners towards greater inner and outer peace. Until then, we hypnotherapists will continue to do our work with individuals and groups, knowing that the personal evolution of the individuals doing the work of transpersonal hypnotherapy is contributing, in a significant way, to the well-being of our community and to the evolution of human consciousness. I will continue to do my small part by training my students in a spiritual form of hypnotherapy that models presence, empowerment, and transformation. And I will continue to give thanks, on a daily basis, for the honor, privilege and grace of the ministry of this meaningful, spiritual work.

## Rick R., CCHT

Rick, an HCH graduate of 2003, had been a successful TV news producer and news director for many years. Later he transitioned into owning a successful catering business. Rick initially took the hypnotherapy training for personal growth. Currently, Rick has a private practice in Sedona, Arizona, working full time as a hypnotherapist, a life coach, and an energy healer. Rick explains how hypnotherapy has changed his life.

"It has been pretty profound. I have always been a pretty accepting person and not a very judgmental person, but I am even more accepting now. I can just sit with people and let them be themselves. As for my daily life, I am still an introvert and that is OK. By embracing my introversion, I am more willing to put myself out there and in that moment, I am not limited to being introverted.

I am more willing to engage other people, even groups of strangers. I feel comfortable most of the time. In the past I was very uncomfortable. I may have had a desire to teach and share things but I couldn't see myself doing it. There was nothing I hated more than standing up and speaking. Since I have taken the training and have been working with clients and teaching, getting up in front of people is the easiest and most fun part of my job.

Doing this work, my patience, ability to trust, my compassion, acceptance, and ability to love have all increased. I felt a shift during the training. I have come to a place where I embrace resistance and shift to a place of being excited when the client is resistant. This has spilled over into my life. When things aren't working the way I want, that sense of excitement begins to come in. I think, 'Whoa. This is going to be interesting.'

I am still growing. Part of the process is to recognize that you are always going to grow. My work with clients has evolved. The more confidence I have, the more I witness the healing working. The more I see it working, the more success my clients and I have.

A big piece of the puzzle shifted into place in doing hypnotherapy, and that is the subconscious mind's pull in creating our reality. It [our reality] is the creation of our subconscious beliefs. Because of my understanding, I am better able to be aware of how I have unconsciously created my reality. By doing my own self-hypnosis and working with my subconscious beliefs, I am more conscious of what used to be subconscious. My consciousness has expanded and I feel more that I consciously create my reality.

Every time I do work with clients, I open up intuitively. And in fact, often times when I am with a client, I tap into some knowing that I was not previously aware of. And sometimes it happens in teaching, too. When I teach my trance breaker group I'll do EFT (EFT is a meridian based energy therapy technique that can be used on its own very effectively or used to support the hypnotherapy process) for forty minutes and then somewhere through the process, I become more open and channel information. My spontaneous, unplanned questions invite in a wider perspective.

Doing this work as a hypnotherapist is inviting me to look at the oneness and how we are all connected. Through the reflections of that oneness [of clients] that walk in the door to my office, I see my practice as a hypnotherapist as a spiritual practice. The big piece of the puzzle is that it is the subconscious. The subconscious is a part of our experience of God or the oneness or the All That Is. Feeling it and embodying it has been the key of the understanding. I can expand out of the human experience to get a bigger spiritual perspective and then to snap back into being human. I can feel reverence, respect and understanding for the human experience without judgment. I think I have always been a healer only now I am owning it.

I learned the power of language. The words I said before and after the trance are just as important as those I say in the trance. My language is important not just in the therapy room with the client: language is important everywhere you speak in your life. And I learned to speak positively, to say what I want, not what I don't want. I learned to go for what I want, not away from what I don't want. I model and teach that it is always okay to be yourself and that you are only responsible for your own feelings. I have moved away from good and bad judgments, in general. Life and your relationship to it, can be effortless. My clients experience returning to their natural state. One of my clients says, 'Doing hypnotherapy is almost like getting rebooted.' Through hypnotherapy you can revert back to the 'original' programming. Doing this work has shifted my consciousness and awareness. And it has shifted the consciousness and awareness even more for my clients. I see that my clients become more spiritually aware. They have a wisdom inside of them that they think they didn't know. They know ... they just forgot they know."

Rick exemplifies *wu-wei* as a facilitator and he also shows how he has deepened his ability in his personal life to work with the energy of what is rather than against it. He is more consciously aware of how he can join the flow of not only his clients' processes but the flow of his own life process. He has opened to accept and appreciate himself more fully and feels that his hypnotherapy practice is teaching him to listen more deeply and to respond more authentically to the way things are.

## Julie L., MFT, CHT

Julie practices as a Marriage Family Therapist in Pleasant Hill, CA. Julie completed the HCH hypnotherapy training in the spring of 2006 and now uses hypnotherapy in her practice. Her personal, as well as professional, life continues to transform through her practice of hypnotherapy.

"Having practiced traditional psychotherapy for several years, I find that hypnotherapy gets clients the results they want faster and more easily. Using both together is extremely powerful. And I love the spiritual and creative aspects of hypnotherapy. I have a lot more fun at work when I use hypnosis.

To help the client access her higher Self, I will often facilitate a process of having the client walk toward, seek out, or call forth a visualization, especially when the client has an unanswered question or a specific need for guidance. I use the visualization as a metaphor for a quest, hopefully heroic! I distinguish the client's higher Self from the egoic self because the egoic self tends to be wrapped in defensive armor. This part is harder to get close to. Often this part doesn't like the client very much. The higher Self is always kind, accepting, and open to connection.

I've become more of my true self, more creative, braver, more playful, lighter. I am more committed to expressing love. In some ways I'm more patient. But I'm also a lot more inclined to cut through bullshit and head into the heart of things. I trust myself more as well as the universe. A good example is buying my house. It's something I've wanted for a long time. And during the course of the training, I realized I could do it and I would receive whatever help I needed.

With my clients I have a stronger sense of spiritual connection. I've always believed that therapy is loving a client into loving themselves, and this (belief) is re-confirmed on a deeper level with hypnotherapy. My view of reality has expanded. I'm more inclined to trust/enjoy/be in the unseen world more often now. And it feels very natural and normal to be there. My spirituality is more solid, which is a little oxymoronic. Being raised as an atheist, I always had a vague sense of spirituality as a kind of soup – with all of us, all of life, floating around in it. I never gave thought to reincarnation or life purpose. Now I experience the soup as a lot more like a stew. The connections between people, animals, things, events, and time are much stronger. I like the idea provided by a Kabalistic rabbi: God, being perfect love, wanted to know what it was to *become* perfect love and we are God consciousness in the act of becoming perfect love.

Through hypnotherapy, my experience of myself as a healer has broadened and validated my perceptions of healing. I've always seen myself more as a midwife – with the client doing all the hard work of birthing herself. Now, though, I see the birthing process as gentler and easier with the client's higher Self facilitating the process.

I hold the work of hypnotherapy as precious and with great honor and respect. I feel sad that so many people live in a fog of fear and lack, lashing out at each other as a result. I try to hold onto the knowledge that as bad as things are, more people are doing better than ever before in history. And maybe we really are in the process of 'becoming perfect love.' I have come to trust more in myself and in the universe. It is fun and feels good to do this work!"

Julie describes how she is more self-actualized in her professional and personal life through learning the tools of spiritual hypnotherapy and incorporating them into her practice and personal life. Her atheist background has transformed into a direct experience of the interrelatedness of all things and a more solid spiritual awareness. Her work as a psychotherapist and healer is more transpersonal through working with hypnotherapy.

## Tammy H., CCHT

Tammy is a single mom of three who grew up in an evangelical Christian community. In the community she trained to be a minister. Tammy has a special gift. She is clairvoyant. She sees and hears spirits of non-physical people, those beings who have passed on and who have not made a complete journey to the light. Before she became a hypnotherapist, she helped people release attached spirits by performing rituals she learned in her church. Her skills and approach to doing the releasement work have changed considerably since doing the training. She works full time as a hypnotherapist, massage therapist, and coach.

"In my hypnotherapy practice I introduce my clients to their higher Self early in the therapy process. I teach the client self-hypnosis and how to access a safe place, get still and quiet, and listen to the higher Self. The higher Self usually responds with a faster pace and the client is responding without judgment.

The process of doing hypnotherapy has given me the ability to flow and to be comfortable with who I am. Instead of living in the past or in my thoughts, I live more who I am now, in the present. There is no resistance and probably the most powerful (thing) is trust. *I* was the one I was learning to trust.

My judgment has turned into more discernment now. I can stay neutral. My vision is clearer and broader. When I took myself out of the judgment seat, then acceptance came too. I have learned to even love the difficult parts of life. [Love]; a little word and such a big experience. If I know I am in the middle of something difficult, then love takes me right to the other side. Love is something that is there in everything.

My experience of being with clients and people now is magical. To watch people begin to heal and transform is a feeling that I love. It has become so familiar, so much a part of my daily life. I used to be withdrawn. I didn't really understand people. Now I understand that they are OK where they are. I no longer feel compelled to try to get out of social situations. I am much more expansive and I just have fun. I know now that reality is a perception. Wherever people are, that's their reality. We create it ourselves.

Spirituality is an energy and a relationship with life, the higher Self, God, and the Light. With my Christian upbringing, I always thought that with spirituality you had to believe a certain way. You had to follow a schedule, follow a routine, follow the rules, and then you had 'spirituality.' Somehow I had separated God and spirituality. Now I know I *live* spirituality more congruently and everything is one. Hypnotherapy allowed me to open up, expand my awareness, expand my own spirituality and my own relationship with it.

Learning to access my higher Self was definitely the first step. I discovered that I am bigger than what I was thinking I am in my head. When I found that out, through the experience of my higher Self and the experience of clients' higher Selves, that was amazing!

Doing this work has allowed me to access expanded states a lot easier. I can enter into prayer and meditation without expectation of failure or success. My spirituality is more about being and feeling what is right and letting information come, rather than fighting against it. Now my experience is that the truth is more *in* me, rather than outside of me. Hypnotherapy allowed me to find that I do have a place and I do have ownership of my experience. My place is my ability to be present and to own it. It is very comfortable.

I allow the wisdom to come thorough me, instead of analyzing it. Being a healer is not a label. It is a way of being. Being a hypnotherapist is an experience, process and intimacy that I can share, in a way that is structured to empower and in a way that can support clients to embrace all these things for themselves. Allow it to come in and do its magic. That's God, that's love, with presence. I recognize that I have always been this love and presence. I just didn't know it until now.

Massage is more of a dance with the physical plane. Hypnotherapy is a spiritual dance. Of course, doing hypnotherapy has affected my body work. I allow myself to know intuitively when I pick up information or I am directed to use a certain stroke or technique. Rather than just following the structure of a massage that I was trained to follow, I follow whatever is there and be with it. I show up and I get out of the way. Now, I am present. It comes through the presence, not through the structure. I recognize that the clients are healers themselves. I can help them find that healing. I love it when the inner light goes on and they figure out that it is they who are the healers, not me or anything I did.

I am very honored to be a hypnotherapist. I always wanted to be a hero, do something heroic: to be a doctor, or a fireman. That never worked out. Now I am a hero: to myself, to my family, and to my clients.

Spirit has taught me to get out of the way and relax. I found out that it is all about that relationship to Spirit. It is all about that we are complete already. We just have to allow it to be seen and to show up. When I stopped fighting that, I let Spirit show me the way. Spirit taught me to get out of the way. And there is always more to learn, new experiences, new lights inside, new directions. Hypnotherapy is an experience. It is presence. It is a relationship with God, the universe, the earth, and with each other. It is an honor to be a hypnotherapist and I want to bring more honor and understanding to this work."

Tammy has wholly embodied the Taoist precept of returning to the state of "uncarved wood." Tammy had to disengage from years of dogmatic religious training in order to return to herself and to trust herself. Because she is naturally very intuitive, when she allows herself to "empty herself of everything," and to "Let the mind rest at peace …" (English, 16), her psychic abilities flourish. I have worked with Tammy twice on paranormal cases where there have been psychokinetic manifestations and both times Tammy has successfully returned to "uncarved wood" by emptying herself of her projections and mind chatter. In this empty state, she did intuitive readings and had accurate psychic perceptions that totally supported the investigations and the healings for those people in the cases, who experienced the paranormal occurrences.

## Julie S., CCHT

Julie took the hypnotherapy training at HCH in the summer of 2000. The following year she began facilitating sessions in the low-fee community clinic while attending the six-month internship program.

"What I liked about hypnotherapy is that you can have an impact on people's lives pretty quickly. I actually began to have a sense in the internship that I could be really good at hypnotherapy by just going into the session and being spontaneous. And being spontaneous was not something that was very easy for me. What started happening was that I realized what spiritual work this is and that was the extra piece that I hadn't had in my corporate jobs.

I recognized the spiritual part (of hypnotherapy) through the transpersonal model that we follow here at HCH. There were certainly experiences that were beyond the individual. There could be glimpses of God for one person and for somebody else there could be a connection with angels or guides. For someone else it might be an overwhelmingly powerful presence, energy, or a connection to nature.

I still remember one exceptionally profound session I had with a young client in the internship. He was a thirteen-year-old boy. His mother brought him for hypnotherapy because he was getting into fights at school. He was a good kid, but he was picking on people. He had this tough-kid bravado. I knew from the intake form that they were not a religious family and he had never done hypnosis before.

In the session he was open-eyed the whole time and he started seeing someone that I could not see in the room. His whole face showed it and then, of course, his voice. First, he saw his dead grandparents. It was very touching to me and it was very touching to him. They were telling him that he is a good boy and that they are looking after him. And this is something this kid needed to hear.

Then, his whole face lit up and he basically said that he saw Jesus. This was not a kid who had a reference point to Jesus. This was a tough kid. He was crying. Tears were streaking down his face. Tears were streaking down my face. He had the biggest smile on his face. He said, 'It's Jesus and Jesus loves me.' It doesn't matter if it was something in his mind or whether Jesus was in the room, which I realize was entirely possible. This experience was beyond my normal acceptance of how things work, so profound, so real. I saw the effect it had on him and I felt the effect it had on me. I was so touched by it and obviously he was. That was something very real. I have had many experiences like this one over the years.

I sometimes have a problem with the terminology, (the 'higher Self.') I often call it 'your wise best self' or 'that part of you that connects with God.' I tell the client when I am doing my orientation, 'There is a part of you that knows what is best for you that is going to guide you through this (process) and that part is going to be activated. That is why you are safe. That is why you are in control.' That wise part is always there. You can just access it more easily in hypnosis.

Doing this work has affected me quite a bit. Knowing that I can do these (healing) things makes me feel more empowered and confident in my life. And, I am definitely more spontaneous. Becoming more spontaneous was a big thing for me. The new spontaneity is in the sessions but there are ways that it carries out into my life, as well. I have more compassion having worked with my clients. I just have to open myself and let it come out. And get out of my own way. And what a blessing when this happens for me and the client. I think that the presence I feel in session is the window. Something happens when I close the (therapy room) door and I am with a client. I go into a different state. It is my best me. I think, 'Wow, that was the exactly the best thing to say at the right time!'

I am finally starting to access my higher Self in my daily life. It is from doing this work and it is from doing my own work. I do have more faith in myself. The miracle that happened in my life is that I actually really do like and love myself now...way more than before I started doing this work. And I will say something else that I very much believe: that whatever is going on with me in my life, the clients that show up have the same issues. My life played out the whole law of attraction. Someone inevitably comes in with a presenting issue that I think has nothing to do with me. Then, in the session they will say something from their higher wisdom or from their guidance that is totally and directly applicable to me. It is almost exactly what I need to hear. I always feel like there is this weird way that I'm there to help the clients; but they are also there to help me. I actually need to listen in the sessions to what they are saying because I don't listen to myself. But when I am in session, I am so completely aware of what is being said that I am listening on another other level and I am taking in the information....it's very helpful. Doing hypnotherapy is like my spiritual meditation practice!

I feel hypnotherapy is the most beautiful, drug-free, natural tool that people could have if they just let themselves but many have all this fear. I want to tell people about it because it changed my life and changed many, many of my clients' lives."

### Rosetta B., CCHT

Raised bicultural with an Italian mother and an American father, Rosetta came to live in the US at sixteen. She married and had four children in her young adulthood. Her life was dramatically affected by the death of a newborn son. The shock of this experience propelled her into the field of child birth education and birth coaching.

Rosetta came to HCH for training primarily because of her interest in past-life therapy. She took a weekend workshop with Brian Weiss and she was hooked on the transformational and healing power of regression therapy. Becoming a hypnotherapist has given Rosetta a connection to others and herself that she never experienced before.

"Being a facilitator and witness to my clients' transformation and healing has changed me. I now understand that in this life I am fulfilling an ancient story of who I am and where I am going next. The story, in the end, is the journey of the progression of my soul. Every client that I work with, and every connection that I make, then becomes a part of my *current*-life story."

For Rosetta, this is the biggest lesson she has learned through doing this work: To deeply and completely love and *accept* self.

"Acceptance of the issues that my clients are confronted with, and acceptance of my own life events and current situations is the goal that I strive for every day. If I don't accept, then I can't really do anything to support change. For me acceptance means making peace with what is and (with) the soul agreements and the lessons at hand.

I have also grown to experience a general level of understanding and acceptance of people that I did not have before. I try to see through people's appearance: their bodies, their (style of) clothes, even their words, and the persona they present in the world. I realize that nothing is really as it seems on the surface. I now know that there are vast and complicated layers to us humans and after peeling off some of the layers, the need to be accepted and loved is always there. I try to smile, and say something kind when I'm interacting with others out there in the world. You just never know what someone is dealing with under the layers."

Rosetta shares her struggles as a new hypnotherapist and what she has learned about the work and herself.

"My client sessions have evolved over the year that I have been in practice. At first it was very intimidating to be so present with another person. The state of this level of presence for me was new. In the hypnotic trance my clients' vulnerabilities and their deep-felt emotions come bubbling up to the surface. At first, being with people in this vulnerable and sometimes fragile state, I lacked confidence in my ability to 'guide' my clients through the processes necessary to get to the healing. I worried that I did not have the proper skills and that I lacked education in psychology. I worried about an issue coming up that I had no idea how to handle. As I became more skilled in the ability to set my own fears aside during a session, my intuition began to open up. As I cultivated an ability to get out of the way and let the process unfold as it may, I began to 'flow' with my clients in trance as a curious observer asking questions that seemed they needed to be answered. I learned that my clients knew what they needed. I began to trust that their process would unfold and that it was not dependent on my having to know the answers for them."

**Jane H., CCHT**

Jane had been a successful film and video producer for forty-two years. In 2012 after inner guidance nudged her forward into a new career, Jane became a hypnotherapist. She was attracted to the connection with people and the ability to share in the healing and inspiration of the work.

"I have actually had the experience of a cliché' – 'It's never too late to learn.' I started the hypnotherapy training when I was 65 and a whole new world opened to me. My coming to this work was because of a request that I made of my Spirit Guides two years previously to lead me to a new path. Now I have re-remembered that I should always ask when I need something and I encourage my clients, friends, and family to do the same.

I must admit that I was spiritually involved in my Catholic faith at a young age. However, the inflexible dictates of the church led me to leave. But I missed the immersion in a spiritual life. My joy in this work is the access I have to spiritual dimensions that I experience in myself and in others, even when they don't realize it. There are times when I am more spiritually aware than other (times) but all I have to do is be still and I feel the connection.

My belief that we continue to exist in another realm after death has gotten much stronger since I started my hypnotherapy training. But what I can't understand is why belief in the afterlife is not more universal when there is so much evidence recorded now, such as near death experiences, out of body experiences, remote viewing, etc. Science is becoming much more involved in examining these phenomena and I am very interested in how they (scientists) view and explain it.

I have loved Buddhism for years and feel quite at home attending meditation community events. I am also very moved by rituals of almost any kind. They reach out to us at a most basic, yet profound, level. But my hypnotherapy practice is grounded in a spirituality in which the work opens up to the world of Spirit where we can commune with the soul of our clients, lost spirits, and the spirits of the departed.

(In the past year) my world has opened up to miracles, a deeper spirituality which I feel every day, and an understanding about the continuation of consciousness.

My compassion has expanded to take in everyone, even those who have harmed me. Making compassion a practice is very freeing in that I don't have to hang on to resentment and negativity. Even when I feel that I am being too critical or judgmental (I'm a type one on the Enneagram), there is a part of me that kicks in to soften my edges. I no longer have to even try to lessen it, it just happens now. I notice this and feel grateful … it's a gift.

I am much more loving. Instead of judging and seeing faults, I see and feel their needs and hurts much more. We are all so vulnerable underneath the armor. I feel privileged when clients open up and trust in me and the process.

(The higher Self is) the place of wisdom, the inner knowing about the right thing to do, the enlightened path to take. There are many qualities that point out the difference between the voice of ego and the voice of Spirit, but I would stress that the higher Self informs us to choose what is for the highest good of all at a soul level while the egoic self is more about selfish interests and comes from an authoritative, controlling place.

The truth is that they (the clients) are doing the healing. My job is to accompany them on their journey of discovery and gently suggest possibilities. Often they will choose a totally different path than I think they should and it can be amazing. Sometimes I get to witness their opening to insights. This might be the greatest joy I get from this work."

**Summary of Interviews**

The stories of these six hypnotherapists are fairly typical of the transformation that occurs for the hypnotherapist when working with a transpersonal empowerment model. For each one, there is an expanded sense of self, a sense that their work is spiritual and transformational by nature for both their clients and themselves, and that they are making a significant difference in the lives of their clients. Because their individual clients are growing and shifting their consciousness, they are making a difference in the collective consciousness. It is evident that, though they may not directly name the Taoist concepts, each is guided by Taoist precepts and spiritual concepts in the style of their work.

## The Transformational and Spiritual Benefits of Going with the Flow and Working with, Rather than Against, Resistance:

Rick R.: "I have come to a place where I embrace resistance and shift to a place of being excited when the client is resistant."

Julie L.: "The higher Self is always kind, accepting, and open to connection."

Tammy H.: "The process of doing hypnotherapy has given me the ability to flow and to be comfortable with who I am. There is no resistance. I show up and get out of the way."

Julie S.: "I actually began to have a sense in the internship that I could be really good at hypnotherapy by just going into the session and being spontaneous. I just have to open myself and let it come out and get out of my own way."

Rosetta B.: "As I cultivated an ability to get out of the way and let the process unfold as it may, I began to 'flow' with my clients in trance as a curious observer asking questions that seemed they needed to be answered. I learned that my clients knew what they needed. I began to trust that their process would unfold and that it was not dependent on my having to know the answers for them."

Jane H.: "The truth is that they are doing the self-healing. My job is to accompany them on their journey of discovery and gently suggest possibilities. Sometimes I get to witness their opening to insights. This might be the greatest joy I get from this work."

## Being Part of a Bigger Energetic Unified Field, Profound States of Knowing and Connecting with the Divine:

Rick R.: "Doing this work as a hypnotherapist is inviting me to look at the oneness and how we are all connected."

Julie L.: "With my clients I have a stronger sense of spiritual connection. The connections between people, animals, things, events, and time are much stronger."

Tammy H.: "Spirituality is an energy and a relationship with life, the higher Self, God, and the Light."

Julie S.: "What started happening was that I realized what spiritual work this is and that was the extra piece that I hadn't had in my corporate jobs."

Rosetta B.: "I now understand that in this life I am fulfilling an ancient story of who I am and where I am going next. The story is the journey of the progression of my soul."

Jane H.: "My world has opened up to miracles, a deeper spirituality, which I feel every day, and an understanding about the continuation of consciousness."

## Expanding our Compassion and our Ability to Love
### Accepting Ourselves and Others as We Are:

Rick R.: "Doing this work, my patience, ability to trust, my compassion, acceptance, and ability to love have all increased."

Julie L.: "Therapy is loving a client into loving themselves and this (belief) is reconfirmed on a deeper level with hypnotherapy."

Tammy H.: "I recognize that I have always been this love and presence. I just didn't know it until now."

Julie S.: "I have more compassion having worked with my clients (and) I actually really do like and love myself now."

Rosetta B.: "For me acceptance means making peace with what is and (with) the soul agreements and the lessons at hand."

Jane H.: "My compassion has expanded to take in everyone, even those who have harmed me. Making compassion a practice is very freeing in that I don't have to hang on to resentment and negativity."

# Part Two

# Spiritual Hypnotherapy Scripts

# Introduction to Using these Scripts

*T*hese hypnotherapy scripts are a resource for all hypnotherapists who want empowering, client-centered processes that have proven to be effective with clients. The series of hypnotherapy scripts are categorized by hypnosis for Body, Mind, and Spirit. In addition, these scripts include how to teach your clients Emotional Freedom Technique (EFT) so that they can effectively use it in and outside of sessions as a support for any presenting issue.

These processes have evolved through working with clients and students at HCH Institute for Hypnotherapy and Psychospiritual Trainings since the 1980s. The techniques are an eclectic blend of Neuro-Linguistic Programming, hypnotic metaphors and stories, and mildly directive and open-ended approaches to hypnosis. Most of the scripts include an interactive therapeutic component that supports insight, expanded self-awareness, and change. Throughout all the processes, however, there is always a transpersonal dimension. These processes not only work with the hypnotee's conscious and subconscious, but also engage the client's infinite, wise, and boundless aspect of higher Self as the co-facilitator or inner therapist. Invoking this wise and healing aspect of Self supports the client in directly accessing the source of healing while in trance.

The introductions to these scripts are written to the client to educate him or her about the hypnotic technique that follows. If you find the content in the introductions helpful to orient your client to the process, you may read the introductions, or use the information and present it to the client in your own words.

Several of the scripts are intended for use at bedtime to support sleep or to induce somnambulistic states of trance. You may use any of the sleep scripts in session as a skill rehearsal to prepare your client to use it as a self-hypnosis processes when in bed.

These scripts are written in second person, and speak directly to the client or hypnotee. If they are used for self-hypnosis, the pronoun should, of course, be changed to the first person. Most of these scripts are hypnotherapy scripts, not hypnosis scripts. This distinction means that they are evocative and interactive. The hypnotherapist will need to allow *long* pauses between suggestions and questions throughout the processes and it is suggested that the hypnotherapist ask the client to report or describe his or her experience during the process. The scripts are therapeutic in that they are empowering and open-ended in format so that the client has the opportunity to have a genuine internally-evoked response that the hypnotherapist can support by pacing and leading the client through her or his inner territory. It is imperative that the hypnotherapist keeps the interactive work open-ended so that the client is not being led into specific responses. *Open-ended* questions, modeled throughout the scripts are the: who, what, why, when, and where questions; not the questions that only require a yes or no response. Open-ended statements avoid leading the client into *specific* representational (visual, auditory, and kinesthetic modalities) systems. Examples of open-ended questions or statements are: What are you aware of? What are you experiencing now? What is going on? Describe what is happening. Share what you are experiencing, etc.

Spiritual Hypnotherapy Scripts for Body, Mind, and Spirit

Notice that the questions ask the client to describe what he is aware of or experiencing rather than assuming that the client is seeing, hearing, smelling, or feeling. Once the client's dominate representational system is identified, the hypnotherapist can pace and lead the client through specific sense modalities.

The hypnotherapist can expect that, at times, the client will have experiences that move away from the script. For example, working with lowering the pain threshold may move the client into a memory of a childhood trauma related to his pain. The hypnotherapist will often have to rely on his or her therapeutic skills to navigate and facilitate the client when an unexpected turn takes place in session. You may always call upon the client's higher Self as the co-therapist and ask the higher Self, "What do you need now?" Following the client's inner direction is always the most empowering and healing response. And once your client knows EFT, you can always have the client tap either in or out of trance, while focusing on any distress that may come from doing provocative, interactive work. Hypnotherapy and EFT work beautifully together. Hypnotherapy brings resources to consciousness to identify which issues need healing or transformation. Then EFT supports the release of energy patterns that are blocking healing and wholeness.

These scripts may be used freely with clients in sessions; however they are copyrighted and are not public domain for recording your own hypnosis CDs to sell or give to clients. All of these hypnotherapy scripts have been professionally recorded with music and ambient sounds and are available as CDs or digital downloads.

The following basic pointers, directed to your client and geared towards past-life, interlife, and future-life sessions, will contribute to achieving success early in the process:

Do not lie down, but sit up while doing the regression. You will stay more alert and be able to interact in the process if you do not go to sleep or become too deeply absorbed into the hypnotic state since the information is usually accessed right beneath the surface of your waking consciousness in an active and engaging state of trance. Depending upon the particular session, if more than one aspect of your past life, interlife, or future life comes to awareness simultaneously, simply choose one on which to focus. You can always explore other aspects of these lives at a later time.

It is a common mistake for people to anticipate that they have to *see* or visualize in hypnosis. Many people report that they do not see anything in a regression. They, instead, know, think, feel, or hear the details of that particular life. All your five inner senses and your intuitive knowing are channels through which you experience these lives. Go with your own natural method of perception. Trust the process and whichever events evolve, even if you feel you are making it up because the content is still coming from within you, that is, from your imagination, which is a reflection of who you are. Your metaphors and archetypes are relevant to your unconscious experience of Self. Give yourself permission to go with whatever comes to you whether or not it makes sense to you at the time. Let go of trying to control or figure it out and allow the process to evolve. If, at some point, you feel stuck and nothing is happening for you, bring forth something from your imagination. You will soon experience that the process becomes more spontaneous and feels more authentic. Know that doing a regression is a skill. The more often you explore past lives, the interlife, and future lives, the easier and more productive your regressions will become.

The following processes are structured based on an understanding of the regression phases that have emerged from thousands of sessions facilitated by myself, other regression therapists, and researchers. Your experience may or may not follow this map. Trust your own experience and intuition and go with what comes to you from your own inner knowing.

These processes, as with any interactive hypnotherapy, may bring up emotions and body sensations for healing. While you can bring yourself out of the process anytime you wish, it is usually a good idea to go through the experience in order to allow an energy release to occur. Try to stay with your experiences to move through and beyond them. You can always use a self-guided experience of dissociating from the body or event by becoming an observer rather than a participant of the events. Simply imagine walking out of the body and floating above the scene to watch the events, in a detached way, as if watching a movie. You may walk back into the body at any point in the process, if you wish. Remember, that whatever may happen in the future, there is no death of consciousness, only a changing of form.

One caution is warranted with any self-guided hypnotic process. It is not recommended that people with mental disorders who are in an unstable mental and emotional state engage in self-guided processes. Rather, they should seek the skill, containment, and support of a trained regression therapist who will guide the process in an individual way, addressing each client's unique needs. Only use this regression process if you are mentally and emotionally stable and functioning in your daily life. As with all provocative hypnotherapy processes, this therapy is not appropriate for people in decompensated, unbalanced, or psychotic states.

## About the Hypnotic Inductions used in these Scripts

The following interactive hypnotherapy processes include several basic induction techniques that I commonly use with my clients. They are:

Eye Fixation Induction with Counting into Hypnosis,
Eyes Closed Induction
Systematic Body Relaxation Induction
Accessing Representational Systems Induction
Space Awareness Induction
Journey to a Safe Place, a Preferred Place, or a Sanctuary Induction

Color Breathing Induction
Activating an Anchor to go into Hypnosis
Body Sensation Induction
White Light Energy Induction
Garden/Aroma Therapy Induction
Body Dissociation Induction

If you have induction techniques that you and your clients prefer, use them along with your own deepening techniques, then pick up the script where the hypnotherapeutic process begins.

## Using EFT(Emotional Freedom Technique) along with Hypnotherapy

At HCH we commonly use EFT and hypnotherapy together and I will usually teach EFT to new clients in the first session for the following benefits:

Usually EFT will work quickly and a new client will have instant relief as well as a tool to use at home for self-help.

If, during a hypnotherapy session there isn't enough time to be complete with the work, EFT will usually smooth out any residual emotions or sensations so that the client can leave the session feeling grounded and complete for that session.

With EFT a client can continue the work at home to reinforce or complete the integration of the hypnosis session.

If a client goes into a difficult memory or emotional state in hypnotherapy, EFT can be used while in trance to clear the trauma and emotional charge and to move through the release in a very supportive, gentle way.

Clients usually tap on themselves. However, in trance, with permission, and if a client is familiar with the EFT tapping points, the hypnotherapist can tap on the client.

# 4. HYPNOTHERAPY for the BODY

## SELF-HYPNOSIS

### Introduction to Self-Hypnosis

*H*ypnosis has been tainted and misunderstood for years. All one has to do is look at the use of hypnosis in Hollywood movies or see a stage hypnotist at a county fair perform, and most of us will avoid being hypnotized. No one wants to be embarrassed because of clucking like a chicken, or lose control and say or do something we wouldn't normally allow.

The truth is that hypnosis is not what most people have been "hypnotized" into believing. So, sit comfortably, take a deep breath, and prepare to have a more accurate understanding of hypnosis.
You experience the hypnotic state many times during the day. Have you driven while daydreaming and forgotten that you crossed a familiar bridge or gone through a tunnel and not been consciously aware of it? If so, you have spontaneously experienced the inwardly focused state of consciousness called hypnosis.

Hypnosis is natural. It is a state of consciousness between waking and sleeping. You may have had the experience of drifting off to sleep and having someone come into the room to ask you a question. Since you are not asleep yet, you can still respond coherently from a relaxed, inwardly focused state. So, if you can go to sleep, you can be hypnotized. The question is: Do you want to allow yourself to be hypnotized?

All hypnosis is self-hypnosis. Contrary to what most people believe, hypnosis involves the use of your free will. You choose to respond to the suggestions given in hypnosis. The "inner hypnotist" is the part of you that says to yourself, "I can and will allow myself to let go and relax." Because your own free will is engaged, you will only respond when you want to respond. Being able to be hypnotized is not the same as being gullible. As a matter of fact, being able to be hypnotized points to a higher-than-normal creative ability and the capability to be the "captain of your own ship," that is, captain of your body, mind, and emotions. When you are in hypnosis you are behind the wheel, driving your own life in more control than in normal waking consciousness. This control emanates from a more expanded and integrated state of awareness.

Hypnosis is a skill. Just as some of us were naturals in grade school when we first swung a baseball bat, some of us are naturals at allowing ourselves to access the state of consciousness that is hypnosis. And similar to hitting baseballs, we can all be coached and taught to go into a hypnotic state.

In a hypnotic state you are more resourceful and creative because you have access to more dimensions and levels of consciousness. You experience yourself as more than your normal waking thoughts, beliefs, and feelings. You are expanded to include access of your subconscious and your higher consciousness. In hypnosis you can access long-forgotten memories, control pain, promote self-healing, and become more intuitive. In

*Spiritual Hypnotherapy Scripts for Body, Mind, and Spirit*

39

hypnosis you are also more highly suggestible to positive suggestions to promote change. By accessing this state, you have an expanded sense of Self, which carries into your conscious daily life.

You remember what you experience when in a hypnotic state. You may experience hypnosis through all of your inner senses by seeing with your inner eyes, hearing with your inner ears, and/or feeling emotions and body sensations. In most hypnotic states you are very relaxed and you return to wakeful consciousness feeling refreshed and renewed. After a hypnosis session you are very likely to continue to think about what you experienced or feel the positive effects of the work you have done as you integrate your new levels of insight and self-discoveries into your conscious self. The positive effects will most often become a part of your conscious awareness and your daily life. The more you access this state, the more positive effects you will have. This accumulative effect is what many of my hypnotherapy students and clients commonly claim.

People have different ways of experiencing the trance state through their inner senses. Many people are primarily kinesthetic in a hypnotic state. These people feel physically and emotionally and often describe having a knowing rather than seeing images. Others experience inner sounds or thoughts in their heads that may come though inner voices or even as impressions or memories of sounds. Some primarily see images, colors, textures, and movements. As you learn how to hypnotize yourself, pay attention to what inner senses are alive for you while in a hypnotic state. Most likely you will have one primary way of perceiving through your inner senses. You may be visual, kinesthetic, auditory, or experience the trance state through a combination of inner senses.

The use of language and the skill of making hypnotic suggestions is crucial in using hypnosis. Here are some basic guidelines and suggestions for writing your own scripts.

- Use the present tense. The subconscious does not register time as does the conscious mind. For the subconscious, there is only the now. Therefore, speak directly to the present moment.

- Make only positive suggestions. State what you want, not what you don't want. For example, if you are doing self-hypnosis for diminishing pain, make a suggestion like, "I feel more and more comfort" instead of, "I do not feel pain."

- Keep the suggestions simple, clear, and direct.

- Include emotion and a positive state of being to your suggestions. For instance, "I enjoy exercising every day."

The script on the following page will guide you through a basic approach for self hypnosis.

To prepare for your hypnotic experience write out three simple, clear, and positive suggestions in the present tense that will support you in relaxing and releasing stress. Some possible suggestions could be similar to these:

"My body relaxes easily and naturally."

"My body is more and more comfortable as I go deeper into trance."

"I enjoy the growing warmth and relaxation in my body."

"Relaxation flows effortlessly from the top of my head and out through the bottom of my feet."

## Self-Hypnosis Script

For learning and practicing self hypnosis find a private place where you can sit comfortably. Make sure that your back and neck are supported and that you sit in an open posture with your legs and arms uncrossed. Before you begin, review the goal for doing this self-hypnosis session and the positive suggestions you have prepared.

When you are ready, focus your eyes on a stationary point in the room across from you. Take a deep breath. Count slowly from one to five. Close your eyes on the count of five or when you are ready.

When your eyes are closed, imagine a color that is comforting and relaxing for you and breathe in this color. Allow the color to move to any areas of your body that you would like to relax more and more. You breathe in the color and you breathe out any tension, discomfort, or stress.

Now imagine a yardstick that is thirty-six inches long. The zero end of the yardstick represents your wide-awake conscious state and the other end at thirty-six represents a deep state of hypnosis. Using the yardstick as a metaphor for your depth and relaxation, a number comes to mind that represents your present depth. If you would like to go deeper, allow each breath to support your softening and letting go. The numbers increase as your depth increases. While you imagine going deeper, the numbers increase. Continue the deepening by imagining that the yardstick becomes a path in nature. You walk along the path. Awaken all of your senses as you explore your surroundings. Feel the sensation of your feet as you walk. Hear your footsteps and notice the sounds around you. Notice the colors and textures of the foliage, trees, flowers, and the sky. Notice the temperature of the air and the sensation of relaxing more and more with each step. Smell the fresh air and the fragrances of the plants and trees that surround you. With each step you feel more and more relaxed. What number comes to mind now?

When you are at a level where you feel receptive and relaxed (usually anywhere between a six to a twelve on the yardstick is deep enough), state the positive suggestions you have written. State them slowly and clearly, and repeat the sequence of suggestions several times. Allow time between each suggestion for their meanings to be absorbed.

When you are finished saying the suggestions, you may either dehypnotize and return to wakeful consciousness or move into another hypnotherapeutic process such as skill rehearsal, pain management, inner-child work, or whatever your focus is for the session. The scripts in this book will teach you how to work with a large variety of focuses for your session. When you are ready to move out of trance, simply count yourself out slowly from five to one. Allow your eyes to open at the count of one.

# HYPNOSIS for STRESS MANAGEMENT

## Introduction to A Hypnotic Vacation

Often taking a vacation can create the time, space, and stimulus to break the stress-filled trance in which we live much of our life.

You may recall that after taking a relaxing vacation, you return to your daily life feeling recharged and renewed. This next hypnosis process will provide you with a virtual vacation that will support you to live more fully in the moment, returning to your authentic self. The effects of this inner change of scene and routine will support your being more relaxed and present when you return to your daily life. You may choose any location for this virtual vacation. Each time you use this hypnosis, you can travel to a different place and have a unique experience. The suggestions are open-ended and will allow you time and space to bring your own creativity and needs into the hypnotic experience.

After using this process several times, with your growing self-hypnosis skills, you can eventually take a virtual vacation on your own anytime, anywhere, without the use of this script. Before going into hypnosis and taking a virtual vacation, have a travel destination in mind or perhaps you will have a surprise vacation to a place yet unknown to you.

## A Hypnotic Vacation

Sit comfortably, adjust your body, and rest your open eyes on a focal point. In synchronization with your out-breaths, count from one to five slowly, and then allow your eyes to close naturally.

Take some time to deepen. Breathing in soothing colors, along with saying your own positive suggestions for deepening, helps you to relax and let go. You naturally and easily move deeper and deeper. You are open and receptive to renewal and balance. You are open and receptive to relaxation and well-being. You are taking a well-deserved vacation and getting a break from your daily activities and concerns. With the planning and traveling behind, you have arrived and settled into your accommodations. Are you traveling alone or has someone accompanied you on this special get-away? Where have you traveled? What do you most want to experience while you are here?

You feel serene and comfortable in this special place where you are free to be and do exactly as you choose. You have a whole day of relaxation and discovery ahead of you. You arrive at the location where you will be spending your day. All your needs are met. How have you dressed and what have you brought with you for the day? What are your surroundings? Take time to be still and take it all in. Notice with all your senses what is around you. Breathe in the air and the smells. Look at the colors. Notice the spatial orientation of the natural and manmade attributes of this place. Notice the lighting, feel the temperature, textures, and the energy of this place. How do you feel being here, right now? If someone is vacationing with you, you may choose to share the initial exploration of this special place or enjoy exploring it on your own.

How will you spend your time today? Will you hike and explore? Would you prefer to find a shady space to read, picnic or rest? Or do you prefer to lounge in the sun? Is there water for swimming? Perhaps you will simply doze and catch up on needed sleep. Do you prefer to be in solitude and quiet or do you share the experience with others? Allow yourself the freedom to be where you want to be and do exactly what you most want today. Step into the scene so that you can feel yourself experiencing this place and this day. Your body takes a vacation. Your breathing is relaxed and easy. Your muscles feel loose and comfortable. You feel a state of well-being in this place.

Your mind is on vacation. It is open, free, and clear. You are present in this moment, fully engaged and enjoying this place, even if you are simply being, and not doing. You are unaware of time. You only know this moment. Everything else is put aside for now. You are present and relaxed and free. You are in this moment, here and now. Feel what it is like to be totally engaged in the now and present with what is within you and around you. You notice with exquisite detail your surroundings and your physical, mental and emotional state of being. You are aware and enlivened. This moment is all there is. Spending the day in this special state is so renewing and acknowledging of what is important in your life: your awareness and your sense of higher Self. This self-awareness is what you bring back from this virtual vacation.

You create an anchor for this self-awareness and presence. The anchor is the phrase, "Right here, right now." Whenever you want to reconnect with this state of being you say to yourself, "right here, right now." The memory of this hypnotic vacation, and the experience of being present in the now, comes back to you. Being in the now supports you in whatever you do during your daily activities of your work and personal life.

Whenever you need to deepen your connection to your higher Self, you are free to take another virtual vacation to another destination. And through connecting with the expanded awareness that comes from taking a break from the trance of your daily patterns and responsibilities, you are able to connect with your greater Self and align with the knowledge that you are able to live from a state of being present in the now. In this state all pressure, tension, and compulsivity to do are washed away and replaced with clear knowing and awareness of BEING and Doing while you are present in the now.

When it is time to return from your inner vacation, you bring back a renewed sense of self and a clear, focused awareness connected to being present in the now. This inner state changes your relationship with everything in your outer life to that of being present in the flow and acceptance of what is right here, right now. Open your eyes when you are ready to come back, feeling at home with yourself.

## Hypnotic Anchoring for Being Calm and Relaxed

This anchoring technique will teach you how to create and reactivate a post-hypnotic cue to help you to be calm and relaxed whenever you are beginning to feel anxious or fearful. Learn this technique and then practice accessing it on your own. The more you practice it, the more deeply learned and readily accessible this state of being calm and relaxed becomes.

For this anchoring, take your right pointer finger and touch the back of your left hand on your pointer finger knuckle. Practice this now. This spot on your left hand will be your anchor for calm and relaxed. Once you have practiced touching your knuckle, place your hands at your side.

Close your eyes. Take a deep breath that announces to your body/mind that you are ready to focus within and let go of the activities and involvement of the day. You are ready to be in this moment. Each breath supports your being present here and now.

Take a moment to think about a time in your life when you experienced the most ideal and wonderful state of being calm and relaxed. Allow yourself to recall the experience and go into the environment of this memory. Step into your body in this memory. Look out of your eyes and see the surroundings. Where are you? What do you see around you? What do you hear in this environment? Are you alone or with others? What time of day or evening is it?

Are you sitting, standing, or lying down? Are you moving or still? What are you wearing? Feel the temperature of the air on your skin and face. Notice your body and the sensations you feel. What does being calm and relaxed feel like? Notice your breathing, What do you smell? Feel the relaxation in your muscles, the comfort in your body. Fill in all the details of this memory so that you experience it fully in this moment, here and now. This memory is very much a part of you. You can access it whenever you want.

As you experience this memory of being calm and relaxed, reach over and touch the left hand pointer finger knuckle just as you practiced it a few minutes ago. Touch it in the same location and with the same pressure. What is the essence. strongest, or best part of this being calm and relaxed? Enjoy this for a moment. You remember this best part of being calm and relaxed and recall it when you next touch your anchor.

Take your finger off your anchor and open your eyes.

Allow your attention to move towards something else in the room as a short distraction that will break the mini-trance you just experienced. Now, test the anchor. While touching your anchor in the way you practiced, close your eyes and go back to your memory of being calm and relaxed. Think about the best part of your experience as you fill in all the details of this calm and relaxed state. Allow all of your senses to come alive. Be in your body and feel the sensations of calm and relaxed, see the sights, hear the sounds, and smell the fragrances. You are calm and relaxed. When you are satisfied that you have accessed the calm and relaxed state, take your finger off the anchor and open your eyes.

From now on, any time you want to feel calm and relaxed, wherever you are, if you are safe to do so, touch your knuckle and close your eyes. Think about the best part of your memory and go back to the calm and relaxed state. Every time you use this anchor the positive effects are more readily available. Practicing using the anchor when you are not feeling anxiety will continue to support your body and mind's learning and remembering of how to be calm and relaxed. It is most effective to use the anchor when you first begin to feel anxiety or fear. The more you use it, the more effective it will become.

# HYPNOSIS for STOPPING SMOKING

## Pre-session Interview for Stopping Smoking

Before teaching EFT or doing the hypnosis processes, ask your client the following questions about his or her smoking behaviors.

- How long have you smoked?

- Why did you begin smoking?

- On the average how many cigarettes have you been smoking in a day?

- How do you feel about the smell of cigarettes?

- How do you feel about the smell of smoke?

- How do you feel about the smell of nicotine on your hands?

- How do you feel about the taste of cigarettes?

- How do you feel about the act of lighting a cigarette?

- What is your experience of holding a cigarette?

- What is your experience of hot air and smoke on the back of your throat and in your lungs?

- How do you feel about the sensation of inhaling smoke?

- How do you feel about needing or wanting to take a break to smoke?

- How do you feel about smoking as a way to deal with negative emotions or stress?

- Have you quit smoking before? If so, what worked for you? What was difficult for you?

- What were the events, thoughts, or feelings that were triggers for starting up again?

- How long have you gone without smoking in the past?

- How long would you need to not smoke now to consider yourself a non-smoker?

- On the average how many hours do you currently go without smoking between the time of the last cigarette in the evening and the first cigarette of the next day? (Know that your body knows how to go without smoking during these hours.)

- Why do you want to stop smoking?

- Who wants you to stop? Why do you want to stop now?

The answers to these questions will be helpful to you in the hypnosis process of reframing.

## Education and Pre-talk for Reframing for Stop Smoking

This reframing hypnotherapy process for stopping smoking will help you uncover and address the needs behind your smoking. Once the needs are known, you will access a wise and creative inner resource to find a more life-affirming way to meet those needs. You will hypnotically practice doing the new behaviors and receive many positive reinforcing suggestions to be smoke-free. You will discover at the end of this hypnosis process what percent of you is ready and willing to be a non-smoker. If your are less than one hundred percent ready to breath air, you still have other needs that must be addressed. You will discover what is between you and being one hundred percent smoke-free and continue to work on transforming yourself.

The needs may be, for instance, fear of failure or a feeling of rebelliousness. After ending this hypnosis session, you can use EFT to tap on whatever is between you and your being one hundred percent smoke free. For instance, "Even though I am afraid to quit because I might fail, I deeply and completely accept myself." Get a SUDS level on how intense the feeling or fear is and when you become aware of any still unmet needs, proceed with the tapping.

You are working towards a change of a deep, lasting level with the reframing process. If you, at any time choose to breathe smoke, use that experience as an opportunity to understand what caused you to smoke by intensely feeling into those still unmet needs. Begin transforming those needs permanently by tapping and finding new ways to more authentically meet your needs the next time you think about smoking.

**Reframing Hypnotherapy for Stopping Smoking**

When you are comfortably positioned, simply close your eyes.

Take a deep breath. Notice when you exhale that your body naturally lets go of tension. Take another deep breath and breathe relaxation into any place in your body that you would like to feel more comfortable. Let go as you exhale. Each breath supports your inner movement, your relaxation, and your well-being. It feels good to take time for yourself to relax and let go of all of the tensions and activity of your day. Throughout this hypnotic process you continue to move to the level of comfort and relaxation that most supports you. Imagine a yardstick that represents your level of relaxation. Zero is your normal open-eyed state and thirty-six is a profound, deep state of hypnosis. What number represents your level now? As you continue to go deeper still, imagine that you are walking along a path in nature. With each step, the number increases and you continue to relax and let go. You are surrounded by the wonderful smells and colors and texture of nature. It is a beautiful day. The air is clean and fresh. Feel your footsteps walking along the path as you take in the beauty that surrounds you. This path leads you to a special place. A place where you are safe and free to be yourself, a sanctuary of beauty and calm. As you arrive at this peaceful place, you take some time to explore the surroundings. Allow all of your senses to discover the wonder of this place. Notice the colors, textures, sounds, smells, and the feeling of being in this place here and now. You are in a place where you are at peace with yourself and your world.

After exploring awhile, you find a place to sit and rest comfortably. You begin to feel so relaxed that you close your inner eyes. You relax more and more, feeling supported by the safety and comfort of this place.

As you rest, you reflect on the fact that in the past you have been a smoker. You recognize that part of you wants to smoke and another part of you desires to be smoke-free as an air breather. In the past, these parts have been in conflict with each other. And now you are ready to call a truce. Access the part of you that has to smoke. This part may come to you as an image, an inner voice, a feeling or a symbol. Ask this part, "What do you want for me?" or, "What are you trying to do or get for me as a smoker?" For instance, this part might be getting a break for you or a way to deal with negative feelings. Ask the part to tell or show you the needs that this smoker part has, over the years, been trying to fulfill through smoking. Keep asking what else, and what else, until the list of needs is complete. Now take some time to make this list of wants and needs that the smoker has recognized. (Dialogue with the client by asking the client to report the needs of the smoker and write the needs down for reference later in the script.)

Thank this part for being willing to speak to you. Know that this part has been doing the best it knows how over the years to meet these valid and important needs.

Now access the part of you that wants to be a smoke-free air breather. This part may come to you as an image, a voice, a presence, a thought process or a symbol. Ask this part, "What do you want for me as a non-smoker, an air breather?" For instance, this part might want longevity and good health, clean breath and smells, or a sense of being free of a habit. Ask what do you want for me? Ask, "What else?" "What else?" "What else do you want for me?" until the list of needs is complete. Take some time now for making this list. Thank this part for communicating with you. (Dialogue with the client to elicit the list of needs and write down the list for future use in this script.)

Now imagine the two parts, side by side. Experience the part that has been the smoker and the part that wants you to be an air breather. Together they equal one hundred percent. In this moment, what percent of you wants to be an air breather?

Now you access a third part. This part is creative, resourceful, infinite, and wise. It may come to you as an image, a voice, a feeling, a thought process, or possibly as a symbol. Ask this part to help you come up with a list of ways that you can actually meet the needs of the part that has smoked in the past. Recall the needs that the smoking part was trying to meet. Your creative part has ideas of behaviors and activities that you can do, instead of smoking, that will actually meet those needs in positive, life-affirming ways. For instance, the need to take a break can be met by going outside, deeply breathing in fresh clean air and by taking a short walk. In addition, the need for managing stress can be supported by using EFT for tapping on the emotions that arise.

This creative part provides positive behaviors for each of the needs. Take some time to experience this process. (Write down the list of alternative positive behaviors in support of meeting the smoker's needs.)

Now ask the part that has been the smoker if it is willing to do these new behaviors. Check for each of the new behaviors, one by one. You have a repertoire of new life-affirming behaviors that this part is willing to do to meet your needs besides smoking. Acknowledging that all of your needs are important and that you can discover positive ways to meet all of your needs is very liberating for you.

What percent of you now is a non-smoker or an air breather?

By meeting your needs with your new behaviors, you are strengthening your ability to choose air over smoke. Every time you think of smoking, a new behavior comes into play that actually meets a need. You find it effortless and enjoyable to do the new behaviors and to breathe air. It is easier and easier with each breath of air and more and more of you is an air breather.

As we are beginning to approach the end of this hypnosis, know that you may tap anytime in or out of this session on any feelings of rebelliousness or holding out, even fear and anger, if they arise. Know that the needs behind these feelings can also be met in loving, life-affirming ways and be smoke-free. You move easily and naturally to one hundred percent of your being smoke-free.

Imagine yourself at a time when in the past you may have smoked. See and feel yourself doing one of your new life-affirming behaviors. Notice how easy it is to choose to breath air rather than smoke. You create a post-hypnotic anchor now that you can use any time to access the feeling of choosing to be a non-smoker and to breathe air. This anchor is the sensation of how good it feels to breathe fresh clean air. The smoke clears from your life and you are surrounded by fresh smells and clean air. You experience your lungs as vital and healthy. You breathe air. The statement that is your post-hypnotic cue is, "I breathe air." Whenever you think about smoking, you say to yourself, " I breathe air." Let yourself take a deep breath of air. Feel the relief of stress and relaxation that comes whenever you take a deep breath.

Bringing these new perceptions and feelings back with you now, I count you out of hypnosis. Five. Beginning to become more alert. Four. Coming back. Three. More and more awake. Two. Opening your eyes. One. You are fully back in the room feeling refreshed and wide awake.

## Hypnotic Skill Rehearsal: Becoming an Air Breather

You take this time for deep rest, renewal, and hypnotic reinforcement that you choose to lead a smoke-free life. Sit comfortably or lie down if you wish to use this hypnosis session while you sleep. Rest your eyes on a focal point of your choice. Take a deep breath. As I count from one to five, allow your eyes to close. One. Your eyes focus comfortably. Two. Continuing to breathe deeply and easily. Three. Noticing your eyes getting sleepy and heavy. Four. Allowing your eyes to close easily and naturally. Five. Now enjoy the sensation of your eyes resting comfortably as you gaze inwards with your inner eyes. Notice what your perceive. You may see darkness or light, movement or stillness, colors, shapes and images or perhaps you perceive a soft inner void. As you look with your inner eyes, you feel the sensations of your body. Where in your body are you the most comfortable and relaxed? As you breathe into the comfortable areas, allow the comfort to grow and spread to areas of your body in which you would like to feel more comfort and well-being. With each breath, you feel flowing waves of relaxation filling your body and resting your mind.

Imagine that you are lying on a buoyant raft and floating on a clear, cool, mountain lake. The sun warms your body. You feel the gentle rocking of the raft as it floats and bobs on the water. You are so restful and calm in this special, private place. You are surrounded by the elements. The beauty and power of nature renews and balances your body, mind, and soul.

As you continue to feel and see waves of relaxation moving through your body, you begin to drift back in time … to a time when you were a child … to a time before you ever tasted or smoked a cigarette … drifting back to a time of your youth when all you know is the child-like natural and innocent state of breathing air. Go back to a happy time, a time of child-like ease of being … a time of being FREE. You allow yourself to step into this memory and to be this child here and now. Feel what it is like to be present and playful. You focus on the moment. As this child. breathing air supports all of your body functions. Breathing air sustains your life force. It is so easy and natural. You don't even need to think about it. Your thoughts, actions, and feelings are expressions of your life force. You are a miracle of creation, precious, healthy, and whole. What is the best part of being a child as you experience your youth? Anchor this experience by putting your right hand over your heart. Whenever you wish to access this innocent pure part of yourself, simply put your right hand over your heart. This child-like innocence is very much a part of you. This child lives with-in you.

Bring this child-part forward to present time, to be with you now. You are protective of this child-like part of yourself. You want to support your well-being by continuing to breathe air. You keep this child-like part free of smoke. You sustain this part by choosing to breathe air.

Become aware of your breathing again. With each breath feel and see waves of relaxation continuing to flow through your body. Now you drift forward in time. Move as far forward as you need to go to acknowledge to yourself that the smoke has cleared from your life and you are smoke-free. You are a non-smoker. You breathe only air. Imagine seeing your future self in a full-length mirror. Notice your posture, your facial expression and the clarity of your eyes and skin. You see a person who is empowered and free. You see yourself healthy and vital. How do you feel as you see yourself as smoke-free? How has your sense of self and your life changed? Feel what it is like as you meet your needs in positive life-affirming ways. You are smoke free. Smoking is far in your past. Your lungs are healthy … your clothes, your breath and hair smell fresh. You have stamina and energy for exercise. You improve your ability to taste and smell. Your circulatory system, organs, and all body functions work optimally with rich oxygenated-blood feeding every cell. Your lungs are healthy. You breathe well. You are healthy and vital. You drink lots of water and eat well. You appreciate your ability to change. You are happy, whole, and in control of your life. You continue to breathe air. You are free now.

Come back to your present self. Take a walk through a typical day in your life being smoke free. See how you incorporate your new life-affirming behaviors into your daily routine. You tap on any physical or emotional challenges. You take time for exercise and delight in moving your body. You take time for yourself. Experience the good feelings of having the tools and ability to meet your needs in healthy and appropriate ways. You are empowered. You are self-loving. Your conscious and subconscious work together for your wholeness and well-being.

You realize that the process of becoming an air breather is loving and natural. You appreciate your inner resources and the skills and tools that support you as you deal with any stress or challenging emotions and thoughts. You have grown and evolved into being more healthy, self-loving, and honoring of yourself. You are free.

Allow these images, words and this deep relaxation to support you on all levels. Know that each time you review this hypnosis process you receive the suggestions and positive images deeper and deeper into the core of your innermost self. You find that these positive suggestions and images are with you on a daily basis supporting your thoughts, feelings, and actions. When you are ready, you may return from this hypnotic state to the activities of your daily life … know that the conscious and unconscious parts of your mind work together in support of your wholeness and well-being in an on-going way. Experiencing this hypnosis process reinforces that you choose to be completely and finally, smoke-free.

# HYPNOTHERAPY for PAIN MANAGEMENT

Pain can be a productive messenger when we need protection; however, when pain is perpetuated and reinforced by negative emotions such as anger, guilt, hopelessness, fear, and anxiety, it becomes self-perpetuating. Pain creates negative emotions. Negative emotions produce more tension and tension produces pain. The following hypnotherapy processes disrupt this pain cycle.

These pain management techniques are intended to be adjuncts to medical treatments and are not intended to replace medical care. It is very important that you have your symptoms of pain examined by a medical practitioner before you use hypnotherapy for pain management so that you are not masking symptoms that need medical attention. By addressing the physical and emotional aspects of pain, by using the amazing energy therapy of Emotional Freedom Technique (EFT), and by aligning with the wisdom and power of your subconscious mind through hypnosis, you can control and even eliminate physical and emotional pain. These techniques can be combined with your prescribed pain medications and are very effective for pain management. You can expect to learn to manage your pain; however, do not stop taking any pain medications without first consulting your physician for direction and guidance.

## Introduction to Pain Management

Pain is experienced on two levels. There are the physical, as well as the emotional, levels of pain. Hypnotherapy will usually work on the emotional level right away and as you relax into yourself more, the physical levels can be managed or controlled.

For this first hypnosis process you will need two pieces of paper and crayons or colored felt pens, pencils, or pens. The language and experience of hypnosis is linked to your ability to experience, with your imagination and inner senses, what you feel, see, smell, taste, hear, and know in an inner way.

You are going to DRAW your pain. This is an important exercise because you need a base level of an inner or hypnotic image before you work with hypnosis about how you experience your pain. If you are in pain right now, draw it the way you experience and perceive it. If you are not in pain at this time, draw the pain the way you remember it at its worst. Consider the location, the size, the shape, texture, color, temperature, movement, density, and even the sound of the sensation. The drawing-the-pain exercise is simply about getting the inner experience of pain out there on the paper. (Draw pain on paper now.)

What is the SUDS (Subjective Units of Disturbance) level between zero and ten of the physical pain that you have just drawn? What is the SUDS level between zero and ten for your emotional pain? Write these SUDS levels down.

Now, on another piece of paper, draw what the same condition would be like when you are pain free. Again, consider the location, size shape, colors, texture, density, movement, temperature, and sound. (Draw an image of "pain free" on paper now.) You now have a map of where you are, where you are going and where you want to be. This pain-free drawing represents a 0 SUDS level for both the physical and emotional pain.

## Lowering the Pain

Sit so that your back and neck are supported with your arms and legs uncrossed. When you are ready, close your eyes. Focus on the sensation of the pain. Where do you feel it? Tune into the location of it. What is the shape of the sensation? What color or colors is the sensation as you experience it? What is the density? The temperature? Is it moving or still? If moving, how does it move? Listen to the sensation with your inner ears. What do you hear? What is the taste and smell of the sensation?

As you focus on these questions, you may or may not get a response to some of them. It is OK. Just notice the ones that you do respond to.

As you experience the sensation now, what is the physical SUDS level between zero to ten? What is the emotional level, from zero to ten?

Now take a deep breath. Imagine the sensation at the level just below the current SUDS level. Moving slightly towards the comfort zone towards zero, imagine the location of the sensation. What is the shape and size of the sensation? What is the density? What is the color? ... the texture? What sounds do you hear? What is the smell and taste? What is the temperature? What number between zero and ten do you give the sensation physically at this level? What number do you give it emotionally at this level?

Take a deep breath. Right before it is this intense, right under this level, moving slightly towards the comfort zone of zero, what is it like?

Become aware of the location now. What is the size and shape of the sensation? What is the color? ... the density? ... the texture? ... the temperature? ... the sound? ... the smell and taste? What number do you give it now physically? What number do you give it emotionally? Right before it is this intense, slightly closer to the comfort zone, what is it like?

With your inner awareness, move through the experience of the sensation again. The location? ... the size? ... the shape? ... the color? ... the temperature? ... the texture? ... the density? ... the movement or stillness? ... sounds? ... taste? ... smell? What number do you give it physically? ... emotionally?

If you are not at zero for both the physical and emotional sensations, continue repeating this process, moving closer and closer towards the comfort zone with each level. When you are at a comfortable level or at a zero physically and emotionally, then go to the next step.

Now that you have moved the sensation to a zero or to a comfortable level, reflect on the movement you have made since beginning this hypnosis process. Choose one mode of experience that you accessed throughout. For instance, maybe throughout this experience you were able to know the temperature consistently, which began as a very hot 9 and gradually moved to a cool sensation at zero. Or perhaps *color* was your strongest mode and the sensation was a black and red 8 that moved down to a sky blue zero, Or perhaps density was dominate for you and you began with a hard baseball at level seven that became a soft fuzzy cloud at one.

When you have chosen your strongest mode, review the systematic changes you perceived from the most intense level to your least intense level. You can now rehearse in your mind's eye and through your inner sensing, your sequence, moving from the highest to the lowest level. Take some time to review and rehearse the sequence now.

In your daily life, whenever you begin to notice the earliest sign of discomfort, you can mentally tune into the sequence and begin lowering the sensations before they become painful. Now practice doing the sequence by imagining that during the day you notice the color or temperature or size and shape of your level three. When you notice it, you take time to tune into the level right underneath a three and breath it into your awareness. Then, move another level lower until you are once again enjoying the comfort zone.

Each time you hypnotically rehearse and use this sequencing in your daily life, you get results faster and more effortlessly. You begin to catch your sensation before it becomes intolerable pain. You are able to manage your emotions and to regulate the sensations comfortably and confidently. You might also imagine that your mode of perception is connected to a dial or dimmer switch. You can move the dial or knob slowly as you lower the sensation to a comfortable level; for instance, moving it gradually from really hot to cool, level by level.

You know that just as in any learning experience of the past, the more you practice using this technique, the more effective and easy it is to use. You look forward to using this method for your own pain management in your daily life and you feel relief increasingly more easily.

Enjoying your success and feeling the comfort, slowly allow yourself to come back into the room feeling awake and refreshed … feeling better than you have felt in a very long time.

## Healing Journey

Note: For this process, you can substitute the gifts with those that are most appropriate for the client.

According to Stanford researchers, Hilgard and Hilgard, up to 30% of pain can be diminished through applying relaxation techniques. The hypnotherapy process that follows supports the body and mind in relaxing and letting go.

When you are comfortably positioned, simply close your eyes. Take a full, deep, cleansing breath. Notice when you exhale, as fully as you can, that your body naturally lets go of tension. Take another full deep breath and breathe relaxation into any place in your body where you would like to feel more comfortable. Let go as you exhale. Each breath supports your inner movement, your relaxation, and your well-being. It feels good to take time for yourself to relax and let go of all the tensions and busyness of your day. Throughout this hypnotic process you continue moving to the level of comfort and relaxation that most supports you.

As you continue to go deeper still, imagine that you are walking along a path in nature. With each step, you continue to relax and let go. You are surrounded by the wonderful smells and colors and texture of nature. It is a beautiful day. The air is clean and fresh. Feel your footsteps walking along the path as you take in the beauty that surrounds you. This path leads you to a special place near a lake: a place from your past, or a place where you have always wanted to be; a place where you are safe and free to be yourself. This place is a sanctuary of beauty and calm. As you arrive at this peaceful place, you take some time to explore the surroundings. Allow all of your senses to discover the wonder of this place. Notice the colors, textures, sounds, smells, and the feeling of being in this place here and now. You are in a place where you are at peace with yourself and your world. Notice the calm, still water and the horizon where the water meets the sky. Walk along the shore of the water and notice the sand and rocks. Find a place to sit comfortably for awhile you relax more and more, feeling supported by the beauty, calmness, and safety of this place.

As you rest your gaze out on the lake and over the horizon, you notice a small hot air balloon floating towards you. The balloon is a rainbow of colors. It is moving gently, smoothly, and effortlessly towards you on the shore. You are curious because no one seems to be in the gondola piloting the balloon. It seems to be purposefully moving towards you as if it will land on the shore. To your delight and amazement, the balloon gently lands next to you on the shore. You rise to greet it and explore it.

Tied to the gondola is a note. It is addressed to you. It says, "Look inside the gondola. These gifts are for you. Allow yourself to receive them deeply and completely into the very depths of yourself. They are what you have been wanting and needing for a long time. "

You reach into the wicker basket. The first gift that you receive is the gift of *being open and receptive*. You make a space within yourself, a space that is open to new ways of perceiving and being with yourself and your body and your mind. This openness is like that of a curious, innocent child. This first gift allows you to be receptive and appreciative of all the other gifts. Feel this openness now.

The next gift is the gift of *growing relaxation* .You begin to feel yourself receiving it now. As you reach out, you feel the relaxation flowing through your whole body. This gift of *growing relaxation* circulates more and more comfort with every breath you take. Feel the calm that is the ground of your being. You are calm and relaxed.

The next gift you receive is the gift of *health and well-being*. You vibrate with balanced, vital energy that nourishes every cell of your body. This energy circulates to places in your body where you want and need more comfort and wellness. Feel it happening now. See it with your inner eyes and know it with your inner knowing. Blood flows freely through your body bringing rich oxygenated nutrients to every organ and body system. The life force flows freely, balancing and nurturing your body's healing. Feel your growing wellness, now.

The next gift you receive is the gift of *forgiveness*. You forgive yourself and others, knowing that anger and resentment are unproductive for your healing and well-being. You choose to come to peace with the past and to be present in the now. It is in the now that you feel forgiveness flow into your body, mind, and spirit. You accept the wholeness of this moment.

Having received these gifts, it is time to let go of all the things in your life that are outworn or inhibiting your healing. Think about which things you choose to release to make more room for the gifts you have just received and allow these gifts to take root more deeply into yourself. Imagine putting all the things you choose to give up in the gondola.

You may want to let go of the clutter in your life, any fear, anxiety, resentment, pain, judgment, anger, outworn beliefs, and limiting attitudes. Place them in the basket. Fill it up. Keep releasing and letting go. Take some time now to allow yourself to let it all go.

When you are complete, you lift up the gondola and the balloon begins to fill with warm air. See it float up as the balloon gets fuller, moving slowly and steadily higher, above the lake and towards the horizon carrying all of the debris out of your life. It finally disappears from view.

You are left with a sense of spaciousness and inner calm. All of the gifts you received have room to be a part of you now. You are open and receptive. You are relaxed and calm. You have health and well-being. You accept and forgive. You are at peace with yourself and present in the now.

Bring these gifts and positive feelings back with you now. Know that they are always with you to enjoy and rely on in your daily life. You create an anchor for these gifts and positive feelings by opening your hands. When you open your hands, palms up, you remember and access this state. The more you use the anchor, the more clear and dependable it is to tune into these gifts that are a part of you now.

You begin your journey back now to wakefulness and well-being. I count you back now from five to one. Five. Bringing your relaxation back with you. Four. Becoming more alert. Three. More and more awake. Two. Opening your eyes. One. You are fully back in the room feeling comfort, refreshed, and wide-awake.

## Hypnotic Analgesia

With practice, this technique for pain management will teach you how to minimize pain by creating a sensation of analgesia or comfortable numbness. Since it masks pain, it is important that you get medical attention to discover what is causing the pain before you use this technique. Hypnotic analgesia is widely used for making medical or dental procedures more comfortable, and is also used in emergency situations to minimize pain until medical attention is available. It can also be used for chronic or acute bouts of pain. With practice, you will have success creating hypnotic analgesia so that you have the benefit of this tool for the rest of your life. The key point to remember is that it is a skill and will most likely take practice.

Sit comfortably and adjust your body so that your head, neck, and spine are aligned. Choose a focal point on which to rest your open eyes across from you on the (wall.) Take a full deep breath. As I count slowly from one to five, allow your eyes to close easily and naturally by the count of five or when you are ready. One. Looking into the focal point. Two. Continuing to breathe deeply and easily. Three. Notice changes in your visual perceptions as you continue to rest your eyes and focus. Four. Your eyes begin to close easily. Five. Enjoy the growing experience of letting go as you continue to breathe in relaxation. Your eyes rest behind your closed eyelids. Gently turn your focus inwards…to see how you feel in your body…to notice where you want more comfort and well-being. Allow yourself to continue to relax and let go throughout this process.

Focus on your abdomen. Imagine a warm sunny light vibrating and pulsing from your belly and moving the vital life-force energy to your dominate hand. Your hand is now filled with the tingling vibration of this light. Your hand and fingers are pulsing and tingling. It is a sensation familiar to you, a sensation of comfortable numbness. This sensation is similar to the effects of a local anesthetic or the sensation of tingling you feel after making snow balls without gloves.

Imagine a control panel in your brain that links up to every area of your body. This control panel adjusts your level of awareness to sensations. You sit at the control panel and dim the link of sensation awareness towards the off position with your dominate hand. With every breath you take, the sensation diminishes to a reassuring, comfortable numbness.

Your hand begins to feel hollow or wooden or as if it is covered by a thick padded glove. You are aware of comfort and tingling only. You give yourself some time to experience the growing numbness … to see, know, and feel it taking place.

As you are confident in the change of your perceived sensations in your hand, your hand begins to feel lighter and lighter and starts to lift or drift upwards.

Your hand moves to another part of your body to transfer the numbness to any area of discomfort. For instance, your hand may move to a sore knee or to your forehead for a headache, or to your jaw for tooth pain. You practice transferring the numbness to different areas. Imagine the numbness in your hand is a special colored liquid. As your hand touches an area, the liquid transfers through the skin of the hand into the area of pain. It flows easily and consistently. As the numbness soaks into the painful area, the numbness grows. You switch the control in your brain to this area of your body to the off position.

You feel changes and enjoy the success of diminishing sensation, of comfortable growing numbness. Take some time for this now.

Each time you practice this hypnotic analgesia, you have more ease and more success in creating numbness. Your confidence grows as you learn to control pain.

You create a post-hypnotic cue that captures the most clear and positive part of your experience. It can be an image, a word, or a sensation. This cue will remind you of your past success and help you to access analgesia again and again, at will. You can practice self-hypnosis to take yourself back into this state to access the analgesia again, whenever needed. In situations where you use analgesia, you may decide to come out of hypnosis with the numbness still in place or it may be better or safer for you to allow all normal sensations to return before coming out of hypnosis. You may choose whatever you prefer on an as-needed basis.

Now, imagine returning to the control switches in your brain. For the closure of this hypnotic process, you move the switches back to the on position and bring back all normal comfortable sensations. Feeling anticipation and even excitement about this new skill, you breath yourself out of hypnosis feeling alert, refreshed and wide-awake. Each breath enlivens and refreshes you as your eyes open and you return to the room.

## Sleep Hypnosis for Pain Management

Sit comfortably *or* lie down if you wish to receive the benefits of this hypnosis while you sleep. Rest your eyes on a focal point of your choice. Take a deep breath. As I count from one to five allow your eyes to close. One. Your eyes focus comfortably. Two, Breathing deeply and easily. Three. Noticing your eyes getting sleepy and heavy. Four. Allowing your eyes to close easily and naturally now. Five. Enjoy the sensation of your eyes resting comfortably as you gaze inwards with your inner eyes. Notice what you perceive. You may see darkness or light, movement or stillness, colors, shapes and images, or perhaps you perceive a soft inner void.

As you look with your inner eyes, you feel the sensations of your body. Where in your body are you the most comfortable and relaxed? Continue to breathe into the relaxation. As you breathe into the comfortable areas, allow the comfort to grow and spread to areas of your body in which you would like to feel more comfort and well-being. With each breath, you feel flowing waves of relaxation filling your body and resting your mind. Your muscles and organs soften and let go. You allow your body to sink into the support of your bed, sofa, or chair.

While breathing in, if you notice any unwelcome or busy thoughts, you can simply let them go as you exhale. Just for this moment, your mind is free and clear … like a breezeless, cloudless sky. Just for this moment, your mind is still and quiet.

Notice any emotions you feel. With the next cycle of breathing, breathe in quiet and stillness and let go of emotions so that your emotional body is like a placid, smooth lake. You become more and more still, more and more comfortable, more and more free.

You continue to deepen and let go with each breath and if you find yourself drifting off to sleep you just go with it … moving into a restful receptive state for your comfort and healing of your body, mind. and spirit. You may listen with your subconscious mind while your conscious mind and body relax and move towards sleep.

Imagine that you are lying on blanket at a beautiful private beach. The sun warms your body. You hear the gentle rhythmic movement of the waves as the water washes onto the shore just barely touching your sandy feet. Feel the comfortable temperature of the water. You are so restful and calm in this special, private place. Allow this place to become real to you now in an inner way. Let all of your senses come alive as you see, feel, hear, and smell your surroundings. You enjoy the feel of this place on your skin, soaking in the beauty and richness of it; and feeling happy to be right where you are now. Let your body take in the vibration of this place. Feel supported and healed by being surrounded by the energy and beauty of this place.

You are surrounded by the elements along with the beauty and power of nature that renews and balances your whole being.

As you continue to feel and see waves of relaxation moving through your body, you begin to drift back in time … to a time when you are comfortable, a time of child-like ease of being … a time of being FREE. You allow yourself to step into this memory and to be this person again, here and now. Feel what it is like to be comfortable and well. You feel the freedom of being in a healthy and balanced body. You focus on the moment. Your thoughts, actions and feelings are expressions of your life force. You are a miracle of creation: precious, healthy, and whole. What is the best part of being this person as you experience your comfort, wellness, and vitality?

Whenever you wish to access this innocent pure, whole, and healthy part of yourself, simply put your right hand over your heart. This child-like vitality and innocence is very much a part of you. This comfort and wellness lives as a real part of you now. You are always able to touch this peaceful stillness in your center. You are safe and connected to your true self. You are accepting and allowing of it all. Your body is vibrating with its own healing energy and well-being.

Feeling peaceful and at ease, know that you can always call forth this happy and well part of you along with this special place. Know that you can call forth the healing power of your breath and your ability to soften and let go.

Bring this peaceful yet powerful part forward to present time to be with you now. In this moment, you feel vital and well again. You are full of hope and possibilities.

Allow these images, words, and this deep relaxation to support you on all levels. Know that each time you practice this hypnosis process, you receive the suggestions and positive images for comfort and well-being deeper and deeper into the core of your innermost self. You find that these positive suggestions and images are with you on a daily basis, supporting your thoughts, feelings and actions. You allow yourself to luxuriate in this deep state of well-being as you drift into a deeply restful sleep. Know that your conscious and unconscious work together in support of your wholeness and well-being in an on-going way. Using this hypnosis process reinforces that you rest well, knowing that you now choose to be completely comfortable, vital, and well.

# HYPNOSIS for WEIGHT MANAGEMENT

## Reframing for Weight Loss

When you are comfortably positioned, simply close your eyes.

Take a deep breath. Notice when you exhale that your body naturally lets go of tension. Take another deep breath and breathe relaxation into any place in your body that you would like to feel more comfortable. Let go as you exhale. Each breath supports your inner movement, your relaxation, and your well-being. It feels good to take time for yourself to relax and let go of all of the tensions and busyness of your day.

Throughout this hypnotic process you continue to move to the level of comfort and relaxation that most supports you. Imagine a yardstick that represents your level of relaxation. Zero is your normal open-eyed state and thirty-six is a profound deep state of hypnosis. What number represents your level now? As you continue to go deeper still, imagine that you are walking along a path in nature.

With each step, the numbers increase and you continue to relax and let go. You are surrounded by the wonderful smells and colors and texture of nature. It is a beautiful day. The air is clean and fresh. Feel the path under your feet as you easily walk along and take in the beauty that surrounds you. This path leads you to a special place, a place where you are safe and free to be yourself, a sanctuary of beauty and calm.

As you arrive at this peaceful place, you take some time to explore the surroundings. Allow all of your senses to discover the wonder of this place. Notice the colors, textures, sounds, smells, and the feeling of being in this place here and now. You are in a place where you are at peace with yourself and your world.

After exploring awhile, you find a place to sit and rest comfortably. You begin to feel so relaxed that you close your inner eyes. You relax more and more, feeling supported by the safety of this place.

While you rest, you reflect on the fact that in the past you have had an issue with weight and food. You recognize that part of you wants to be your ideal weight and another part of you desires to be free to eat whatever and whenever you want. In the past, these parts have been in conflict with each other. And now you are ready to call a truce. Access the part of you that craves food, overeats or eats to deal with emotions. This part may come to you as an image, an inner voice, a feeling or a symbol. Ask this part, "What do you want for me or what are you trying to do or get for me through food and eating?" For instance, this part might be rewarding you, or helping you to manage stress or negative feelings like anxiety, boredom, loneliness, or anger. Ask this part to tell or show you the needs that this overeater has, over the years, been trying to fulfill through food. Keep asking what else, and what else, until the list of needs is complete. Now take some time to review this list of wants and needs that the overeater, emotional eater, or heavier part has prepared. (Ask the client to share the list of needs with you and write them down.)

Thank this part for being willing to speak to you. Know that this part has been doing the best it knows how over the years to meet these valid and important needs.

Now access the part of you that wants to be in your body at its ideal weight. This part may come to you as an image, a voice, a presence, a thought process or a symbol. Ask this part, "What do you want for me?" For instance, this part might want good health and more physical stamina or energy. Or perhaps this part wants to wear certain types of clothes comfortably and freely. Continue to ask, "What else, what else, what else do you want for me?" until the list of needs is complete. (Ask the client to share the list of needs with you and write them down.) Take some time now to review this list. Thank this part for communicating with you.

Now imagine these two parts, side by side. The part that has had the issue with weight or food and the part that wants you to be lighter and free of cravings. Together they equal one hundred percent. In this moment, what percent of you wants to be your ideal weight?

Now you access a third part. This part is creative, resourceful, infinite, and wise. It may come to you as an image, a voice, a feeling, thought process, or possibly as a symbol. Ask this part to help you come up with a list of ways that you can actually meet the needs of the part that has had the food and weight issues in the past. Recall the needs that the overeating part was trying to meet. Your creative part has ideas of behaviors and activities that you can do, instead of emotional eating, that will actually meet those needs in positive, life-affirming ways. For instance, the need to take a break can be met by going outside and taking a short walk. The stress that leads to emotional eating can be diminished by using EFT, Emotional Freedom Technique. EFT can also be used to transform a specific food craving.

The creative part comes up with positive behaviors for each of the needs. (Ask the client to share the list of alternative behaviors and write them down.)

Now ask the part that has been the emotional eater or the overeater if it is willing to do these new behaviors. Check for each of the new behaviors, one by one. ( Read the list to the client and one by one find new behaviors for each need.) You are discovering a repertoire of new life-affirming behaviors that this part is willing to do to meet the needs besides eating. Acknowledging that all of your needs are important and that you can discover positive ways to meet all of your needs is very liberating for you. What percent of you now is ready, willing, and able to support your ideal weight and healthy eating now?

By meeting your needs with your new behaviors you are strengthening your ability to make healthy food choices. Every time you think of eating, a new behavior comes into play that actually meets a need. You find it effortless and enjoyable to perform the new behaviors and to eat healthy, small amounts of foods that satisfy and fully support your body's physical needs for nutrition. It is easier and easier to carry out these new behaviors with each food choice. And more and more of you is on board making healthy food choices day after day and meal after meal.

As we are beginning to approach the end of this hypnosis, know that you may tap anytime in or out of this session on any feelings of rebelliousness or holding out, even fear and anger, if they arise. Know that the needs behind these feelings can be met in loving, life-affirming ways. You move easily and naturally to one hundred percent of you being ready, willing and able to make ongoing healthy choices of food and balanced healthy eating behaviors.

Imagine seeing and feeling yourself doing one of your new life-affirming behaviors. Notice how easy it is to make healthy food choices. You will create a post-hypnotic anchor now that you can use any time to access the feeling of choosing to be a healthy and balanced eater. This anchor is the sensation of how good it feels to have your parts aligned and committed to healthy eating. You release the heaviness from your life and you feel light and energetic. You experience your body as vital and healthy. The statement that is your post-hypnotic cue is, "My body and mind are satisfied with healthy foods in small portions." Whenever you think about eating, you say to yourself, " My body and mind are satisfied with healthy foods in small portions."

Take a deep breath of air. Feel the relaxation and relief of stress that comes from knowing that you are in alignment with your choice to be satisfied with healthy foods in small portions. Bring these new perceptions and feelings back with you now. I count you out of hypnosis. Five. Beginning to become more alert. Four. Coming back. Three. More and more awake. Two. Opening your eyes. One. You are fully back in the room feeling refreshed and wide-awake.

## Reframing Hypnosis for Exercising

When your body is comfortably seated, simply close your eyes.

Take a deep breath. Notice when you exhale that your body naturally lets go of tension. Think of a color that is comforting and relaxing for you. Breathe in this color. See and feel this color moving into any areas of your body that would like to be more comfortable and relaxed. This color softens and relaxes the muscles and organs. Each breath supports your inner movement, your relaxation, and your well-being. Each out-breath releases tension or discomfort. It feels good to take time for yourself to relax and let go of all the tensions and concerns of your day. Allow yourself to be present in this moment, noticing your breath, feeling your body, hearing my voice, and any other sounds. Throughout this hypnotic process you continue to move to the level of comfort, enjoyment, and relaxation that most supports you.

As you continue to go deeper still, imagine that you are walking along a familiar path in nature. With each step down the path, you continue to relax and let go. You are surrounded by the wonderful smells, colors, and the beauty of nature. Breathe in the cool, clean, fresh air. Hear the sound of your footsteps on the path as you easily walk along and take in the beauty that surrounds you. This path leads you to a special place; a place where you are safe and free to be yourself, a natural sanctuary of beauty and calm. As you arrive at this peaceful place, you take some time to explore the surroundings. Allow all of your senses to discover the wonder of this place. Notice the colors, textures, sounds, smells, and the feeling of being in this place here and now. You are in a place where you are at peace with yourself and your world.

After exploring awhile, you find a place to sit and rest comfortably. You begin to feel so relaxed that you close your inner eyes. You relax more and more, feeling supported by the safety of this place.

As you rest, you reflect on the fact that in the past you have had an issue with exercising. You recognize that part of you wants exercise and another part of you feels unmotivated, tired or simply too busy to exercise. In the past, these parts have been in conflict with each other. And now you are ready to call a truce. Access the part of you that avoids exercise. This part may come to you as an image, an inner voice, a feeling, or a symbol. Ask this part, "What do you want for me or what are you trying to do or get for me through avoiding exercise?" For instance, this part might be wanting more time to relax you, or it may feel over committed with present obligations for use of your time, or it may simply feel too tired or be uninterested in exercise. Ask this part to tell or show you the needs that it has been trying to fulfill. Keep asking, "What else and what else?" until the list of needs is complete. (Ask the client to share the list and write it down.) Now take some time to review this list of wants and needs of this part that doesn't want to exercise.

Thank this part for being willing to speak to you. Know that this part has been doing the best it knows how over the years to address its feelings and meet these valid needs.

Now access the part of you that wants to be physically fit. This part may come to you as an image, a voice, a presence, a thought process, or a symbol. Ask this part, "What do you want for me?" For instance, this part might want a strong, toned body, physical stamina, or more energy. Perhaps this part wants to move through life with more flexibility and ease. Ask this part, "What do you want for me?" Ask, "What else, what else, what else do you want for me" until the list of needs is complete. (Ask the client to share this list and write it down.) Take some time now for reviewing this list. Thank the part for communicating with you.

Now, imagine the two parts, side by side: the part that has resisted exercise and the part that wants to exercise with all the benefits. Together they equal one hundred percent. In this moment, what percent of you wants to exercise?

Now, you access a third part. This part is creative, resourceful, infinite, and wise. It may come to you as an image, a voice, a feeling, thought process, or possibly as a symbol. Ask this part to help you come up with a list of ways that you can actually meet the needs of the part that has resisted exercising in the past. Recall the needs that this part was trying to meet. Your creative part has ideas of behaviors and activities, which you can do, that will actually meet those needs in positive, life-affirming ways. For instance, the need to relax or take a break can be met by going outside and taking a short walk. Or the stress that leads to lethargy can be managed by using EFT. The creative part comes up with positive behaviors for each of the needs. Take some time to make a list of positive ways to meet these needs. ( Ask the client to share the list and write it down.)

Now ask the part that has been resisting exercise if it is willing to do these new behaviors. Check for each of the new behaviors, one by one. You have a repertoire of new life-affirming behaviors that this part is willing to do to meet the needs. Acknowledging that all of your needs are important, and that you can discover positive ways to meet all of your needs, is very liberating for you.

What percent of you now is ready, willing, and able to support your exercising now?

By meeting your needs with your new behaviors, you are strengthening your ability to live a more vital and balanced life. Every time you think you are too tired or too busy to exercise, a new behavior comes into play that actually helps you deal with your low energy or time management. You find it effortless and enjoyable to perform the new behaviors and exercise to support the physical, mental, and emotional benefits of exercise and movement. It is easier and easier to choose revitalizing movement over lethargy. And each day more and more of you is focused, motivated, and committed to exercise.

As we are beginning to approach the end of this hypnosis, know that you may tap anytime in or out of this session on any feelings of rebelliousness or holding out, even fear and anger, if they arise. Know that the needs behind these feelings can also be met in loving, life-affirming ways. You move easily and naturally to one-hundred percent of your being ready, willing, and able to make an ongoing commitment to exercise.

Imagine seeing and feeling yourself doing one of your new life-affirming behaviors and enjoying exercising regularly. Notice how easy it is to perpetuate your exercise routine. You create a post-hypnotic anchor now that you can use any time to access the feelings of consistently exercising and enjoying its benefits in your daily life. This anchor is the sensation of how good it feels to be in a vital fit and healthy body. You feel energetic and light. You experience your body as vital and healthy. The statement that is your post-hypnotic cue is, "I exercise my body. My body is vital, energetic and fit." Whenever you think about having low energy or being lethargic, you say to yourself, "I exercise my body. My body is vital, energetic and fit." Let yourself take a deep breath of air. Feel the stress relief and relaxation that comes from knowing that you are in alignment with your choice to exercise your body to be vital, energetic, and fit.

Bring these new perceptions and feelings back with you now. I count you out of hypnosis. Five. Beginning to become more alert. Four. Coming back. Three, more and more awake. Two. Opening your eyes. One. You are fully back in the room feeling refreshed and wide-awake.

## Introduction to Hypnosis and NLP for Healthy Eating and Exercising

In this next process, Neuro-Linguistic Programming (NLP) will support the re-wiring of your language, thought, and behavior patterns and hypnotic skill rehearsal will program and reinforce effective routines for healthy eating and exercise. By changing your eating habits and getting regular exercise you will influence the efficiency of your metabolism to lose and then maintain your weight. Hypnosis and NLP are self-help tools for your own healing and transformation. It is recommended that you check with your healthcare practitioner before you follow any self-help weight management or exercise program.

# Hypnosis and NLP for Healthy Eating and Exercising

Sit comfortably with your eyes closed. Notice your breathing. As you breathe in, your abdomen rises. And as you breathe out, your abdomen falls. Focusing on your breathing in and out and the rising and falling of your abdomen calms your mind and body. While your body settles, notice where in your body you feel the most warmth. Notice where in your body you feel the most relaxation. With your next few breaths, imagine the warm and relaxed areas begin to expand throughout the rest of your body. With each breath, you feel more and more warmth and relaxation, reminding you of times when you have basked in the sun. With the spreading warmth, all your muscles begin to relax. The tension melts away. Discomfort subsides. Your mind becomes more focused and still. You are open and receptive to mental images and suggestions that support your health and well-being. You align with the wisdom of your higher Self and the power of your subconscious mind. Each time you listen to this hypnosis, you reinforce these suggestions and they are exponentially more effective. Knowing that your higher Self supports and protects you in responding only to suggestions that are for your highest good and well-being, you receive these suggestions freely and openly.

You now have a loving relationship with your body and food. When you eat, you are mindful of what you eat, when you eat, and how you eat. By being mindful of these three things, your relationship to food and your routines around food, change to support your body's ideal health, weight, and metabolism. You respect what your body has to say and you give your body what it needs, whether that is lots of water, healthy food, or a loving response to your emotional needs. When you are hungry or you are thinking about eating, look down to your right with your inner eyes. Listen to what your body is saying to you. It will speak with sensations, emotions, images, or words. Is your body feeling hungry for food? Or is it emotionally hungry for something? Is it anxious, angry, lonely, or wanting a break? If it is emotionally hungry, use EFT to work with your emotional needs. If your body is physically hungry, look down to your left with your inner eyes and ask your body what nutrition it needs to satisfy your hunger.

After your body responds, look up to the left to see the well-prepared, healthy food you will eat for your body. See the appropriate portions, the colors and textures of the food.

And finally, look up to the right and see yourself eating and enjoying the food. You see yourself eating slowly and chewing your food completely. You know that eating slowly is not only more enjoyable, but the food begins to digest while you chew it, and your brain has time to get the signal that you are eating and receiving the nutrition that your body needs. When you eat mindfully, the brain has ample time to recognize when you are full. You eat to live and no longer live to eat. You see yourself eating at the table without distractions. You are mindful of how delicious and satisfying every bite is. You savor the textures, the smell, and the flavors of each bite. You stop eating when you no longer feel hungry.

Imagine yourself looking down to the left again. You feel physically and emotionally satisfied. You feel self-love about the choices you have made.

Being mindful that your body communicates to you, you are exquisitely aware of the difference between physical and emotional hunger. Following the physical hunger signals, you feed your body small meals more often during the day, never allowing your body to get over hungry.

When you make food choices, you balance your diet with lots of fresh fruits, vegetables, and proteins. You limit your carbohydrate intake, eating only small portions of carbohydrates and whole grains. You avoid processed foods and sugar. You drink lots of clean, fresh water. You drink water in the morning, during the day, and before each meal. Water assists your body in being fully hydrated and in flushing out toxins and old fat cells. Water is life. You hydrate your body well.

Eating several small meals each day allows your metabolism to work more efficiently. Your body digests the foods well, allowing your body to receive all the nutrients it needs. Shopping for and preparing food is a loving ritual. You enjoy planning your meals because eating healthy foods is such a joy for your whole being.

Remember when you were a child and you played your favorite sports and games? You moved your body without even thinking about it. Because your body remembers that moving is fun and easy, you exercise regularly. You choose physical activities that you enjoy and engage in them several times a week. Brisk walking feels wonderful. It is great to be outdoors, breathing in fresh air and feeling the temperature of the air on your face and arms. You find ways to add walking to your daily routine. You walk up stairs, park farther away from your destination and whenever possible you take a walk break during your workday. Your body gets leaner and stronger each week. You exercise for stamina and strength. Moving your body regularly and quickly boosts your metabolism. Your body burns fat and builds lean muscle. You see and feel the changes on a weekly basis. Your clothes are looser, your energy level is higher, and your immune system is strong. You are motivated and positive. Each healthy choice makes it easier to make another healthy choice. One small change is like a drop of water that turns into a waterfall. It all begins with one small change, with one drop in a glass until your glass is full.

You are empowered and self-loving. You are light and free. You are slim, strong, toned, and fit. In this image of yourself, you have the knowledge that you did this. You are in a bright place where all of you is in alignment as a healthy, slim you.

Every time you repeat or recall this hypnosis session and each time that you follow these life-affirming practices, you grow in confidence and self-esteem. You love yourself and your life. You are filled with gratitude to your higher Self for the support you receive on a daily basis for your healthy, vital life.

So, in a moment, I am going to count you back from five to one when you will be fully awake and ready to return to activity … knowing that something deep within you has changed … that you have focus and determination to act on these changes. Five … Four … Beginning to reorient … Three … Feeling your hands and legs … Two … Ready to open your eyes … One … Back in the room.

**Introduction to Hypnosis for Boosting Metabolism**

In the previous skill rehearsal we hypnotically programmed daily routines and behaviors for healthy eating and exercise.

In this hypnotic process you will receive positive images and suggestions for using mind over matter. Your higher Self will boost your metabolism so that your body more efficiently metabolizes fat and builds lean muscle.

**Hypnosis for Boosting your Metabolism**

Sit comfortably and focus your eyes on a stationary spot across from you. While your eyes rest on your focal point, take a few deep breaths. I will count slowly from one to five. By the count of five, or when you are ready, allow your eyes to close naturally and easily. One, breathing deep and easy breaths. Two, letting go as you exhale. Three, feeling inwardly focused and more relaxed. Four, comfortably and naturally closing your eyes, Five. Now that your eyes are closed, take a moment to notice a growing sense of peace and stillness within you. Imagine that above your head is a star of clear light that glows and illuminates your body and the auric field around you. This pure, warm light engulfs and penetrates your physical body, balancing, harmonizing and revitalizing each cell in all of your body systems. See and feel this balancing taking place. Each breath supports you and allows you to focus and let go of the rest. Your higher Self, the infinite wise part of you, is represented by this clear light. Throughout this hypnosis, your higher Self deepens and modulates your level of trance so that you are open and receptive to positive suggestions for an increased and efficient metabolism. Your higher Self knows what is best for you and takes charge of working directly with your subconscious and body allowing positive and healthy effects to come from this hypnosis. In this state, as the light moves through and around you, your higher Self has influence over your consciousness and all the programs that influence the metabolic functions of your body. Increasing your metabolism helps you to effectively process food and to efficiently burn excess fat in your body.

Imagine a representation of your higher Self at the controls of your body functions. The control can be represented by any metaphor that works for you. Perhaps it is similar to a rheostat that increases or dims a light bulb, or maybe it looks like a thermometer where the levels are delineated by a color that moves up incrementally to show increased metabolic activity. Or maybe your metabolic rate is represented by a moving needle on an image similar to a speedometer. Your higher Self works with whatever metaphor is right for you to increase your metabolism. Your higher Self increases your metabolism now. It increases to the perfect level to boost your energy and burn fat more efficiently than ever before. Your metabolism continues to increase until it reaches the maximum efficiency for your weight loss needs. You see, feel, and know that even now, your metabolism is increasing. And as your metabolic functions are optimally controlled, so is your set point for weight loss. Notice the representation through your metabolic register or dial. Notice how it is moving. You are galvanizing your metabolic rate. It is more and more efficient. Even now, your body is responding. Your controls also set your ideal body size and weight. You metabolize and release old fat cells easily. Your body builds lean muscles.

Day after day, when you first awaken, you check in mentally to adjust and reset your metabolic controls. Day after day, your higher Self makes any necessary adjustments to your metabolic functioning to support your energy levels and weight loss. Your higher Self completely supports your choice and decision to create your ideal body size, weight, and energy level through healthy eating, regular exercise, and working daily with your metabolic controls. You boost and maintain your metabolism to the most efficient levels for you. And once you reach your ideal weight, your higher Self continues to adjust your metabolism to maintain this weight.

You stand in front of a mirror dressed for the day. Your image reflects a vital, fit, and lean body that you have earned through healthy living. You maintain your highly efficient metabolism by mind over matter, healthy food choices, and routine exercise. You feel light and energetic. You are healthy and vital. You love and care for your body. Your higher Self supports you every step of the way as you live a long and healthy life. You use a post-hypnotic anchor regularly during the day that reinforces this hypnosis, your efficient metabolic rate, and all of your positive thoughts, feelings, and behaviors. This anchor is the phrase "Healthy Living." Whenever you think or say the phrase, "Healthy Living," you activate and reinforce all of the positive suggestions that support your active metabolism, choices, and behaviors. The words, "Healthy Living," activate being vitally healthy and fit.

Feeling the benefits of your metabolic boost and being excited about the changes it makes in your life, it is time to return to your wakeful state. Breathe your way back into the room, allowing each in-breath to vitalize and energize you. Beginning to become aware of your body. Focusing on the sounds in your surroundings. Feeling more alert. Opening your eyes and coming back into the room. Allow your eyes to fully open when you are ready.

## Sleep Hypnosis for Reinforcing Healthy Living

After preparing for sleep, lie in your bed with the lights out. Allow yourself to sink into the mattress, feeling the support and warmth of your safe and comfortable bed. Imagine lying in a swinging hammock. It is a warm summer night. You are in a beautiful garden. Smell the fragrances of jasmine and the roses that surround you and listen to the relaxing sound of trickling water from a fountain close by. The moon is full and the sky is clear. Watching the starlight flickering through the leafy canopy of trees, you begin to feel drowsy and relaxed. You have had a busy day. And it feels so good to let go of all activities and thoughts as you rest right here, right now. You are safe and protected in this special place. You drift, more deeply, more and more comfortably into a calm state of inner peace. Your mind clears with each movement back and forth. You are ready for sleep. While you sleep you have positive, loving visions. You feel aligned and clear in thought. Your multi-dimensions of self are working together in harmony for your highest good and well-being.

A wonderful hypnotic dream unfolds. You are standing in front of a mirror. See yourself the way you are. And with this image of how you look, the size and shape of your body, the expression on your face, you also see with your inner knowing all of the choices, habits, and behaviors, that over the years, have contributed to your size and shape. You know from your deep inner knowing that you have within you all you need to make new choices and to create new behaviors that include your healthy way of life. Now, turn around and look into another mirror. In this mirror you see a transformed you. This you is trim. This you is vital and healthy. This you has a life routine that consistently supports exercise and eating right to support your ideal weight. You admire yourself in the mirror, appreciating how you look and feel. Now, step into this mirror and become this person that you see. You are in this healthy, lean, and trim body. You feel energetic, flexible, and strong. Your day includes mindful eating. You listen to your body by looking down to the right. If it says you are hungry, you look down to the left to find out what nutrition your body needs. And then look up right to see the food it wants in the appropriate portions that are deliciously prepared. Then, you look up to the left and see yourself enjoying the food, chewing it completely and eating it slowly. See yourself being completely satisfied and well-nourished.

You support your metabolism by eating small meals throughout the day. If your body tells you that the sensations are due to your emotions, not hunger, you use EFT to tap on whatever you feel. You tap out any cravings or distracting thoughts that mask your feelings. You listen and respond to your body lovingly and appropriately. You know that your feelings and your needs are real and that they deserve your attention and appropriate response. Additionally, you boost your metabolism. Every day you check your control room and have your higher Self make any adjustments that are necessary to know your metabolism works efficiently and optimally in creating and maintaining your ideal body and weight. Your metabolism works optimally to create energy and burn fat.

You support your efficient metabolism with regular exercise, doing activities you enjoy. You feel good after moving your body, increasing your blood flow, and recharging your energy level. Water is life. You drink lots of fresh, clean water before you eat and many times during the day to hydrate and flush toxins out your body.

Now look behind you and see that the old image of you in the first mirror is shattered. All of the old habits, cravings, lethargy, procrastination, negative beliefs, and defeating self-talk are gone. You have truly begun a new life and discovered your whole and healthy self.

You are balanced, in control, and self-loving. You enjoy being your self and living in your body. You make healthy choices in support of your vitality and health. And when you sleep, you rest well knowing your higher Self creates loving, empowering, and healing dreams that reinforce your desire and will to be fit, trim, and healthy. Sleep well with these healing dreams.

And when you awaken, it is a new day. You joyously, naturally, and easily choose the behaviors and mind set of healthy living.

# HYPNOSIS for SURGERY

Your higher Self, in all of its wisdom, is guiding you and supporting you and allowing you to receive these positive suggestions into the very depths of your subconscious mind.

This journey will take you to a wonderful place of healing and renewal. Enjoy this process and know that you are safe every step of your journey. Imagine yourself on a beautiful island, a paradise surrounded by healing blue-green water and warm moist air that you breathe in deeply. You are supported and surrounded by a tropical lush green forest with flowers all around you. The land, the rocks, and the mountains are covered by green plants and beautiful flowing waterfalls. Imagine walking down a path by a waterfall, hearing the sound of the water, and feeling the freshness cooling your face.

You continue to walk in nature surrounded by the wonderful fragrances of flowers, and the sound birds and water. With each step you take, you move deeper and deeper within. As you continue to walk, you get closer to the beach. When you arrive, you walk along the shore, feeling the sand in your toes, feeling the sun on your body, and seeing the sun sparkling on the water. You hear the sound of the ocean and the waves flowing in and out. You walk into the warm water and lie on your back and begin to float. Looking up into the blue sky, you see the seagulls soaring above you. You feel the lightness and buoyancy of this floating and it takes you deeper and deeper still. Your body rocks gently back and forth with the movement of the water. You are free. You are safe and secure. You are held and supported by the buoyancy of the water.

After floating awhile, you swim ashore, leave the water and walk slowly across the sand. Feeling the warmth of the sand on your feet and the sun on your back, you begin to walk into a tropical garden. While you walk through the garden, you enjoy the smells of gardenia and plumeria. You pick a flower to carry with you as you walk. As you smell the flower, you become more and more relaxed. The palm trees sway gently and you feel the light breeze on your skin. Tropical birds sing their beautiful songs. Eventually you approach the waterfall. As you step into and under the waterfall, the cool water flows over you, washing away all stresses and concerns.

As you move out of the water, you sit comfortably on a warm rock. You are in a state of peace and harmony, feeling in tune with nature and all that surrounds you. The distant sounds of the ocean continue to sooth and support you. The moving in and out of the waves is in sync with the in and out of your breathing. You are at one with yourself and the world. You feel the peace, beauty, and harmony that surrounds you. You are profoundly at peace and are safe. You are at one with the heart and soul of mother earth.

After resting, you continue to walk following a stream to the edge of the forest. The light is changing and the late afternoon shadows are longer as the day unfolds.

You discover a very intriguing place. A place you have never noticed before. As you approach it, you become aware of a vibration of love and healing. As you approach this dwelling, you discover that it is a healing temple. You are greeted by people with loving faces and smiling eyes dressed in ritual like robes. You are received into this temple knowing that it is time for you to receive the healing that you need.

As you are guided into the temple, you are taken to a special room where you are prepared for this healing ritual. You are cleansed and anointed with healing oils. You are guided to a wonderful place where bedding has been prepared for you. You lie down comfortably. There is soft lighting and calming music surrounding you.

As you lie down, you close your eyes and you become aware of angelic presences that are here to support you and protect you during this healing process. You ask for them to support you on this journey to good health. These angelic beings will guide the doctors and other healers to do their very best during this healing procedure. These healers are turned over to their higher Selves. They are guided with the highest skill and highest intention to do the best job possible to support your healing and wellness. You are comforted knowing that they, too, are supported by spiritual presences and guides as they work.

You are safe, you are cared for, and you are protected. Your immune system is strong. Your body, mind, and spirit are aligned so that this healing procedure has optimum positive results. You experience quick healing and minimum discomfort. Your body responds well to all medications. After the procedure, you metabolize medications easily. You have minimum swelling. And because in quantum reality, there is no time or space, you imagine folding time as you move to a state of complete health and healing. You have fully recovered from this healing process. The angels of good health release you from any and all fear and bring you courage, confidence, and strength. You know that they have guided you here to this healing process to improve your health and well-being. You know that they guide you and protect you through this process every step of the way.

The outcome of this healing is wonderfully supporting you on all levels. It is all in divine order. You receive more energy, more vitality, and health having gone through this ritual. You recover quickly and completely. You maintain a positive attitude and state of mind. Your angels are with you every step of the way. It is time for your healing now. It is all in divine order. And even if you are sleeping through this healing process, your higher Self is with you and is protecting and supporting you every step of the way.

Eventually, this procedure is complete and you allow yourself to sleep, supporting the healing and recovery process. Taking as much time as you need, when the time is right for you, you begin the journey back to full wakeful consciousness. You have a healthy immune system, a vital life force, and a sense of comfort, ease, and well-being. You see and feel all the benefits of this healing journey. You drink lots of water and feed your body nourishing food in support of your healing. You have a positive attitude and perspective. You appreciate your ability to trust yourself and the universe and to continue your healing on all levels from this moment forward.

Now you begin your journey back, having said your goodbyes to all of your healing helpers. Come back to wakeful consciousness when you are ready. All you have to do is breathe your way back. Bring back with you a renewed sense of well-being and a sense of appreciation for all the seen and unseen helpers that are with you, supporting you every step of the way.

# 5. HYPNOTHERAPY for the MIND

## HYPNOTHERAPY for INSOMNIA

*I*f you are using this script, you are most likely one of the forty million Americans who suffer from insomnia on a regular basis each year.

With regular use of the techniques included in this book, you can be free of your sleep difficulties. Together, hypnosis and Emotional Freedom Technique are effective tools for reducing or eliminating insomnia.

For the most effective results in eliminating your insomnia, first learn about sleep hygiene and some simple behavioral choices you can make to support your ability to sleep. Next, work with the Emotional Freedom Technique or (EFT) process. EFT may be used anytime during the day, at night before bed, or in bed during the night if you are not sleeping. EFT can clear your sleepless patterns, worries, physical or emotional pain, or agitation that inhibits your ability to relax and let go of mind chatter and distress. EFT can also clear your energy system and symptoms so that your body and mind are poised to fall asleep and stay asleep naturally and effortlessly.

After learning and practicing EFT, use the insomnia hypnotherapy processes while in bed. Use whichever hypnotherapy technique you prefer or alternate using them for variety. After repetitive use of the techniques and practicing the sequences of the processes, you will eventually be able to hypnotize yourself to sleep by allowing your "inner hypnotist" to guide you.

## Important Pointers for Sleep Hygiene

According to the health website, http://www.medicinenet.com/sleep/page6.htm#sleep_hygiene, here are several behavioral guidelines that may help you to overcome insomnia:

"Before bed, avoid watching movies or TV programs that may create anxiety or worry.

Avoid caffeine in the evenings.

Avoid alcoholic drinks before bedtime.

Sleep as much as you need to feel rested; do not oversleep.

Ideally, exercise 20 minutes a day at least four hours before bedtime.

Avoid forcing yourself to sleep.

Keep a regular sleep and a waking schedule.

Don't go to bed hungry but avoid large meals and excessive fluids before sleep.

Avoid doing work in your bedroom or having clutter or distractions in your bedroom. Make your bedroom an inviting, soothing, and safe place.

Do not smoke before bed or in bed.

Adjust your sleep environment: lights, temperature, noise, etc.

Resolve your worries before you go to bed."

## Systematic Relaxation for Enhancing Sleep

This relaxation process is intended to be used when you are in bed and want to sleep. You can begin your night of sleep with this process or use it to assist you in sleeping again if you awaken. Repeatedly using this relaxation process will teach you the skill of relaxing and letting go. The more you use it, the more you will cultivate the skill of becoming more and more relaxed. Relaxation will assist you in letting go into sleep.

After adjusting your sleep environment and preparing yourself for bed, lie comfortably in your bed. Position your body so that it is supported and as open as possible. If you are comfortable to do so, lying on your back is ideal. Now is the time for you to connect with the wisdom of your body, mind, and spirit, along with your natural abilities for sleep.

When you are ready, simply close your eyes. Take a few deep breaths. Begin to notice your body and any areas where you would like to be more comfortable and relaxed. Begin to breathe into those areas now. Imagine that each breath softens the muscles and brings the flow of blood and life force into those muscles and organs as a way to support your releasing and letting go. Now image a color that you associate with comfort and well-being. Breath this color in with each inhalation and direct this color into your body. You begin to feel more and more comfort and you are more and more relaxed.

Continue to breathe in your relaxing color with each inhalation. You are breathing in relaxation with your in-breaths and you are releasing and letting go of the busyness of your day, along with any stress or any physical or emotional discomforts as you exhale. Imagine that you breathe out discomfort and past experiences of sleeplessness. Breathe out everything you want to release and set free when you exhale. Breathe in the relaxation. Let go of the rest as you exhale. As you continue to breathe, you begin to experience your body is filled more and more with the color of well-being and relaxation.

You continue to deepen and let go with each breath and, at any time, if you find yourself drifting off to sleep you just go with it … moving into a restful receptive state for your comfort and healing of your body, mind, and spirit … You may listen with your subconscious mind while your conscious mind and body relax and you move towards sleep.

Focus your awareness on your toes. Breathe into the areas of your toes. Imagine that your toes are filling with the color of comfort and relaxation as you inhale. Simply think or imagine it is happening, feel it or possibly even see it. As you exhale, any stress or restlessness moves out from the bottom of your feet like sand moves through your fingers … filling your toes with comfort and well-being … emptying your toes of tension.

Focus on your feet. Breathe relaxation into your feet. See and feel the muscles, tendons, and bones softening and letting go. All tension and discomfort flows out the bottoms of your feet as they are filled with the lightness of comfort and well-being. Your feet keep you connected to the earth and allow you movement through your daily life.

Moving to your ankles, feel and see the comfort flowing up your body into your ankles as tension and any discomfort dissipates and softens … filling your ankles with the color and sensations of comfort.

As you focus on your body, you can hear my voice but may not hear my words and you can drift off into the deeper quieter perceptions that come with sleep.

Focus on your calves and shins. Acknowledge how your legs bring mobility to your life. Give your calves and shins your loving focus and attention and breathe in appreciation for their carrying you through your life. Allow all muscle fatigue and tension to move down your body and out the bottoms of your feet … dissipating stress … bringing in a new sense of balance and well-being.

Focus on your knees, which bring you flexibility and the ability to change direction in your life. Your knees are surrounded by the color of relaxation. You breathe in this color … softening the muscles and nurturing the tendons and cartilage with each breath … releasing and letting go of all tension to flow out from your feet.

Now bring your attention to your thighs and the muscles which carry you through your day. Appreciate their strength, their hard work. Give them rest now. Allow the muscles to soften and let go. There is nothing to do, nowhere to go. Be present here and now in this moment. Simply *rest*.

Moving up to your abdomen … softening your belly with each in-breath … having a gut knowing of how natural and easy it is to let go. Remembering how natural and easy it is as a child to sleep when you are ready to rest and let go.

Now place your attention on your buttocks and lower back, breathing the color of relaxation into the muscles … softening, resting, growing in comfort and well-being. releasing and letting go.

Moving up your back and into the area of your heart, diaphragm and lungs … filling the space of your upper body with a growing sense of comfort and lightness … feeling a spaciousness; that there is space between every cell in your body … filling the space with your color of comfort. See it flowing in you and through you, and letting go of all the rest.

Focus on your shoulders and arms. Seeing all tension flow down and out your fingertips. Replacing the space of your shoulders and arms and hands with the light of your soothing color, with comfort. You rest well knowing that your muscles and bones are in complete comfort and that you are well.

Your attention moves to your throat and neck. Fill your throat with the sensations of growing relaxation and comfort. Feel an openness in your throat … an ease of breathing … a growing sense of peace and safety … trusting in your natural desire to rest well … knowing that your body appreciates and responds to your letting go.

Fill your jaw, temples, and mind with the knowingness that your body is more and more relaxed … that you are at peace with yourself and the world. Rest well, knowing that even now your body begins to renew itself. Notice that your mind can rest, as well. When you are aware of thoughts, they drift by like leaves on the surface of a stream. They come and they float away.

And even if the surface of the water is moving and has the coming and going of leaves, you can imagine seeing below the surface into the deeper, quieter pools where there is a darker calmness and spaciousness … a restful place of deep quiet. You have the freedom to choose where you want to be. You focus on what you want for yourself now in this moment. You let go even more and more into a natural, deep state of comfort and restful sleep.

You remember being a small child and how naturally your body and mind know to rest when you are tired. You sleep when you need rest. Imagine being that child now. Choose to be in the safety of your bassinet or crib or in the protection of your parent's arms. Feel the ease and comfort of letting go into sleep now. You sleep deeply. Your body rests in comfort and well-being. You dream healing dreams. You sleep easily and deeply. You awaken in the morning refreshed and renewed. You sleep like a baby. Your body and mind know how to flow into the wonderful and restful state of sleep. It is as natural as breathing. And when you awaken in the morning, you appreciate the wonderful ease and your natural ability to dream healing and inspiring dreams … looking forward to the next night of sleep … knowing that your body and mind remember how to sleep deeply and well. You bring into your daily life a renewed sense of trust and well-being.

While you rest, you take a break from all the past stresses and concerns. You are on vacation from the routines and patterns of your life. You are away from all the daily distractions, responsibilities, and demands. Where do you most want to be now … in the tropics, the mountains, a desert oasis, by the ocean, in a garden, at a cabin in the woods? Go to the place where you most want to spend restful time; a place of beauty and peace … a place of renewal. You are in a place where you lose track of time and you experience your life unfolding moment to moment. Be on vacation now. Let all of your senses support your enjoyment of this moment.

Look around you at the surroundings. Take in the colors, textures, and sights. Smell the fragrances and feel the temperature of the air. Listen to the sounds of nature and the sounds of silence around you. Feel supported and nurtured by this place and your surroundings. Already, you are feeling the natural, growing sense of comfort and well- being.

Find a place to lie down or recline on a lounge chair, a hammock, possibly on a sofa or a bed. Make yourself comfortable as you feel even more letting go.

It is that magical time of twilight. The sun is going down and there is a stillness in the air. The sky is brushed with the last illumination of the sun's rays and is glowing a deep blue.

Project your awareness into the deep blueness. Surround yourself with it like a comforter of blue. Imagine that, in front of you, you slowly draw a large white circle on the blueness. Draw it now. … Imagine the large circle in front of you. Inside the circle, using your cursive writing, slowly in a big sweeping script, in white letters, you write the word "sleep." Focus on each letter as you write it. Feel the rhythm and flow of your arm and hand movements as your write: S…L…E….E…P. Take care to write the word inside the circle. Imagine the word there now. *SLEEP*.

Now, using your other hand, very carefully imagine erasing the word by tracing slowly over letters. Erasing the S…L…E…E…P. Inside the circle is clear, vast blueness. Look and feel into the depth of the circle. Once again, in rhythmic sweeping cursive writing, draw the word, *sleep*. … S…L…E…E…P. Take your time. The white letters are inside the circle. Luxuriate in the flow and the movement of writing, taking care to stay in the circle. *SLEEP* is right in front of you, carefully drawn. See, feel, and hear the word, *SLEEP*. Enjoy the effects of this wonderful state and the meaning and feeling of whiteness on the deep blue. Using your other hand in the same sweeping and rhythmic movement, very slowly, with care, trace over *SLEEP* as you erase one letter at a time S…L…E…E…P.

A clear deep blueness remains.

You lose yourself in this flow of movement, sound, and sight … taking care, drawing the word, one letter at a time … seeing the whiteness on the deep blue … staying inside the circle … S…L…E…E…P. *SLEEP*… erasing the word with the slow, sweeping movement of your other hand. The letters disappearing right in front of your eyes … S…L…E….E…P. Nothing to see, nothing there. Gone. Vast blueness. You continue with the flow of drawing the word, one white letter at a time. S…L…E…E…P. See it appear in front of you, however fuzzy, however indistinct. *SLEEP*. And then slowly erase the word. Tracing over the letters carefully, one at a time. … Watch it disappear. S…L…E….E…P. … dancing in front of you, like a cloud in the breeze, like a bird in the sky. Now you see it. Now you don't. Now you hear it. Now you don't. Now you feel it. Now you don't … back and forth … white over blue … only blue. You are surrounded by the comfort of blueness. Drift and expand into the vast blueness in front of you… around you. You become the flow of the letters, You become S…L…E…E…P. You are asleep. You sleep. Resting well in the vast blueness. Resting well. A…S… L…E…E…P. Now you see it … *aSLEEP*. Now you hear it … *aSLEEP*. Now you feel it …. *aSLEEP*.

Now you are the vastness … the blueness. … Go into the blueness. Become the vastness asleep … asleep well. Stay with the rhythm, the back and forth as long as you like as short as you want … on vacation … loosing time, letting go, expanding self, resting well, asleep now. You are letting go into sleep now. … deeply … comfortably … resting well.

All is well.

# HYPNOTHERAPY for ANXIETY

The most common issue, by far, that clients present in my practice as a focus of therapy is anxiety. Experiencing anxiety can include many fearful emotions and physical symptoms. There are several types of anxiety disorders in which symptoms range from feelings of uneasiness to immobilizing bouts of fear. While these hypnosis processes are not intended to replace individual medical and psychological treatment, you can use the techniques and processes to learn to manage your symptoms of anxiety and you may likely shift the energy and thought patterns that keep your symptoms in place. I use and teach these anxiety management techniques with my clients and hypnotherapy students with consistently good and sometimes profound results. With regular use of these processes, you can hope for relief from the frequency and intensity of your symptoms and you may even control them for good. If you feel unsafe or too overwhelmed to use these techniques on your own without a therapist as your guide, I encourage you to seek professional assistance. If your physician or therapist is treating you for anxiety, consult with them before you use this program.

What is your anxiety like? Is it a general and almost daily state of worry and tension? Is it linked to specific memories, thoughts, and triggers, or primarily bouts of fear for short periods of time? No matter what your symptoms are, these energy therapy and hypnosis techniques can shift your energy, helping to alleviate your symptoms and cultivate a state of calm, well-being.

## Space Induction Hypnosis for Anxiety and Fears

Sit in a safe place where you have privacy and will not be interrupted. Uncross your arms and legs and position your body so that your back is comfortably supported. Adjust your headphones and test to make sure you are hearing a comfortable volume. Close your eyes.

Become aware of the space between your hands.

Become aware of the space between your shoulder blades.

Become aware of the space between your right elbow and your left knee.

Become aware of the space between the top of your head and the ceiling.

Become aware of the space between your in-breath … and your out-breath.

Become aware of the space between your feet and the floor.

Become aware of the space between the phrases that your hear.

Become aware of the space between the right side of your body and the wall on your right.

Become aware of the space between your heartbeats.

Become aware of the space between your eyebrows.

Become aware of the space between your thoughts.

Become aware of the space between your eyes and your closed eyelids.

Become aware of the space between your heart and the person most dear to your heart.

Become aware of the space between your body and the chair or sofa.

Become aware of the space between the outside of your skin and the inside of your body.

As you become aware of the space, notice where in the space you feel the most comfort and relaxation.

Begin to fill more of the space with this feeling of comfort and relaxation. Allow it to grow and flow into all other areas of your body. Focus on the places where you had been holding tension, tightness, or fear.

Allow the comfort and relaxation to soften these areas. Allow the space to expand as the tension dissipates and dissolves like clouds becoming more amorphous, lacking shape, lacking form … clearing and softening … opening and expanding … growing in spaciousness and comfort.

Become aware in the space of any fear or anxiety that remains. Focus on it and where in the space it lives.

What do you perceive in this space? Is it a sensation … a thought … an emotion … an image … a memory? Stay with it. Focus on how it occupies this space as a part of your awareness now. Watch it. Feel it. Stay with it. Notice it in relation to all of the other space in you and around you. Breathe into it. Embrace it. Allow it to be. Notice how it changes. How it responds to your being present with it … allowing it.

You are not the tension. You observe it, but you are not it. You are the witness, the observer of the space. You are not the fear. You observe it but you are not it. Continue to observe and watch. What do you experience in the space now? Stay with it. Watch it. Notice the energy clearing and releasing. Notice that there is more and more space. Be with the spaciousness … the openness … the calmness and well-being.

As you feel more and more space, with what do you wish to fill the space?

You fill the space with trust.

You fill the space with peace.

You fill the space with love.

You fill the space with a calm deep inner experience of being safe.

Now allow whatever you choose to fill the space.

Become aware of the space between your hands.

Become aware of the space between your shoulder blades.

Become aware of the space between the top of your head and the ceiling.

Become aware of the space between your in-breath … and your out-breath.

Become aware of the space between your feet and the floor.

Become aware of the space between the phrases that you hear.

Become aware of the space between your heartbeats.

Become aware of the space between your thoughts.

Become aware of the space between your eyes and your closed eyelids.

Become aware of the space between your body and the chair or sofa.

Become aware of the space between the outside of your skin and the inside of your body.

As you become aware of the space, notice where in the space you feel the most comfort and relaxation, the most trust and peace and love. Bring these qualities back with you now as you slowly open your eyes and return to the time and space of your life … bringing trust, peace, and love back with you. In this time and in this space … all is well.

## Sleep Hypnosis for Anxiety with Tree Metaphor

After lying in bed and adjusting your body so that you are in a comfortable, safe, open position, turn out the lights and close your eyes. If you have already created your hypnotic anchor for calm and relaxed by using the anchoring process, then activate your anchor, or go to your best memory of being calm and relaxed. This memory becomes your time and place for a hypnotic vacation in a place of peace and safety and beauty. This is a place where you are free to be at peace with yourself and the world. Step into the environment of this place. *Be* in it. Look around you. See the colors, feel the textures, and notice the areas of open space and sequestered and protected areas. Find a place where you can lie down and rest, perhaps on the grass, on a lounge chair, a bench or on a hammock … a place where you feel protected and safe. Notice the temperature and the fragrances of the air. Listen to the peaceful sounds around you or become aware of the stillness and silence.

Each breath you take is relaxing and comforting. You breathe in relaxation and breathe out the rest. Imagine a soft breeze blowing through your hair and over your arms and a soft tinkling of wind chimes soothing and comforting you. With each thought and each breath, you are becoming more and more relaxed. All tension is flowing out from the bottoms of your feet with each exhalation. You breathe in relaxation and let go of the rest.

While you rest and relax, you reflect on nature and being in nature, and you remember a time and place when you felt a connection or attraction to a particularly special tree. Remember this tree now … and know that trees have a unique wisdom to share. Trees don't talk; but they do have a great deal to tell us. We can learn from trees what they know innately. And this tree can teach you much about yourself and what it means when you are rooted and safe.

Imagine what it would be like to be this tree. You have sprouted and grown in a place where you thrive. All of your needs are met so you can be safe and strong through your whole life. You send roots down into the earth and you receive all you need: sun, air, water, and earth-rich nutrients. Daily, you tap into your source that gives you life and nourishes the Self. You are so stable and rooted that you weather all changes and seasons. You survive and thrive through the storms and the droughts. You bend with the wind and move through the changing seasons of your life with ease. You know that there is a time for everything, that all things change, and you change with the times. You understand that you are a part of the natural rhythm, which comes with life. You trust this rhythm to bring you what you need, when you need it, even if you are not consciously aware of it.

Is the tree aware of what it wants and needs, or does it simply be with what is and grow with each moment to express its tree-ness and its innate capacity to grow with the flow of what is? You survive and thrive through all changes, branching out, adapting, and growing through it all. You store up strength and energy to thrive through the storms and droughts of your life. Your trunk is a core of stability that is strong, dependable, and constant. Your branches are a protective cover, providing a place to rest. You branch out with new possibilities for being calm and relaxed and safe in your life. You are rooted in the experience and knowledge that you are safe to be right here, right now. You blossom in your potentials and enjoy the bounty of your life. You are a part of the greater All That Is. You trust your place in it all. You rest well, knowing you are safe, here and now. You sleep well through the night knowing that in the morning, when you awaken, you greet the new day with a sense of wonder and trust of what is. Rest well.

# INNER FAMILY

## Introduction to Creating the Inner Family and Healing the Inner Child

As children, we all have needs that must be met appropriately and consistently for us to thrive and become self-actualized as adults. If our needs are not met, or they are met erratically or inconsistently, we may develop traits or characteristics that are our defensive attempts to meet our needs. Many of our dysfunctions or coping styles are the consequence of these unmet needs and our responses to our childhood. Working with the inner family and our inner child is a therapeutic approach to intrapsychically begin meeting those nagging needs and to create corrective emotional experiences that have a lasting effect on who we are and how we function and respond in our relationship to ourselves, each other, and our daily lives.

Learn how to use EFT before you do the hypnosis processes so that you have a way to transform any patterns or emotions that come up during your daily life and you have a way to resolve emotions or memories that may not be resolved through the hypnosis process.

Also, before you begin the inner child work, do the hypnotic processes first in order to create a new inner father and mother so your inner child will have the resources available for inner parenting. If you grew up without one parent or were adopted, imagine the inner father and/or inner mother as a person(s) who was a representative figure of that parent; a step parent, teacher, neighbor, or uncle, for instance.

If you are using the following scripts for self hypnosis and you begin to feel overwhelmed, seek the support of a professional mental health practitioner who can support you by pacing and containing your process so that you are safe to do the work.

Special thanks to Dr. Ronald W. Jue, Ph.D, for permission to use his inner family processes.

## Hypnosis to Create the Inner Father

Sit comfortably. Adjust your body so that your back and head are supported. Close your eyes and take a deep clearing breath. Breathe in relaxation with your in-breath . . . and breathe out any discomfort, tiredness, or stress with your exhalation.

With each cycle of breathing, imagine breathing in the positive part of what you want to feel and letting go of what you wish to release with each out-breath. With each cycle of in-breath and out-breath you become more and more relaxed.

Imagine that you are in a safe and beautiful place. You are surrounded by beauty and positive energy. You feel at home and protected. Look around you and take in the surroundings. Notice the colors and textures. Breathe in the air as you notice the temperature and the fragrances. Notice the time of day and the quality of lighting and shadow around you. Listen to the sounds around you. Take it all in. You feel supported by this special place. You are safe.

You find a place to sit awhile. As you relax, you invite your inner child to join you. Notice your inner child. How old is your inner child? What is he or she wearing? What is the expression on your inner child's face? What is his or her body posture and what is it expressing? As you observe your inner child, what do you perceive that he or she needs?

Imagine your father standing in front of your inner child. Notice how he is dressed, his facial expression and his body posture. What does your father's state of being communicate to the child? How does your inner child feel standing with his or her father? Where in the inner child's body or in your body do you feel the response to your father? What do you feel? What does the response communicate to you about the relationship you share?

Standing with your father, is your *father's* inner child, who is about the same age as your inner child. Notice your father's inner child's dress, his facial expression and his body posture. What does this child's state of being communicate? What does he need?

Standing with your father's inner child is *his* father, who is your grandfather. Imagine that your grandfather has all of the awareness, skills, and resources to parent and lovingly support your father's inner child. Imagine that your father's inner child has his needs met appropriately, lovingly, and consistently. Notice how your father's inner child responds. Your father's inner child begins to grow up. As he develops, his needs are met appropriately, lovingly, and consistently, day after day, week after week and month after month. He grows into a man. He is a man who experiences his wholeness and in his wholeness he has plenty of love and attention and wisdom to share. And as an adult, he is present, giving, and engaged as a parent. Your father's inner child has grown into a new, healthy, loving inner father for your inner child. Your new inner father has the time, skills, and resources to meet your inner child's needs. Notice your inner child standing with his or her new inner father. Notice your inner child's facial expression and body posture. What is your inner child experiencing now? From this moment on, whenever your inner child needs attention, protection, holding, appropriate boundaries, and love, your inner father is present and engaged in parenting.

And as you think back to your father's inner child and any past unmet needs, you can hold a new level of perception. How do you feel towards your father now? You understand more about how he grew into the father he became.

You make a place in your heart where your inner child and your newly-healed, whole, and self-actualized inner father live. This place is where they relate and respond to each other from an experience of wholeness and healing for your inner child. Your inner child's needs can now be supported and met in loving, appropriate, and consistent ways.

## Hypnosis to Create an Inner Mother

Sit comfortably. Adjust your body so that your back and head are supported. Close your eyes and take a deep clearing breath. Breathe in relaxation with your in-breath … and breathe out any discomfort, tiredness or stress with your exhalation.

With each cycle of breathing, breathe in relaxation and breathe out the rest. With each breath, you become more and more relaxed.

Imagine that you are in a safe and beautiful place. You are surrounded by beauty and positive energy. You feel at home and protected. Look around you and take in the surroundings. Notice the colors and textures. Breathe in the air as you notice the temperature and the fragrances. Notice the time of day and the quality of lighting and shadow around you. Listen to the sounds around you. Take it all in. You feel supported by this special place. You are safe.

You find a place to sit awhile. As you relax, you invite your inner child to join you. Notice your inner child. How old is your inner child? What is he or she wearing? What is the expression on your inner child's face? What is his or her body posture and what is it expressing? What is your inner child's state of being? As you observe your inner child, what do you perceive that he or she needs?

Imagine your mother standing in front of your inner child. Notice her dress, her facial expression and her body posture. What does your mother's state of being communicate to the child? How does your inner child feel standing with his or her mother? Where in the inner child's body or in your body do you feel the response to your mother? What do you feel? What does the response communicate to you about the relationship you share?

Standing with your mother is your *mother's* inner child, who is about the same age as your inner child. Notice your mother's inner child's dress, her facial expression and her body posture. What does this child's state of being communicate? What does she need?

Standing with your mother's inner child is *her* mother, who is your grandmother. Imagine that your grandmother has all of the awareness, skills, and resources to parent and lovingly support your mother's inner child. Imagine that your mother's inner child has her needs met appropriately, lovingly, and consistently. Notice how your mother's inner child responds. Your mother's inner child begins to grow up. As she develops, her needs are met appropriately, lovingly, and consistently, day after day, week after week and month after month. She grows into a woman. She is a woman who experiences her wholeness and in her wholeness she has plenty of love and attention and wisdom to share. And as an adult, she is present, giving, and engaged as a parent. Your mother's inner child has grown into a healthy, loving mother for your inner child. Your new inner mother has the time, skills and resources to meet your inner child's needs. Notice your inner child standing with his or her new inner mother. Notice your inner child's facial expression and body posture. What is your inner child experiencing now? From this moment on, whenever your inner child needs attention, protection, holding, appropriate boundaries, and love, your inner mother is present and engaged in parenting.

Place a hand over your heart. Feel that the fullness of your heart is the home where your inner family dwells. Whenever you want the support of your inner family for your inner child, you can place your hand over your heart to call forth your inner father or mother to meet your inner child's needs. And as your child's needs are met lovingly, appropriately, and consistently, your inner child experiences more wholeness, balance, and health.

And as you think back to your mother's inner child and any past unmet needs, you can hold a new level of perception. How do you feel towards your mother now? You understand more about how she grew into the mother she became.

You make a place in your heart where your inner child and your newly-healed, whole, and self-actualized inner mother live. This place is a place where they relate and respond to each other from an experience of wholeness and healing for your inner child. Your inner child's needs can now be supported and met in loving, appropriate, and consistent ways.

## Introduction to Hypnosis for Healing Your Inner Child

Use this hypnotherapy process for healing your inner child *only* after you have created your new inner father and mother so that the inner family resources are in place to support the re-parenting of your inner child. In this hypnosis process you will focus on a present time and a current issue that is problematic in your daily life. For example, maybe you feel anxious facing authority figures at work and you would like to be more comfortable and confident. Perhaps your primary relationships bring up constant fears of abandonment and you would like to feel more trust. Possibly you no longer want to be defensive and angry whenever you feel criticized. Or maybe you want to stop taking on responsibilities for others with the usually unfulfilled hope that they will meet your needs in return. Any pattern in your adult life that feels like an outcome of your childhood needs not being met is a potential focus for this inner child process. You may repeat this process for any pattern or behavior that you would like to change.

If you have severe neglect or abuse in your background, it may be necessary for you to work with the guidance of a trained mental health practitioner so that you are supported, paced appropriately, contained, and feel safe to do the inner-child work. Do not use this process alone if you are feeling overwhelmed when working with your inner child.

## Hypnosis for Healing the Inner Child

Choose an experience from your recent daily life that you will use as a focus for this hypnosis session. Work with an experience that brought up emotions, perceptions, or behaviors that you feel represent an expression of your defenses or maladaptive qualities that are in some way rooted in your childhood.

What is the focus for your session? When you are ready to go into hypnosis, sit comfortably with your back supported. Take a deep breath. Notice your lungs filling and your belly extending as you breathe in air. As you exhale, imagine letting go of all the tension in your body. Breathe in relaxation and breathe out any discomfort or stress. After a few breaths, you notice your eyes blink naturally and when you are ready, allow your eyes to close. As you sit, feel your body supported by the furniture and your feet comfortably positioned on the floor.

In your imagination return to your safe place or if you prefer, go to another inner landscape where you are protected and surrounded by beauty. With all of your senses, experience your surroundings. See the colors and textures, smell the clean air and fragrances, and hear the sounds around you. In this moment, right here and right now, you are safe. As you explore and appreciate your surroundings, find a place where you can sit and rest. Feel the energy and support of this special place as you reflect on your focus for this inner-child work. Close your eyes as you sit and reflect. Using your anchor for your inner father and inner mother, know that they are with you and available to assist you in this inner-child work.

Now invite your inner child to join you. As your child-self arrives, begin to communicate through eye contact, loving touch, or words. ... Welcome your inner child into your safe and protected space. Tell the child that you and the inner parents are here to support the child in having his or her needs met and that this meeting is an opportunity for healing. Ask the child to take your hand and invite him or her to take you back to the childhood event or memory that is most directly responsible for the current issue in your life. Tell him or her that in an inner way, the child may finally begin to have his or her needs met. Where in your body do you feel the sensations or energy related to this issue? What emotions do you feel? What thoughts come up as you talk to yourself about this concern?

As you take the child's hand, I will count from one to ten. By the count of ten, you will be back in a childhood memory or event related to the present time issue. One. Focus on the body sensations. Two. Moving back in time. Three. Going to a childhood event. Four. Opening to healing the memory. Five. Following the emotions back in time. Six. Back in time. Seven. An event or experience that you can heal. Nine. And ten. You are in another time and place in your childhood. Focus on yourself as the child, step into the child body, and experience it. How old are you? Where are you? What is happening around you? What are you doing? How do you feel? Notice if you are alone. If you are with others, who they are?

Using all your senses, experience being the child. Perceive from your child awareness. What is it that you need in this experience? Invite either the inner mother, inner father or both inner parents to be present for the child. The inner parent knows what this child needs more than anyone in the universe. This inner parent has the time, tools, resources, and wisdom to be with the child in a way that supports the child's needs. Perhaps the child needs safety. The parent can protect the child or take the child out of the environment to the safe place. Perhaps the child needs love and attention, or the child needs to understand something about what is happening and the inner parent explains the truth of what is happening. The child has only to be the child. A parent is there to do what parents and capable adults do and the child finally gets to be safe, loved, understood, and accepted just as he or she is, simply for being. Your child self feels loved and his or her needs are met in positive ways.

Imagine, day after day, your inner child, is supported, heard, honored, cared for, and loved, consistently and appropriately. How do you feel now? Imagine your child growing, learning, and evolving with daily support and attention, feeling loved and safe. What is your experience now?

Allow this experience of having your needs met to fill you completely, touching all aspects of who and what you are, filling every cell of your being. What is a word, phrase, or image that comes to mind that expresses the essence of the best part of your child's experience now? This best part becomes your anchor to this new connection to your inner parent, to this feeling and to knowing that your needs are now met in this deep inner way. And any time, in your daily life, that you are aware of your inner child's patterns being activated, use this anchor as a way to connect with your inner child and to parent your child lovingly and appropriately in that moment. Your inner child is safe, loved, understood, and honored. Your inner child's needs are met.

Know that each time you work with your inner child, you are supporting your inner child's evolution, healing, and well-being. Slowly, when you are ready, come back to the room and open your eyes.

# DREAM WORK IN HYPNOTHERAPY

## Introduction to Dream Work

You will spend one-third of your life asleep and, while asleep, much of your time dreaming. Working with your dreams can be fascinating and enlightening. Hypnosis and self-hypnosis tools can open the door for remembering and working with your dreams. There are five stages to dream work: having a dream, remembering the dream, journaling the dream, writing down impressions and initial comments about the dream, and finally, doing the dream work. The hypnotic processes on dream work will help you to move through all five stages of dream work. Your dreams are truly a doorway to accessing the archetypal and spiritual realms, to a deeper self-awareness, to increasing your problem-solving skills and for learning and healing. Since the state of hypnosis is between the waking and sleeping states of consciousness, using hypnosis for dream work can greatly enhance remembering dreams and the work of uncovering their wisdom. Dream work will inform, inspire, and enhance your connection to Self. Welcome to the adventure of working with your dreams.

## Types of Dreams

Once you are remembering your dreams, you will discover that there are a variety of dream types and each dream has several levels of meaning.

### 1. Daily life

Some dreams are related to your daily life. A dream can relate to events or situations that are a part of your normal activities. These dreams often have familiar people, environments, and memories from your past or present-life circumstances. These dreams may support dealing with the anxieties of your life or helping with problem solving about those things you consciously or unconsciously worry about in your waking life. Dreaming about past events will likely be connected to things that are needing attention and healing from that period of your life. In these daily-life types of dreams, we are trying to process or organize what happened or will happen and these dreams often give us creative approaches or solutions to problems.

### 2. Recurring dreams

Recurring dreams are the psyche's way to demand our attention. In my dream work experience, a recurring dream will usually stop once the dreamer has taken the time to work with the dream and understand the messages the dream offers. Also included in this category of dreams is what is called a serial dream. These are dreams that have the same theme, characters, or feelings that have continuity and seem to evolve from dream to dream. These dreams are like sequential chapters in a book. Serial dreams will often be bookmarks for the dreamer to understand her own growth and evolutional process.

### 3. Nightmares

Nightmares are potent dreams that also have the effect of getting the dreamer's attention. Most dreamers who have nightmares usually awaken so they are sure to remember the dream. When the dreamer works with the nightmare and understands the important messages the dream offers, the fear generated from the nightmare can be transformed into wisdom and healing. What appears to be the "boogeyman" in the dream can be a dream helper who "wakes up" the dreamer to something that is important and needs attention.

### 4. Spiritual or other dimensional dreams

Some dreams are spiritual or other dimensional. Dreamers have this type of dream when they have a premonition, share a visitation with a person who has just died, who the dreamer did not consciously know is dead, or have dreams that bring guides or spiritual messages to consciousness. Also, in this category are dreams that may be past-life memories. These dreams often leave the dreamer with a feeling of clearly having "been there;" a feeling that the dream is as real or more real than the waking state. Spiritual dreams may also put us in touch with archetypal aspects of ourselves. They may also teach us about those parts of ourselves that are our shadow aspects, which are disowned, avoided, or projected out onto others or the world.

5. Lucid dreams

In lucid dreams the dreamer is aware that he is dreaming and is able to direct the dream consciously for a positive outcome in the dream experience. Lucid dreams are empowering, teaching people how to bring the sense of empowerment into their daily lives.

## Guidelines for Working with Dreams

- We dream to become more awakened in our life. All dreams bring into consciousness something of which you are not yet aware.

- Dreams may have many levels of meaning for the dreamer.

- All aspects of the dream are parts of the dreamer, as well as representing aspects of his or her inner or outer life in the past, present, or future.

- Symbols in a dream may have standard meanings; however, those meanings may not fit the dreamer's experience of the symbols in the dream. Also, because symbols have different meanings in different cultures, the standard cultural meanings may not symbolize the same concepts for each person's dreams.

- Dreams speak in the language of metaphors, symbols, and archetypes.

- Often words or details in your dreams will have double meanings.

- Only the dreamer can know the meaning of her own dream. A person who offers an interpretation for someone else's dream needs to own that she is interpreting the dream through her own projections and filters, as if it were her own dream.

- Dream work engages the dreamer to arrive at her own sense of understanding through her unique aha! experience. The dreamer knows when she has realized the teaching and meaning of her dream because she feels it and knows it through her body.

- It is important that dream work is used as one tool to guide you in your life. It is inappropriate to assume that all dreams tell you what to do. They will, however, give you encouragement to explore your options and choices and act as sign posts along the way.

## Introduction to Hypnosis for Remembering your Dreams

The first challenge in working with your dreams is remembering them. Here is a simple hypnosis exercise you can do before bed to activate your dream source, the Dreamweaver, the transcendent Self, that has all-knowing awareness and wisdom. This exercise helps to bring your dreams to consciousness when you awaken. Be persistent in listening to and using this hypnosis at bed time. Through this process you are working to program your capacity to dream and remember your dreams. If the door to remembering your dreams has been closed for a long time, it may take awhile to loosen the rusty hinges so that the door opens easily and effortlessly each night. Place a pad of paper and pen next to a lamp on your bedside table. This paper will be your dream journal.

## Hypnosis for Remembering your Dreams

After preparing for sleep, lie comfortably in your bed. It is time to set all of the activities and focuses of your day aside. You are looking forward to an enjoyable night of restful and renewing sleep and wonderful dreams. As you lie comfortably in bed, notice where, in your body, you feel the most comfort and well-being. Breathe into that area and imagine that comfort begins to expand throughout your body moving to any areas where you want to experience more comfort. You breathe in relaxation and as you exhale, you release any tension and business of your day. Now it is time for you to let go and relax. Close your eyes.

Imagine you are walking on a gentle, sloping path down a hillside. The path winds easily through a forest. With each step along the path, you take in the beautiful surroundings and move deeper and deeper within. Your senses come alive as you walk. Look at the colors and textures of nature. Feel the stability of the earth beneath your feet. Hear the sounds of the forest around you. As the light of the late afternoon sun glows through the trees and ferns, you enjoy many shades of fresh green and rich-colored earth tones. Breathe in the moist fresh air … and as the sun sets, you feel the cooling temperature on your face and arms. You can barely hear your footsteps as you walk on the moss-covered path.

After walking for some time, you see a small structure through the trees. You are intrigued to discover a dwelling so deep in the forest. As you approach the structure, you have discovered what feels like a very special and sacred place. The structure is a small temple. As you enter the walkway to the door, there is a carved wooden sign that reads: Welcome to Dreamtime. Your Dreamweaver awaits your arrival. As you enter, you will be between the worlds of wakefulness and sleep and you are able to communicate with the part of you that orchestrates your dreams.

Tingling with excitement and anticipation, you approach the tall, wooden door. You release the latch, open the door, and step inside. What a wondrous place. Hundreds of twinkling candle flames illuminate the room. In the center of the room is a smiling presence, who emanates love and good will. You approach the figure and discover someone who seems very familiar to you. You meet the part of you that creates your dreams, your Dreamweaver. In this meeting your Dreamweaver and conscious self learn to communicate, to build trust and an on-going relationship to enhance your dream life and your ability to remember your dreams.

Your Dreamweaver welcomes you and invites you to look around the room. Your eyes have grown accustomed to the candle light and you are able to see many doorways along the walls. Your Dreamweaver communicates that each doorway leads to a specific kind of dream. Each door has a symbol, word, or picture that represents the kind of dreams to which the door leads. For example, one door leads to dreams that are connected to your growing up and childhood events that want healing and resolution, while another doorway leads to dreams about past lives. The next doorway leads to dreams that connect you to people and animals who have died and who wish to communicate with you. Another door leads to problem-solving and life-direction dreams. There are many, many kinds of dreams that you will explore in your dreamtime and many wonderful teachings, discoveries, and healings await you through these doors to your dreams. After showing you the doors, your Dreamweaver takes you lovingly by the hand and guides you to a luxuriously appointed bed. You lie down on a thick comfortable, mattress. You are ready to sleep now.

You ask your Dreamweaver to send you dreams that will bring you messages and teachings that will support your healing and growth. You ask for support from the dreamer in remembering your dreams so that the dreams may communicate their messages to your conscious self. In this relaxed state, you have more direct access to a focused awareness and you are open to receive these helpful and empowering suggestions.

Your Dreamweaver stands by your bed while you sleep, supporting you and guiding you through the doors and into dreams while you sleep. Your Dreamweaver becomes more and more active while you sleep and you remember your dreams. As soon as you awaken, lie quietly for awhile and tune into your feelings, images and any words or impressions that are still with you from dreamtime. Then, reach for your dream journal to record any impressions or details of whatever dreams that you have brought back to conscious awareness. Record any emotions, body sensations, words or phrases, and impressions that come out of your sleep and any details, stories, characters, events, or environments you remember. You journal anything even if it is only a vague memory or impression. You journal with words and drawings. Your regular dream journaling communicates to your unconscious that you are earnest about wanting to remember and work with your dreams. Your commitment to dream journaling opens the door to remembering your dreams. You imagine awakening and reaching for your dream journal. See and feel that you are writing on the paper, recording and honoring each detail or dream fragment that comes. At a later time, you review the dream and write down comments and questions you have about the dream for future dream-work sessions. You write in your dream journal each time you awaken, and the door to remembering your dreams opens wider and wider each night.

In the days and weeks ahead you remember your dreams easily and with more and more detail. You appreciate your Dreamweaver's help as you remember and work with the wisdom of your dreams. Each time you go to sleep, you are excited that your dreamtime is more and more accessible to you upon awakening. And knowing that a dream is already waiting at a door to dreamtime, you allow yourself now to drift off to sleep. You rest comfortably. You sleep well. You remember your dreams.

## Introduction to Hypnotic Dream Work

Doing dream work in the non-ordinary state of consciousness of hypnosis has many advantages over doing dream work in the normal wakeful state. Since dreams occur in the altered state of sleep, and hypnosis is the liminal consciousness between wakefulness and sleep, the dream and wakeful consciousness can more easily and directly communicate. Also, in the hypnotic state, you have a more direct access to the intuitive and the higher Self's insight and knowingness. The state of hypnosis gives us access to more right brain and symbolic awareness that is closer to the language of dreams and in hypnosis, we can move out of the way from some of our blind spots and mental blocks.

In dream lingo, the main character in each dream is called the dream ego. Sometimes the dream ego is clearly your daily self and in other dreams it may appear as another person, animal, or even an inanimate object. The dream ego is the dreamer's self image or the consciousness of the one having the dream. You will do most of your dream work from the dream ego perspective, but you may also become other dream characters or a symbol in the dream to understand their messages and meanings.

You do not need to have a complete dream to engage in dream work; work with any dream image or fragment that intrigues you; however, only focus on one dream at a time. Before beginning the hypnosis process to work with your dream, choose and review a dream from your dream journal and make a list of specific questions about the dream. You will have time to focus on these questions in the dream-work hypnosis. There will be many different levels and aspects of your dream to explore in the following hypnosis process. Some aspects may not be relevant to every dream. You may do the segments sequentially or skip any segments that are not relevant to your dream. After practice, you will naturally learn these processes and have the ability to take yourself into self hypnosis to facilitate your own dream work. Now get ready for some enlightening dream work and fun!

## Hypnosis for Working with your Dreams

Work with this process after meeting the Dreamweaver.

For this hypnosis process have your dream journal handy so you can take notes after the session. After adjusting your body so that it is supported and sitting up comfortably, close your eyes. Begin by breathing in a few deep, clearing breaths. Imagine a yardstick in front of you that represents your level of hypnosis. The zero end represents your conscious state and the thirty-six end represents a profoundly deep state of hypnosis. For this hypnosis process the level between six and eighteen is ideal because you will be interactive through the dream work. Imagine the yardstick and the number that represents your beginning state of trance. With each breath, the numbers representing your depth increase on the yardstick. Keep breathing in relaxation and letting go with each exhalation. Now imagine the yardstick becomes a path and you are walking along the path carrying your dream journal. A page is open to the dream that you will focus on in this dream work session. Each step you take supports your movement along the yardstick. You go deeper and deeper with each step. You enjoy the surroundings as you take in the scenery, the smells, and the sounds around you. You check the level of your depth as you move along at your own pace, breathing in and out and moving deeper and deeper along the way.

After moving along on the path for awhile, you discover a beautiful and private resting place. You are delighted to see that your Dreamweaver awaits you to assist you with this dream work session. You find a place where you sit together comfortably.

You hand your Dreamweaver your dream journal which is open to the page of the dream, which is the focus for this work and you ask for assistance in understanding the dream. Dreamweaver nods and smiles as a sign of support. While doing this dream work process, if you need support, you may ask your Dreamweaver for help.

You begin the dream work by re-entering the dream. Dreamweaver asks you to close your eyes and touches your shoulder. You are back in the Dreamtime temple standing before one open door. You step through the doorway that leads back into this dream. You are standing in the environment and setting of the dream. Use all of your senses as you revivify and recall the dream. See and feel the surroundings. What is it like to be in this dream again? By reentering this dream, you have access to all of the details and particulars of this dream. Take some time to focus on the over-all map of your dream. What are the actions of your dream ego? What does your dream ego do and what does it avoid doing? How does the dream ego feel throughout the different phases of the dream? What attitudes or beliefs does the dream ego have?

In this dream, what are the challenges and the conflicts? What are the resources and successes? What is resolved and unresolved in this dream?

What questions does this dream evoke? What are the themes in this dream? How does this dream map overlay onto your daily life? How does it overlay onto your inner life? How does the map of this dream overlay onto what you need more of in your life?

Now you focus on talking with the dream figures. With which dream character or dream object would you most like to speak? Call that figure forward. What does the figure feel like or look like? Is it familiar like anyone or anything you know? You ask questions and await a response that may come through an inner voice, an image, telepathy, inner knowing, or through feelings. You ask, "Why are you in my dream? How do you relate to my outer life? What part of me do you represent? What do you want me to know about why you are in this dream? What do you want to happen in this dream? How did you get into the situation of this dream? What do you want from me?" Now ask any other question of the dream image. Receive what comes. Are there any other dream figures with which you wish to speak? If so, you can dialogue now. Your dream figures or images may also dialogue with each other for an expanded view of the dream and more than one point of view. Share what comes.

Now you focus on symbol amplification by choosing one important symbol that stands out to you in this dream. Bring this symbol forward. Focus on it while you continue to relax. Work with your breathing to let go even more, allow this symbol to come alive for you and develop in your awareness. How does the symbol appear physically in the dream? Notice its colors, textures, shape, sounds, voice, words, and energy. What are its qualities? What is its essence? What are its functions in the dream? How do you feel when in its presence? What does it remind you of in your daily life? What does it bring up for you? What is this symbol communicating to you right now? What does its presence in your dream communicate? In what ways is this symbol connected to your past, your present, and your future?

Are there any other dream symbols with which you wish to work? You may amplify these dream symbols and dialogue with them, as well. What do you experience?

To further expand your understanding of this dream, focus on the following questions and receive what comes:

- What are you not yet seeing or understanding in this dream?

- What is this dream asking of you to carry out in your daily life for healing?

- What does this dream show you about your beliefs or attitudes?

- What is this dream teaching you about yourself and your life?

- What else would be helpful to know about this dream?

When you feel complete with receiving responses to these questions, thank your Dreamweaver for the support. You will clearly remember this dream work session. Take time now to slowly open your eyes and come back into the room. From all that you discovered about the dream and yourself, what title do you give this dream? What does this dream teach and heal? Journal about your dream.

The last dream work exercises will be appropriate to do on your own after you have integrated this dream work session. Give yourself a few days and come back to revisit this dream and dream journaling. Respond to the following thoughts and questions in your dream journal as dream-work activities: If you were to rewrite this dream, how would it change? If the dream were to continue to a resolved ending, how would it end? You can also rewrite the dream as a myth or a story, incorporating all that you have learned and discovered through the dream.

Based on your insights and learnings, contemplate the changes you would like to make in future dreams as a way to support your evolution and growth. Then do the dream-manifesting hypnosis process to incubate a dream that expresses a transformed dream ego. Finally, in your daily life, consider using affirmations, intentions, and actions to change any parts of yourself that you have met in your dreams that need support and transformation to express more wholeness.

Dream work can become a mainstay to your ongoing process of self-discovery and growth into manifesting and living a more whole, self-actualized life. You are well on your way.

## Introduction to Advanced Dream Work

The purpose of these advanced dream work techniques is to enhance your self-awareness and to support your ability to be more self-actualized in your daily life. I recommended that you work with the Remembering your Dreams, Meeting your Dreamweaver, and Hypnosis for Working with Dreams processes first to become comfortable with the basics of dream work before using these more advanced dream work scripts. The advanced dream-work hypnosis processes are intended for people who regularly remember their dreams and have at least some basic dream-work practice.

In using these hypnosis processes to enhance your dream life and dream work skills, you will need to keep your dream journal by your bedside, as you will be writing down your dreams upon awakening. The single most important key to remembering and enhancing your dream life and dream-work experience is your commitment to write down your dreams. Daily dream journaling primes your unconscious to become engaged and involved with dreaming and remembering your dreams. Over time, your dream journal will give you an overview of your dream themes and patterns and will also give you perspective on your own evolution, healing, and growth.

When you journal, write in present tense and in first person from the perspective of the dream ego, the one having the dream. One helpful dream journal technique is to use a spiral notebook and to write the dream or draw images and impressions on the right side of the notebook and to leave the left side page blank for taking notes and writing comments from working with your dream.

The first interactive hypnosis technique that follows is a process to use, seed. or manifest a dream to help you with an issue that is alive in your daily life. You can do this process in session with guidance, and then use your self-hypnosis skills at home on your own before bed. You will meet with your Dreamweaver, the part of you that orchestrates your dreams, and ask for help in manifesting a dream that will bring you teaching or healing in response to a specific concern. The second advanced hypnosis process includes guidelines for lucid dreaming and hypnotic techniques to help you build and program lucid dreaming skills. These hypnotic lucid dreaming processes will soften the boundaries between your waking and dreaming consciousness so you can activate the capacity to lucid dream by being aware that you are dreaming and to begin to direct your dreams in empowering and creative ways. Lucid dreaming helps you to live the dream of your waking life with more awareness, empowerment, and fulfillment.

## Introduction to Hypnosis to Seed or Manifest a Dream

Use this process once you are regularly remembering your dreams. The purpose of seeding a dream is to ask your Dreamweaver for a dream to help you with a question, decision, relationship, concern or issue in your life to which you want to bring understanding, insight and healing. For instance, you might ask for a dream to help you with direction around a life transition, or you might ask for advice on dealing with a health issue. Perhaps you can ask for a dream that will give you inspiration and insight into moving forward with an art project or feeling blocked in some other area of your life. Or possibly, you want to seed a dream to activate your spiritual growth and awareness. Before you proceed with this hypnosis, have a clear focus in mind. Write down your request for the dream in your dream journal. Also, write down any thoughts you may have about why manifesting this dream will be important and meaningful to you in your life. If you do not receive a dream the first night after doing this hypnosis, then do this process for a few more nights. The dream may take some time to be incubated before it comes to you. Be patient and persistent.

The following hypnosis process programs the subconscious to work with your Dreamweaever or transcendent Self to bring you insights and transformation. Dream manifesting will not necessarily result in a direct answer to a question since dreams are symbolic and are filled with many levels of meaning.

After you manifest an incubated dream, you have the joy of working with the dream to discover the many possibilities and gifts the dream presents.

After receiving the wisdom of the dream you have an opportunity to choose whether to follow any guidance or insight by taking action and living out the healing and teaching of the dream. Do not be over simplistic or too literal and throw caution out the dream door by saying this dream told you what to do. Use dream work as one touchstone in your decision and choice-making process. The Hypnosis to Seed a Dream that follows works with images and metaphors that continue the hypnotic journeys form the basic dream-work processes to cultivate more advanced dream work skills. You can experience this process in session and then use your self-hypnosis skills to repeat it on your own before sleep.

## Hypnosis to Seed a Healing or a Teaching Dream

While lying in bed and ready for sleep, close your eyes. Notice your body. Where in your body are you the most comfortable and relaxed? As you breathe into those comfortable and relaxed areas, imagine the comfort growing and spreading to other areas in your body that want to relax and let go. Imagine the comfort is growing with each in-breath and any discomfort and tension moves out from the bottoms of your feet as you exhale. Continue to breathe in relaxation and breathe out the rest as you become more and more still and you become more and more relaxed. The space of comfort and relaxation continues to grow and expand throughout your body. You look forward to sleep and to the guidance, inspiration, and healing of the dream that awaits you.

While your body continues to soften and relax, your mind becomes more still and focused. Imagine that you carry your dream journal with you as you once again move onto the path into the forest. Take in the surroundings. It is evening and the path ahead is illuminated from the glow of the Dreamtime temple that you have visited many times. See the surroundings. Smell the trees and plants as you breathe in the cool oxygenated air. Feel the sacredness of this special time and place as you approach the temple now and return to this safe and trusted place. You are free to access your wisdom and whole Self here. You are free to open the doors to dreamtime. Anticipating your return, your Dreamweaver welcomes you at the door. Feel and see the beauty in this special place. The walls are illuminated with the flickering candlelight. There is an energy of peace and vast possibilities here.

In these supportive surroundings, you sit together on chairs while you communicate. Your Dreamweaver listens attentively as you explain your purpose for the meeting. Thank the Dreamweaver for the on-going support in dreaming and remembering your dreams. Tell the Dreamweaver about the need behind your current request. You ask for help in manifesting a healing or teaching dream that will inform, teach, inspire, and bring healing to this concern or situation. Show the Dreamweaver your dream journal and read your intention and request. How does the Dreamweaver respond? Listen with your ears, eyes, body, and heart. Does the Dreamweaver have any advice or requests for you? Assure the Dreamweaver that you will work with any dream that comes, working towards more self-awareness and understanding. Take time now for any further dialogue and exchange. You receive what comes in whatever way it comes.

When you are complete with your communications, it is dreamtime. You are guided to get into bed. Knowing that the preparations for a healing dream are in place, you easily and effortlessly move into sleep. And while you sleep, your Dreamweaver waits for the appropriate time in your dreamtime to take you to the door of the dream woven to meet your request. In the right moment in dreamtime, you walk through the open door and meet the characters, setting, symbols, messages, and feelings that are the guidance of your dream. Sleep knowing that the unfolding of your path is guided by the support of your Dreamweaver, your wise, transcendent Self. You look forward to journaling and then working with your dream to discover its gifts and wisdom. You are grateful for dreaming as a tool in order to live more fully awakened as your whole Self. Sleep well.

## Introduction to Lucid Dreaming

In our waking life, we normally experience several levels of awareness. We can be fully self-aware and conscious, partially self-aware, or unconscious. Just as in waking life, there can different levels of awareness in dreaming. The goal of lucid dreaming is to develop the ability to become conscious enough in a dream to be aware that you are dreaming and to interact in your dreams to create desired outcomes. Having the ability to lucid dream creates positive effects in your waking life of feeling more empowered and self-confident to interact with the content and process of living in your daily life.

The first skill of lucid dreaming is <u>mindfulness</u>. It begins by asking ourselves in a dream, "Am I dreaming?" Here are some specific things you can do after asking the question, "Am I dreaming?"

In your dream, look at a watch, and look again. In dreamtime the numbers or face of the watch may display strange characters or be distorted. You may, instead, look at your hands. In a dream they may not be recognizable as your own. Perhaps you look in a pool of water, a window or a mirror to see your reflection. In a dream the reflection is often distorted, blurred, or unrecognizable. Reading something in a dream may have content or writing that changes while you read.

Another method is to pre-arrange and hypnotically practice using a symbol in your dream as a signal that you are dreaming. One dreamer uses her power animal, a butterfly, as a cue to realize that she is dreaming. Another person uses the sound of her favorite instrument, a flute, as a clue to become aware that she is in a dream. Choose a signal or cue for yourself and practice responding to it in your hypnotic skill rehearsal for lucid dreaming.

The second skill of lucid dreaming is being able to <u>recognize dream signals</u> to know that you are dreaming. One way to recognize your dream signals is to look carefully at your past dreams for themes or patterns, things that commonly recur in your dreams. For instance, do you have dream themes of doing activities like talking on the phone to someone who has passed, or cleaning house in formal dress, or planning a class you will teach, or playing catch at a particular beach? Recognizing your dream signals will help you remember your dreams and can be a cue to ask yourself, "Am I dreaming?" Practice asking yourself this question during the day to become more lucid in your wakeful state and you will condition yourself to ask the same question and become lucid in your dreams. By comparing your wakeful perceptions to those in dreams, you will begin to notice distinctions, intrinsic to wakeful consciousness versus dream reality.

If an anomaly occurs in your dream, you can use it as a signal that you are dreaming. For instance, experiencing that your body is flying, feeding a tortoise a hamburger, exploring Pluto in a convertible, or playfully swimming in a pool with a piranha would be good indicators that you are having a dream.

Sometimes dreamers awaken from a lucid dream prematurely. Stephen LaBerge, a well known lucid-dream researcher, proposes two ways to prolong a lucid dream: The first is to rub one's hands in the dream to activate the brain in producing the sensation of rubbing hands rather than the sensation of lying in bed coming into awareness. The second is to spin the dream body to engage the brain in activating rapid eye movement, which can extend a phase of rapid eye movement sleep, the state of sleep consciousness most directly related to lucid dreaming. In hypnosis you can skill rehearse using these lucid dreaming tools so that when you are in the actual dream state, they will be more readily available in your dream consciousness and you will be more prepared to access these skills.

The following hypnotic processes have the purpose of programming and activating your capacity to participate in a lucid dream. Use the Lucid Dreaming Skill Rehearsal anytime you like and the Hypnosis for Lucid Dreaming when in bed, right before sleep. Be persistent and patient as you cultivate the skills, benefits, and joys of lucid and interactive dreaming into your dreamtime. Many of the images and metaphors used in this Hypnotic Lucid Dreaming Skill Rehearsal will be familiar from using the other dream work scripts. Repeating and reinforcing these images and metaphors continues to program you for dream work success.

## Hypnotic Skill Rehearsal for Lucid Dreaming

For this lucid-dreaming skill rehearsal hypnosis, sit comfortably with your back and neck supported and your arms and legs uncrossed. Make sure that your back and neck feel supported and sit with your arms and legs uncrossed.

Close your eyes. Take a few deep, clearing breaths. Feel a growing sense of relaxation moving through your body and more and more stillness in your mind. Any tension or discomfort flows down your body, out your hands, and through the bottoms of your feet, like sand through your fingers. Experience a growing sensation of comfort and well-being. Allow yourself to be right here, right now. This moment is all that is. Enjoy it. Luxuriate in the now.

Imagine that you have prepared for bed and your day is ending. You look forward to a restful night filled with empowering dreams. You especially look forward to your lucid dreams. As you crawl into bed, you feel the clean, cool sheets on your bare feet and notice that you are already feeling relaxed. Your body is comfortable and supported by your pillow and mattress. You enjoy your body's stillness as your thoughts begin to quiet and slow down. You welcome restful sleep.

And now you begin to dream. The dream unfolds bringing you visions, sounds, smells, feelings, and interactions. The dream theme is familiar to you. Your mind, dream body, and emotions are engaged in the dream and you ask, "Am I dreaming?" You look at your hands and realize that your dream body hands are not those of your daily life. You recognize that you are self-aware in your dream. You are aware that you are dreaming. So that your lucidity stays engaged and focused in the dream, you rub your dream-body hands together or you spin your dream body around. You stay engaged in the dream and focused on your lucid dreaming. You are enlivened, expanded, and empowered. You direct your dream by interacting with the dream figures, the dreamscape, and the content and story of your dream. You communicate what you wish to express. You move around in the dream to where you wish to go. You are creative and resourceful in this dream. You communicate with the people and symbols in your dream. You are creating your own dream. You enjoy the freedom, the awareness, and your self-empowerment to choose the events, characters, direction, and outcomes in your dream.

And when the dream is complete, you remember the dream in order to record it in your journal upon awakening.

You look forward to sleep and dream time knowing that your skill increases each time you participate in a lucid dream. Your success and skill as a lucid dreamer exponentially increases with each experience of lucid dreaming. You lucid dream more and more frequently.

Knowing that this skill rehearsal and all of these positive suggestions support your success and growing skills as a lucid dreamer, you return to the room refreshed and renewed as I count you back from five to one. Five. Four. Three. More than halfway back. Two. And eyes open now. One.

## Sleep Hypnosis for Lucid Dreaming

You are ready for sleep and you look forward to wonderful lucid dreams. Adjust your body in bed so that you are comfortable and ready to relax. Take a few deep breaths. You begin to settle in and let go. Feel the comfort of your bed and pillow supporting your body as you breathe in relaxation and breathe out the activities and busyness of a full day.

While you continue to soften and relax, imagine that you are once again walking on the path approaching the dream temple, the place in which you connect with the part of you that orchestrates your dreams, your Dreamweaver. Each step you take is a step towards sleep and wonderful dreams. Your inner senses explore the surroundings as you get closer and closer to the dream temple. You have arrived. As you open the door to enter, you discover that flickering candles illuminate the temple and reflect light off the many doors that are the passageways to your dreams. You are comfortable here. This is a familiar and safe place. Your Dreamweaver has been waiting for you, welcomes you with a smile and guides you to the dream bed to rest. You are ready for sleep. Dreamweaver stands protectively and patiently by your bedside and awaits your letting go into sleep … drifting deeper with each breath … fully letting go, go to sleep.

While your physical body sleeps, your dream body accompanies the Dreamweaver to a special door in the temple leading you to a lucid dream. Dreamweaver says to you, "As you walk through this door into a dream you retain your self-awareness. You dream the dream and know that you are dreaming. You experience the dream as you actively create it. Walk through the door. Experience the dreamscape. Where are you? All of your senses explore the dream environment. What do you experience around you? What colors, shapes and symbols are present with you now? Who is with you? What are they doing here? What do you smell? What do you hear? And how does your dream body feel?

You ask the question, "Am I dreaming?" Notice your hands. Clearly, you are dreaming. Rub your hands together or spin your dream body to stay in the dream. You begin to interact and engage with the dream characters, symbols, and the dreamscape. The dream unfolds as you wish. You are the artist and your dream is the canvas. What do you want? Where do you wish to go,? What do you bring to your dream for the most delight, healing, and learning? And so it is … you actively create and interact. While your body sleeps, you are self-aware in your dream.

You can heal, learn, and teach. You can feel, remember, discover, and know. You can transform, evolve, and grow. You can BE. Enjoy being aware that you are aware. You orchestrate this dream. You are free to create the dream and outcomes you want. You are empowered as you direct your dream. You delight in the creative expression of this lucid dream. You continue to be aware that you are aware.

When your body awakens, you journal your dream, knowing that many more lucid dreams are born from these dreams you choose to create.

# 6. HYPNOTHERAPY for the SPIRIT

## HIGHER SELF HYPNOTHERAPY

### Introduction to Higher Self Hypnotherapy

In these Hypnotherapy for Spirit processes, you will become familiar with and trusting of your own innate wisdom and intuitive knowing through connecting with the guidance of your higher Self. Your higher Self is loving, empowering, supportive, gentle, and wise. It is the part of you that is creative, resourceful, and all-knowing. It is your divine nature and Spirit. This aspect is very different from the egoic parts that want control, are judgmental, demanding, and put pressure on you to perform or "do it right." It is through contacting the higher Self that healing and transformation take place.

### Higher Self Hypnotherapy

Sit comfortably and adjust your body so you are open, comfortable, and your back is supported. Take a deep breath … and notice how you can relax as you exhale. Continue to breathe deeply and comfortably. You let go of all the concerns of your day with each exhalation. With your next deep breath and exhalation, simply close your eyes. Gaze into the space between your eyes and closed eyelids. Notice what you perceive there. Notice any lightness or darkness. Notice colors, shapes, any movement, or stillness. Imagine looking beyond what you perceive as you let go of the busyness and activities of your day.

As you breathe, imagine a color that feels comforting and soothing to you. Breathe this color into your body, focusing on areas that want to be more comfortable and relaxed. Each color-saturated breath supports the expansion of comfort and the letting go of tension and discomfort with each exhalation.

Imagine a natural environment where you can be for awhile … a place of peace, protection, and beauty … a place where you are safe. Go to this place now. You are surrounded by the beauty and the energy of this place. Allow all your senses to come alive. See and feel the colors and textures around you, Feel the temperature of the air on your face, arms, and hands … and smell the fragrances in the air. Notice the quality of light and shadow around you as you experience this time of day or evening. Listen to the sounds of any animals, insects, and birds that are present. Notice if there are any sounds of water in the surroundings. You are at peace here. You are at one with yourself and your place in this world. Continue to take in your surroundings … feel, smell, see, and hear what surrounds you. Fill in all the details of what you experience being in this place, here and now. Fully enjoy this moment of beauty and relaxation.

*Spiritual Hypnotherapy Scripts for Body, Mind, and Spirit*

Find a place to sit and rest as you take in all this place has to offer you: balance, renewal, and perfect peace. Imagine that as you sit with your eyes closed, you breathe in the pure air and energy of this place … this sanctuary for your body, your mind, and your spirit. Your higher Self is kind, offers loving energy, and support.

In this state of restful inner awareness, you call upon the part of you that is infinite and wise, the part of you that is your higher Self. You experience this part as an image, a feeling, a presence, a knowing, or an inner voice. Your higher Self is kind, loving energy and support. What do you experience now? How does your higher Self make itself known to you?

Be with this energy and awareness. Know that it is always available for you to access. Know that its purpose is to guide, empower, and support you on your path of this life.

What do you wish to ask your higher Self? In what ways do you need guidance or insight? Take some quiet time to communicate through words, feelings, symbols, images, and inner knowing. Receive what comes. If you have a special concern or need, present it to your higher Self. Ask for specific guidance and support. Ask your higher Self to show you what you need to know about this concern in your life.

Your connection to your higher Self is not limited to this state of consciousness. Your higher Self can communicate with you throughout your daily life and in your dreams, as well. Now that you have communicated directly with this wise aspect of yourself, ask it to come to your awareness at any time that you would benefit from its guidance and support. How will you know when your higher Self is communicating and encouraging your growth and development? How will you know when your higher Self is informing you or nudging you in the direction of your highest good? You experience how your higher Self will get your attention and how you can begin to become more and more aware of its presence in your life. What does your higher Self communicate to you about what you need?

Imagine you are in a situation a few days from now when you are in need of direction, encouragement, or support. Step into the situation. Imagine being there with all of your senses. Feel yourself, see out of your eyes, and hear what you are saying inwardly to yourself, or listen to the conversation you are having if you are with someone else. Naturally and easily, you become aware of the presence of your higher Self. It gently nudges you to pay attention and you are aware of it being with you and within you as a resource for support. You remember to listen to and to freely accept its empowerment and guidance. You choose to respond in a way that supports your wholeness and well-being and the wholeness and well-being of others. You connect with and respond from your higher Self's wisdom and perspective. From experience, you learn to trust your higher Self. It always affirms divine order and the good of the whole.

You find that the more you access and listen to this divine aspect of yourself, the more connected to it and in communication with it you are. You look forward to many, many experiences from your higher Self and to the integration and growth it promotes within your being. Your awareness and sense of Self continues to expand through your connection to your higher Self.

Knowing that each time you listen to this hypnotherapy process, the voice of Spirit becomes stronger and stronger, and your relationship with your higher Self grows in strength and clarity, you look forward to changes in your outer daily life. You live more effortlessly in the flow of your own highest good and the divine.

It is time to begin the journey back to wakeful consciousness. You return with a strong inner connection to Self, a renewed sense of well-being, and clarity of mind. Come back slowly as I count you back from five to one Five. Beginning to return. Four. Becoming more alert. Three. More than halfway back. Two. Your eyes opening. One. Back in the room feeling alert and fully awake.

## Introduction to the Inner Healer

The Inner Healer process is intended to be used as a self-care adjunct to your regular medical care; it is not intended as a medical treatment or as a substitution for medical care. All hypnosis is self-hypnosis and all healing that comes from the use of mind/body hypnotherapy healing is healing that is generated within your Self. This self-hypnosis will introduce you to your Inner Healer and support the ongoing development of your relationship to your own abilities to support your own healing from within.

## Inner Healer Hypnosis

Now is time for you to connect with the wisdom of your body, mind, and spirit and your natural abilities for self-healing.

Sit in a comfortable place with your back supported and your arms and legs in an open and receptive posture. When you are ready, simply close your eyes. Begin to notice your body and any areas where you would like to be more comfortable and relaxed. Begin to breathe into those areas now. Imagine that each breath softens the muscles and brings the flow of blood and life force into those muscles and organs as a way to support your releasing and letting go. Now imaging a color that you associate with comfort and well-being, breathe this color in with each inhalation and direct this color to the areas of your body that you wish to support. You begin to feel more and more comfort and you are more and more relaxed.

As you experience a growing sense of comfort and well-being, imagine that you are walking along a path in a redwood forest. You feel the softness of the rich forest loam under your feet as you walk and you smell the aromatic fragrances of the trees and plants along the way. It is late afternoon. You enjoy the play of light and afternoon shadows on the path as you walk. You hear a profound silence and occasionally the forest birds. You are at peace in this wonderful place. You are sustained by the stabilizing ground beneath your feet and the fresh oxygen-rich air. You move deeper into the forest.

While you travel on, you notice that the sun is beginning to set. The light is becoming dim. You are deep into the beauty and quiet of the forest. And yet, far off in the distance you see a glow of warm light and hear a faint sound of chimes and bells. You are curious about what this could be, so deep into the forest. You travel deeper at your own comfortable pace … continuing to enjoy the sights, the sounds, and smells.

The glow of light gets brighter and the beautiful sounds of chimes and bells become clearer and more audible. You are moving towards the light and sound.

Around the next bend on the path you see the source. There is a small temple ahead. It is glowing with light, surrounded by lush ferns and colorful flowers. You hear the sound of a garden water fountain that is near the open front door. As you get closer, a smiling robed figure steps into the illuminated doorway to welcome you. It is as if your arrival has been expected. The greeter explains to you that you have come to a very special healing place. A place where you are assisted in having the skills, resources, and support to heal yourself.

You feel the loving presence of your greeter as you are guided into the temple. You are taken into a room containing a bath filled with oil scented healing waters. There is soft music and candlelight. Your greeter leaves the room. You disrobe and climb into the warm bath. You close your eyes, enjoying the fragrance and feeling of these healing waters on your body. You begin to relax even more and drift off into a wonderful dream-like state.

You become aware of a presence. This presence is your Inner Healer. It may be an image or a voice or a feeling. How does your Inner Healer make itself known to you now? It has come to assist you in your balancing, healing, and renewal. You are incredibly connected to each other. Your Inner Healer knows exactly what you need. You invite your Inner Healer to use all of its skill, wisdom, abilities, and resources in support of you now.

The Inner Healer may become transparent and move energetically into your body to the areas and sites wherever support and healing are needed. Your Inner Healer begins making changes, working if necessary, like a surgeon, or a magician, or working like a spiritual deity with energy and the light of divine grace. The Healer has all the tools and skills necessary to heal. You receive needed changes in your body structures. Your body is cleansed and balanced. Your body functions and organs are restored to perfect functioning, just the perfect amount of life-force energy is generated and maintained. Circulation is balanced and you are restored to comfort and well-being. New fully functioning cells are developing. Debris is eliminated from your body. The tissues are renewed, and the flow of energy is stimulated and restored. Describe the changes you see and feel taking place.

You feel and see the healing taking place. Your body, mind, and spirit work together with your Inner Healer in this healing ritual. You take as much time as you need to feel and see that the healing is taking place right here, right now. What are you experiencing?

You appreciate this special time and focus on yourself and your current needs. You receive many benefits from this healing exchange. You look forward to experiencing all of the lasting benefits coming with you. The water, light, and music that surround you support your healing, as well. All toxins are released. Full balance is restored.

The healing ritual is coming to completion for now. You may either say goodbye to your Inner Healer and know that you will meet again or you may ask your Inner Healer to stay with you as an unconscious, on-going, and continuous support of your wellness needs as you return to your waking state.

You become aware that your greeter has returned bringing you a clean towel. You are asked to step out of the water, dry yourself, and dress for your return journey. Your greeter awaits you at the temple entrance.

When you are finished in the bath area, you walk towards the entrance of the temple feeling light and balanced. You give thanks to your greeter for the healing opportunity to meet with your Inner Healer and for sharing this special healing place. You know that you may return at anytime you wish. You are surprised to discover when you exit the temple that the forest and path are illuminated with early morning sunlight. The path is surrounded by the morning activity of birds and small forest animals. You enjoy the cool morning breeze and the warmth of the sunlight on your hands and face. You are feeling well and at peace.

You are ready to meet the rest of your day. You return from this journey feeling better than you have felt in a long time. You return with all the memories and benefits of this healing journey and your work with your Inner Healer .

I slowly count you back now to waking consciousness from five to one. Five. Four. Three. Two. One. Wide awake and renewed.

# HYPNOTIC ENERGY BALANCING

Behind every aspect of who you are is energy. Your energy system can be flooded with too much energy or depleted. You will be guided through a series of processes and techniques that will balance your energy system and empower you to take charge of your own energetic domain by maintaining effective energetic boundaries. Learning to ground your energy allows you to be more present in your body and energetically protected, contained, and focused. You will learn to balance the major chakras or energy centers of your body. Clearing stagnant, negative, or disruptive energy from your auric field will be presented as well as how to perform energetic clearings in specific environments. You will also learn an on-the-go technique you can do during the day when you need quick psychic protection.

Before you begin using these processes, consider in what ways you are having difficulties with your energy system and set some goals for yourself. For instance, do you feel hypersensitive and bombarded with energy when you walk into a room? Do you, on a regular basis, feel emotions that you believe are not your own that you empathically pick up from people around you? Are you scattered and have difficulty focusing? Do you feel emotionally numb and stuck in certain areas of your life? While any of these symptoms could be related to psychological or physical issues, there is also always an energetic component. And since we are primarily energetic beings, working on an energetic level can often shift the psychological and physical states. So, as you set your own energetic goals, give each symptom a number from zero to ten that represents the difficulty or intensity of the problem. Zero is no difficulty and ten is the most intense difficulty. Use this zero to ten gauge to evaluate and track the changes you experience as you begin to take control of your energy system. After practicing these processes for awhile, you will eventually be able to do these processes for yourself, anytime and anywhere. The more you use them, the more healthy and dependable your energy system and energetic boundaries will be.

The grounding and chakra-balancing hypnosis processes and the environmental and auric-clearing techniques are instructions that you can facilitate on your own.

## Introduction to Chakra Balancing

Chakra is a Sanskrit word that translates into a turning wheel or disc. Chakras are described as being shaped like multi-colored lotus petals. They are energy centers that are connected to main organs, endocrine glands, physiological functions and expressions of different aspects of psychic or spiritual power. They are often referred to as power centers. Chakras are invisible to the physical eye but are often visible to clairvoyants or palpable to clairsentients. There are seven major chakras and many minor chakras in the human body. Imagine the chakra is like an aperture in the lens of a camera that can open and close. If a chakra is too open there may be a draining or depletion of energy and an experience of energetic exhaustion. If a chakra is too closed, there may be an experience of blockage, resistance, or numbing related to the corresponding body functions and expression of consciousness. Balancing the chakras helps to restore the inflow and outflow of energy, bringing the energy system into harmony, and the body, mind, and spirit into balance.

In this visualization and guided process you will learn about each of the seven major chakras and how to bring them into balance. After doing this process with the help of this script for awhile, you will be able to balance your chakras on your own anytime and anywhere, as needed. Knowing how to balance your chakras is an important tool to support and maintain your energy hygiene and well-being.

## Chakra Balancing

Sit comfortably with your back supported. Close your eyes and take a few deep, clearing breaths. This is a time to balance and harmonize your body, mind, and spirit. This is a time for Your Self.

Focus on the base of your spine, the center of the root chakra represented by the element of earth. It is related to your physical needs, instincts, and survival. Imagine the rotating disk at your root chakra. How open or closed does it look or feel? In your mind's eye, or in your thoughts, imagine a dial that is connected to your root chakra. Imagine a gauge on the dial that represents how open or closed your first chakra is now. With your imagination, turn the dial to adjust the opening of the chakra so there is a perfect balance of the flowing in and out of energy. Awaken this chakra. While you adjust the dial, breathe in the color red: the color of physicality, of manifesting, of dynamic presence. Smell the fragrance of a red rose and experience the flavor or smell of a fresh, crisp red apple. Vibrate with the energy of red. Hear red, the C note on the scale. This chakra brings us grounding, health, prosperity, security, and an ability to be present in our body, here and now. Feel and see the balancing taking place. Breathe out stuck, or stagnant energy. Breathe in new revitalizing energy. See the chakra balanced and moving in harmony with All That Is. You are safe. Your needs are met. You are present right here … right now.

Focus on the area of your abdomen, your sexual organs, and your lower back. This second center, the sacral chakra, is represented by the element of water. It connects us to others through movement, sensation, feelings, and desires. When balanced, this energy center supports our fluidity, flexibility, sexual fulfillment, self-gratification, and grace.

Imagine your sacral chakra now. How open or closed does it look or feel? Turn the dial to balance it so that there is an equal expression of giving and receiving of energy. Focus on the color orange as you breathe into the sacral chakra. Smell an orange, taste it. See the orange color in an autumn leaf or a sunset. Hear and vibrate with the note D. Awaken and enliven your sacral chakra. Stay with the balancing. See and feel the changes taking place. You have the ability to express your sensuality and creativity with fluidity and grace.

Focus now on your upper abdominal area, the power center or solar plexus. This chakra is represented by the element of fire and relates to your personal power and your ability to empower others. It rules our metabolism, our will, and autonomy. When balanced, it brings us energy, trust, spontaneity, and balance of power. As you focus on your solar plexus chakra, how open or closed does it look or feel? Adjust the dial so that it is balanced. Breathe the color yellow into this center. Breathe in energy to revitalize, breathe out extra energy to clear it. Use the dial and find the balance, the giving and receiving of power. Smell and taste the color yellow. See the sun, a lemon, a daffodil. Awaken the chakra. It vibrates with the note E on the scale. Focus on the balancing. The inflow and outflow of energy. You express your power by honoring yourself and others.

Focus on the area in the center of your chest, the heart chakra. A balanced heart chakra supports our abilities to feel compassion, a deep sense of love, and connectedness. It is related to the element air, along with our self-acceptance and the acceptance of others. The heart chakra corresponds with the sense of touch. As you focus on your heart chakra, notice how open or closed it is and use the dial to begin to balance the opposites in your life: the giving and receiving of love, the male and female, the light and shadow, the self and others. As you adjust the dial, breathe in the color green. Smell the freshness of spring grass, breath out old, excess energy and revitalize it with the new. See and feel the balancing taking place. Listen to the vibration of green, the F note on the scale. Awaken this chakra. Your heart is open and balanced. You have the ability to give and receive love. You are compassionate and centered. You love and accept yourself the way you are.

Focus now on the area of your throat. The throat chakra represents your ability to express and create. It is related to the sense of hearing, language, and sound. When the throat chakra is balanced, you have an authentic voice and express your truth. How open or closed is your throat chakra? Use the dial to balance it. Breathe in the color blue while it is balancing. Vibrate in the blueness and the note G. See the light blue sky and a robin's egg. Awaken this chakra. See and feel the balancing taking place, breathing in and out to balance the wheel. Your creativity has an outlet and is a part of your daily life. You express your truth and authentic self through all you do, say, and who you are.

Focus now on the center of your forehead, your third eye or brow chakra, the center of seeing, intuition, and knowing. It is related to the properties of Light and Vision. When our third eye is balanced our intuition is working to support us in seeing the truth and getting the big picture. Your third-eye chakra is associated with the color indigo, a deep midnight blue, almost violet. Breathe in indigo now. Imagine the color of the sky at dusk. Breathe in the color as you check the dial of your chakra and begin balancing the third-eye center. Awaken this chakra, opening to your intuition, vibrating with the A note of the scale. You have clear seeing and knowing.

Finally, focus on the area at the top of your head, the crown chakra. This center is pure spiritual awareness and pure consciousness: the seat of your higher Self. The crown chakra is our connection to timelessness and the dimensions beyond our physical form. It is the opening to being all-knowing, wise, and beyond time and space. Through it we connect to the Divine within ourselves and the universe. Awaken this chakra. Check the dial for your crown chakra and begin to balance the flow and movement of the energy. Breathe in a glowing color of purple. See a glistening amethyst, feel purple, and vibrate with the B note on the scale. Experience the Divine within. You are connected All That Is.

One by one you again move through the seven chakras making any small adjustments on the dial. Beginning with the red root chakra, checking to see and feel that the first chakra is balanced and making any adjustments necessary. Then, check the orange sacral chakra, refining the dial so that it is perfectly balanced. Moving up to the yellow solar plexus chakra, make any minor adjustments on the dial so that the inflow and outflow of energy is balanced and harmonized. Moving to the green heart chakra, adjust it so there is a perfect giving and receiving of love. Then make any necessary adjustments to the blue throat chakra, perfectly balancing the inflow and outflow of energy. Your expression is true to yourself and balanced. Now making any subtle adjustments to the indigo third eye, you access inner knowing and seeing with your inner eye. Finally, make any subtle adjustments to the glowing purple color of your crown chakra, your connection to All That Is.

Now all the colors of the chakras are flowing up your spinal column forming a rainbow of light, sound, and vibration connecting all of the energy centers into one vast expression of your wholeness. Experience red, orange, yellow, green, blue indigo, and purple streaming through the center of yourself, connecting all chakras. Feel all centers working together in harmony, as a full expression of your whole and total Self. See and feel the totality, the connection to self, and to All That Is. You are a divine expression of energy. You are balanced and in tune with your true Self.

Bring this balanced energy and expression of your wholeness with you as you slowly open your eyes and return to your waking conscious state feeling whole, relaxed, and balanced. Carry this state forward for the enjoyment of the rest of your day.

## Introduction to Grounding and Protection

Grounding is an important energy practice for many reasons. It helps you to shake off any energetic fallout from dealing with daily challenges, and it shifts your focus and awareness to the present. Grounding can raise your energy so that you are more balanced and protected. It can be similar to a grounding wire that allows excess energy to flow safely and freely out of your system.

Practice this grounding technique after you have any experience of an energetic disruption, when you are tired and need to recharge your energy system, or to prepare and protect yourself before you do face any challenges or attempt any healing work. Grounding is also helpful for anyone who experiences anxiety or difficulties staying focused and present. The following is one technique for grounding.

## Grounding and Protection: How to Be in your Body Right Here, Right Now

You can do this grounding technique sitting or standing up, preferably outside. Close your eyes if you are comfortable to do so.

Either standing or sitting, take a deep breath. Hold it and then let it go. With your feet flat on the ground, imagine that each exhalation sends roots through your body and out of the bottoms of your feet. These roots are growing and going deeper into the earth with each out-breath. The roots grow through the top soil, through the bedrock and into the underground waterways, growing deeper and expanding outward.

As the roots grow deeper and deeper into the earth, you receive the benefits of the earth's energy through them. Your body absorbs the rich nutrients, the constant and dependable energy of mother earth. Your roots continue to grow to the very center of the earth where the fiery core of our earth mother provides us with all our needs. This earth energy rises up through the roots and into your body, bringing energy that stabilizes and balances you. The warmth relaxes any tension and renews your body and mind. Open to it and receive it now. Bring this energy fully up into your body from the bottoms of your feet, filling you with the warmth that energizes and renews, moving through each muscle and organ, filling your body and spilling out the crown chakra. When the earth energy moves out the top of your head, it flows upwards and onwards into the sky, leafing out like branches into the heavens.

And now, these branches absorb the light of the moon and stars, and this light of the sky streams down into the top of your head, filling your body with starlight and moonlight … moving into each muscle and organ … pulsing through each vein and artery … filling your body with light. Your body is radiant in this light, vibrating with the energy of the heavens.

Now imagine with each in-breath you bring in the earth energy through your feet, through your body, and out the top of your head. With each out-breath, you pull in sky energy through the top of your head and out the bottoms of your feet … mixing and balancing the earth and sky, the mother and father, the male and female … collapsing opposites … creating a perfect balance of the yin and the yang. Continue to breathe, following the flow of these energies that balance and support, that renew and recharge, energy that supports your being present right here, right now. When you are ready, you can open your eyes. Take a minute to adjust as you gently move back into activity. Notice how you feel.

## Triangles of Light: Clearing your Auric Field

This process comes from the channeled writings of Alice Bailey.

This technique is useful for clearing your aura of any energetic patterns and debris that can inhibit your forward movement, growth, and evolution. It is also an energy clearing technique for spirit releasement. While sitting, begin by saying aloud this declaration:

*I am the Soul*
*I am the Light Divine*
*I am Love*
*I am Will*
*I am Fixed Design.*

*In the wisdom of the Soul I place a soul star six inches above my head, as a representation of my higher Self. In the wisdom of the Soul, I place a vortex of energy around my body starting six inches above my head, moving into the earth, 30 feet beneath me.*

After stating the declaration aloud, focus on the star of energy above your head and imagine a line of light moving from the star to a point six inches in front of your third eye, And from the point in front of your third eye to a point in the center of your head, then up from the center of your head back to the soul star forming a perfect right triangle. Imagine drawing this triangle of light, over and over again. The light is opening the third eye and flushing all debris from this chakra with each drawing of the triangle of light. Find a comfortable pace for yourself as you keep drawing the lines of light in this right triangle pattern, until you have a constant flow of triangles of light moving in this pattern. Debris is releasing from the chakra and being cleared from your auric field by the vortex, then grounded in the earth. On a daily basis take time to say this declaration and do the visualization until you experience that the third eye chakra is clear and balanced.

Using this same pattern, state the declaration and make right triangles of light for your throat chakra. Sending lines of light from the soul star to a point six inches in front of the throat, into the center of the throat and straight up to the star. Take a few days or as much time that it takes to practice this on a daily basis until the throat chakra intuitively feels or looks clear to you. Remember that as you do this visualization, the vortex will continually release debris from your auric field. Repeat this pattern for each of the seven chakras. The entire process could take weeks or a month or more. Each person's energy system is different. Over the days and weeks, notice any changes that you feel as you bring this process to completion. Over time you can expect to feel clearer, more perceptive, and more empowered.

## Environmental Clearing

This environmental clearing technique can be used for your own environments or you can clear environments for others. You may do this process by yourself, but doing it in a group exponentially increases its effectiveness. This technique is ideal for clearing a home, office, garden, or blessing a new space.

To prepare for the clearing, you will need the following tools:

- noise-makers such as bells, whistles, drums, flutes, horns, or pots and pans to bang together

- If you are working in a group, each person will need a noise-maker.

- fresh flowers

- small glasses or flower vases

- You will make one small flower bouquet for each room being cleared.

- small votive candles, one for each room

- safe candle holders to allow burning until candles are naturally extinguished

Before you do the clearing, set clear intentions for what kinds of energy you want the space to support. For example, do you want the space to support healing, creativity, harmonious relationships, peace, and introspection? Or do you want productivity, financial abundance, personal growth, and expansion? Take time to write down your intentions because after the space has been cleared, you will focus on them.

After preparing the tool and intentions, go to the area closest to the center of the space you will clear. In a house or building go to the main area of the living or working space. Bring your noise-makers and gather all of the people doing the clearing together. The facilitator will make a statement about the intentions for the clearing and the blessing of the space so all who are present can focus on the intentions.

The facilitator begins the clearing or space blessing with this statement, filling in the right descriptive words for the space you are clearing. While the following declarations are made aloud, all participants visualize the star and vortex.

This process was channeled and is the transmission of Djwal Khul. (Two Disciples)

*We are the Soul*
*We are the Light Divine*
*We are Love*
*We are Will.*
*We are Fixed Design.*

*In the wisdom of the Soul, we place a soul star 30 feet above this house as a symbol of the soul energy and highest good of all who gather here.*

*In the wisdom of the soul, we place a vortex around this house, starting thirty feet above, moving into the earth thirty feet below. This vortex serves to clear and protect this space and all who are present in this space are grounded, focused, and protected and the highest good comes to all. We ask the nature spirits on this property to keep the vortex moving knowing that the energy that is cleared and released becomes the energy available for their creative use and evolution. There is now an energetic ecology in place for the highest good of all.*

After stating these declarations, have the participants take the noise-makers and move around the perimeter of the space making noise to break up the old energy patterns. The louder, the better. In a building move along the floor and the top of the walls, move into closets and around doorways and thresholds. People can be assigned particular areas or you can have a free-for-all with each person going through the whole space. Have fun, knowing that the sound is literally disrupting and breaking up energetic configurations, thought forms, and stagnant or inharmonious patterns. It may even wake up ghosts or confused spirits. Have fun and be playful and rowdy. When everyone feels complete with this phase of the clearing, re-gather in the central area. People can share their experiences.

Then ask people to take a bouquet and candle to each room, creating a small altar of beauty and light. Gather together in the central area again after the altars are in place. If an outdoor space is being cleared, create the altar in the central area of the space. Then the facilitator will restate the intentions for the space, making sure that all understand the intentions. At this point, the participants go through the space again, only this time all of the walls, doorways, closets, cupboards, and nooks and crannies are blessed with the intentions. Participants may chant the intentions, lay hands on the walls and thresholds, or use healing symbols or crystals to imbue the space with blessings and positive intentions. Bless the area of the altar in each room as well.

Have people gather again when the clearing is complete to share their experiences. If you like, it would also be a good time to socialize and to share some refreshments in order to celebrate the clear energy and new beginnings for the people who live or work in the space.

Let the candles burn until they go out and enjoy the flowers in each room until they are no longer fresh.

Periodically, the occupant or caretaker of the space can say the declaration and do the visualization to enhance its ongoing clearing and protection and also to reinforce the intentions for the space.

## On the Go Psychic Protection

Use this technique on the go anytime you quickly need to activate protection. Your eyes may be closed or open. The more you practice this method, the faster and stronger the effects.

Imagine a glowing light of brilliant white in your solar plexus. See or feel it as a glowing, pulsing warmth. The light begins to fill your body. It expands into all areas both above and below your solar plexus, filling your body and limbs completely. The glowing light fills in any weakened areas or tears in your aura by creating psychic bandages of protection in those areas which are weak or injured. The light strengthens the boundaries of your physical body and fortifies your auric field creating a bubble of while light as protection. This bubble is only permeable by positive helpful energies. All unwanted energy bounces off, protecting you from any harm or ill will since only positive loving energies can penetrate this globe of Light.

# HYPNOTIC REGRESSION THERAPY

## Introduction to Experiencing Past-Life Regressions

There are many benefits from experiencing past-life regressions. Exploring past lives can bring healing, understanding, and resolution to current-life issues of phobias, relationship difficulties, physical conditions, questions of life's purpose, and a direct experience that we create our realities by the choices we make. Interestingly, one does not have to believe in reincarnation or past lives to benefit from the process of participating in a past-life regression. Commonly, what people experience as past lives will often arise spontaneously through dreams, *déjà vu,* forms of somatic therapy, meditation, and during hypnosis sessions. Having a past-life experience does not prove that there are past lives. While past-life researchers like Ian Stevenson are interested in showing that the soul survives physical death and that the soul can remember, often spontaneously, being in other bodies, times and places, my interest as a past-life regression therapist is pragmatic. Does the process help, heal, and empower us in the here and now? I can say, from over thirty years of experience conducting thousands of group and individual sessions, that past-life therapy often supports healing and transformation when no other therapeutic modality will help. This script provides you with a past-life regression process that is open-ended for repeated use in order to explore any past-life connections to your current-life questions, concerns, and issues. Know that doing a regression is a skill. The more lives you explore, the easier and more productive your regressions will become.

## Past-Life Regression for a Current-Life Question, Concern, or Issue

Before you begin this regression, it is important to take a moment to clarify for yourself the question, issue, or concern that you will use as a focus for this past-life exploration. Past-life therapy is most fruitful when the focus is an issue for which you have some emotional charge or real concern.

After you have chosen a focus, sit comfortably with your back supported. While you are seated, rest your eyes on a focal point across from you. While you focus your eyes on your spot, take a deep breath. Your deep breath will support the beginning of your letting go into a state of consciousness where you are able to access past-life memories and events.

As I count slowly from one to five, allow your eyes to close naturally by the count of five or when you are ready. One. Continue to breathe slowly and deeply. Two. Letting go with each exhalation. Three. Breathing into areas of your body where you would like to feel more relaxation and comfort. Four. Noticing changes as you allow your eyes to close. Five. As you continue to deepen and expand your awareness throughout this hypnotic process, your higher Self knows exactly the appropriate depth to create and what it is that will support and benefit your healing and transformation. Turn yourself over to this infinitely wise aspect of yourself. Relax into knowing that your higher Self is accompanying you every step of the way. Know that you are protected and safe and that you will only remember what you are ready to know and heal.

Continue to breathe fully and slowly and imagine the color red. Remember the color of a crisp, red apple, or winter berries, or possibly a piece of red clothing that you enjoy wearing. Think red. See and feel the color red as you breathe it into the base of your spine … filling your body with the vibration of red … the color of grounding … of aliveness … of being embodied.

Now imagine the color orange. Remember the color of a ripe persimmon, an orange chrysanthemum, a brilliant orange, an autumn tree. Think orange. Breathe in orange as you focus on the area right below your belly. See and feel the vibration of orange ... the color of creativity, procreation, and sensuality. Allow it to fill your body as you continue to relax and let go.

Experience the color of yellow. Recall the glow of the warm sun … the color of a ripe lemon. Breathe yellow into your body as you focus on the area of your solar plexus … the area right above your belly. This is the seat of personal power and the center through which you empower others. Fill it with the thoughts, feelings, and vibration of yellow … continuing to expand, balance, and deepen.

Imagine the color of green as you focus on your chest and heart area. See and feel the freshness of new leaves in spring and freshly mowed grass. Fill your heart with the healing and new beginnings of green. Continue to deepen, soften, and let go.

Imagine the color of blue. Breathe in the blueness of a clear blue sky … of deep clear blue water. Focus on your throat, the area of communication and self-expression … breathing in blue, balancing, relaxing, and letting go … deeper still.

Focus on your forehead while you imagine purple: an amethyst … a plum … the purple sky as dusk … See and feel purple as you breathe it into your forehead, softening and deepening with each breath.

And now imagine the brilliance of pure white as you breathe white light into the area right above your head … balancing and expanding your awareness, connecting to your soul awareness, your greater knowing, your higher Self.

Focus now on the question, issue, or concern you wish to explore. Notice where in your body the energy of this concern lives. Notice the thoughts and feelings you have around this issue. Take this concern with you as you notice a path in front of you. Now all of the colors you breathed into your body begin to stream out of your body in sheets of rainbow colors forming a path of color and light in front of you. Step on this path. Feel the support and vibrations of these rainbow colors under your feet. Walk along this path, allowing all your senses to notice the surroundings. Take in what you see around you … listen to the sounds in your surroundings … feel the sensations of the temperature and the growing sense of relaxation in your body as you move along the path. Breathe in the fragrances of the air. As you walk, this path turns into a very special bridge … a bridge of rainbow light … a bridge into the past life most directly related to your present life concern and issue. Approach the bridge and step upon it. Feel the vibration of all the colors of the rainbow supporting you and transporting you through time and space.

As I count from one to five, you move back in time … back to the past life … standing in the body of that past life most directly related to your present life question, concern, or issue by the count of five. Your higher Self is guiding you. One. Back through time and space. Two. To the past life most relevant to your concern. Three. Breathing your way back. Four. And five.

You are standing in your past-life body in another time and place. Allow all of your senses to come into play. Become aware of your feet. Are they covered or bare? If covered, what are you wearing on your feet? Notice the size of your feet. Are they large or small? Become aware of the size and shape of your body. Are you male or female? What is your height and stature like? How old are you? If you are wearing clothes, what are they made from? Notice the colors, style, and texture of the clothing you wear. What does it feel like to be in this body at this time? What is your physical energy like? What are you feeling and thinking at this moment? What is it like to be you?

Now become aware of your surroundings ... where are you now? Allow all of your senses to see, feel, smell, and hear what is around you. Are you inside or outside? What time of day or evening is it? Are you alone or with others ... if others are with you, who are they and what are they doing? And what are you doing at this place here and now? What is your purpose for being here?

In this state of consciousness, you are free to move forward or backward in time in this past life, as needed. Move now, as I count to three, to the dwelling where you live. One. Two. Three. What is your dwelling made of? Describe the structure or architecture. In what kind of environment or terrain do you live? Explore your home. Notice your furnishings. Experience the feeling of being in your home. Where do you sleep? Where do you eat? With whom, if anyone, do you live? If you live with others, who are they in relationship to you? How do you feel towards them? What plants and animals are in your surroundings?

In your home, what role do you play? What are your daily responsibilities and chores? Who prepares the food? What do you typically eat at the beginning of each day? What is it like to live the daily life you live? Where do you spend most of your waking time? Move into this environment now. With whom do you interact on a daily basis? What do you do with your time and energy most days? What are your skills, your gifts, and attributes? What are your difficulties and challenges? How do you feel about your relationships with the people in your daily life?

Experience being with the most significant person in your past life. Who is this person in relationship to you? What is the circumstance of your relationship? How do you feel towards this person? How do you interact? How do you perceive this person feels and interacts towards you? What is the most significant event that you share? What is the consequence of this event in each of your lives? How does this event affect you and your life circumstances and your relationship?

Move now, as I count to three, either forward or backward to a significant experience in this past life. an experience that in some way has affected your current life. One. Two. Three. Where are you now? What are you aware of? What is happening? Who, if anyone, is involved? What are you doing? What is your response or reaction to this situation? How do you perceive others respond or react? What is the consequence or effect of this event for you and for others? What life circumstances do you have as a result of this experience? What decisions or beliefs do you have as a result of this experience? What physical and emotional effect do you have from this experience?

Move now, either forward or backward in time, to a significant event in this past life that is happening either socially, politically, or environmentally that impacts your life. What is the time period? In what culture and geographic location do you live? What race or nationality are you? What are your attitudes, experiences, and beliefs as a part of this culture? How does this social, political, environmental, and historical time affect you, your attitudes, beliefs, and your sense of self? What significant historical events happen during your life?

In the next few moments of non-directed time, experience anything else about this past life that your higher Self brings to awareness. Allow your higher Self to guide you into and through the experience.

Now as I count to three, move into the death experience of this past life. One. Two. Three. What is the circumstance of your death? How old are you? What is the cause of your death? Who, if anyone, is with you when you die? What do you experience at the moment of death? What happens after death? What do you experience next? Move to the state of consciousness and being between lives. What do you experience?

From this state you have access to all-knowing soul awareness. Experience an overview of the past life you just explored. In what ways is it similar to your current life? How is this past life connected to your current-life question, concern, or issue? Consider the challenges, skills, the relationship dynamics, the fears, and the gifts. What was the main purpose or lesson of your past life, and how does it relate to your current life? Is there any part of that past life that seems unfinished? Look into the soul of the person who was your most significant relationship? Do you recognize the person as being someone in your current life? If so, who? In what ways is the relationship similar? How is it different? Be aware of any carryovers between you from the past life. What agreement do you have between you in your current life?

If your past-life self could communicate with your current-life self, what would he or she wish to say to you? If your current-life self could communicate with yourself from the past life, what would you say to him or her? Look into the play of cause and effect between your past and current life. What do you see? What are you here in your current life to learn, complete, and experience? How are you progressing with your soul work in your current life? What do you need to know to support your learning and growth?

In this state beyond time and physical space, you may, if you choose, access wise guides of light to assist you in healing the past and in empowering you in your current life. Take a few moments to meet with any healing or wise beings who can bring their special skills and resources to support you now. See and feel the healing taking place. Know that you will remember the details of this past-life regression and these details serve your understanding, acceptance, and forgiveness of the past and your empowerment, trust, and growing awareness of yourself in the presence of the here and now of your current life.

Bring all of the benefits of this experience back with you now to your conscious, wakeful state as you return, alert and wide awake, while I count you back from five to one. Five. Becoming more alert. Four. Feeling your body. Three. Taking in a deep enlivening breath. Two. Eyes opening. One. Back to the here and now. Take a few moments to stretch, to reacclimate to your physical body, and transition back into activity.

## Exploring a Past-Life Relationship

In this regression you will have the opportunity to either explore a present life relationship of a person whom you believe you also might have known in a past life, or explore the dynamics or patterns of current-life relationships to find out how the pattern or dynamic is related to a past life. You may have a person or a situation in mind that you wish to explore, or you can ask your higher Self to bring one into focus during the hypnotic induction and deepening, choosing a relationship that would be most helpful to explore.

Sit comfortably. Take some time to adjust your body so that your back and neck are supported. When you are comfortably positioned, simply close your eyes. Become aware of your body. Notice the places in your body where you feel the most relaxation and comfort. Breathe into these areas and allow the comfort to spread to any areas of your body where you want to experience more peace. Allow each breath to soften tension and expand sensations of relaxation and well-being.

Imagine you are walking along the shoreline of a beautiful beach. You may revisit a beach that you know, or you can allow your imagination to create a beach. All of your senses take in the details of the beauty that surrounds you. Feel the texture and temperature of the sand beneath your feet. Notice the fragrance and temperature of the fresh sea air. Take in the sounds of the waves washing up on the beach. You may feel the water wash over your feet as you walk along the water's edge. Notice the contrast of colors between the sand against the water and the water against the sky.

You know that your higher Self, the infinite and wise aspect of your consciousness is with you, in an inner way, on this walk and journey, protecting you and guiding you each step of the way. Enjoy being in the moment, in the here and now.

Looking down the beach you become aware of the silhouette of a person in the distance walking towards you. The person begins to look familiar. You recognize this person's walk and stature. As you approach each other, you recognize who it is, and you realize that this person also recognizes you. When you meet, you greet each other in whatever way is appropriate for you both, and begin to walk together along the shoreline, side by side. Notice what it feels like to be with this person. What do you feel in your body? What emotions do you feel? What is your level of comfort or discomfort when you are together? When you hear the tone and quality of voice and spoken words of this person, what is your response?

Spiritual Hypnotherapy Scripts for Body, Mind, and Spirit

Reflect on your history together. What roles have you played in each other's lives? What are the gifts that have come through this relationship? What are your challenges?

As you continue walking, you discover an entrance to a small cave along a sea wall of rocks and sand. Your higher Self is nudging you to enter, as you discover that this cave is a portal into a past life that you shared. You enter the cave and see that there are many different symbols on the cave wall. Each symbol represents a different soul journey, a different lifetime. Your higher Self takes you over to one particular symbol and urges you to reach up and touch it. As you touch it, you are transported through time and space. And by the count of five, you are standing in another time, place, and body. One. Your higher Self guiding you. Two. Back farther and farther. Three. More than half-way there. Four. And five.

You are standing in the body of your past life. Become aware of your feet. What are the size and shape of your feet? Are they covered or bare? Allow your awareness to move up and through your body. What is your stature? … your gender? How old are you? Become aware of your hands. What is the color and texture of your skin? How do you use your hands on a daily basis to interact with your environment … the people around you … and in the daily activities of your life? How does it feel to be you? What are your thoughts and emotions? Experience the embodiment of being this person in the here and now.

Now allow your focus to move into your surroundings. Where are you? What are you doing in this place? See, feel, hear, and know the details of your surroundings.

Move into an experience of being in the presence of the significant person in this past life with whom you have a relationship or dynamic in your current-life. Move into an interaction with this person now: One. Two. Three. Become aware of this person's presence. Is this a male or female? What is the age of this person? What does the person look like? What do you feel when you are with this person? What is your relationship? Hear the person calling you by name. Hear yourself call this person by name. What roles do you play in each other's lives?

Move now to a significant experience or interaction you share with this person as I count to three. One. Two. Three. What is happening now? What is the circumstance of this interaction? What external events are affecting you both? What internal experiences affect you? What are your feelings, thoughts, and responses? How do you perceive this person is feeling, thinking, and responding? What is the consequence of this event for you? … for the other person? How does this event affect your relationship? How does your response to this event affect your relationship?

Move forward in time to another significant event between you as I count to three. One. Two. Three. Where are you now? Take in your surroundings with all of your senses. What is happening? What is happening in your relationship at this time? How are you each affected? Take time to explore any details of this event and its effects in your lives and in the feelings between you?

In what culture and time period do you live? What is happening around you socially, politically, and environmentally? What discoveries and historical events happen during your life? In what ways do any of these events affect your relationship with yourself and your significant person?

Now move to the event of your death. What is the cause of your death? Where are you and what do you experience? Where is this significant person when you die? What do you feel about the relationship and this person as you die? Move through the death of your physical body now. What are you aware of? Where do you go and what do you experience at the moment of death?

Move now into the state of consciousness between lives. From this expanded state you have higher Self-awareness about the purpose of the life you just experienced. Look specifically at the relationship. What is complete between the two of you and what is unfinished? In your current lives how are you playing out any of the unfinished dynamic? In your current lives, how are you sharing any of the positive influences of your past-life relationship? What soul agreements do you each share with the other? What lessons do you each teach and learn?

Become aware of the play of cause and effect and how it is the result of the roles, responses, and choices you made. What new choices do you wish to make in your current-life relationship? What do you wish to say to this person either now from your higher Self to his or her higher Self, or person-to-person in your daily life? What does this person's higher Self wish to say to you?

What do you know now through doing the past-life regression that changes your understanding, forgiveness of yourself or the other, and your acceptance? How do you feel about this person and your relationship now?

In the interlife, you both receive healing. Guides are available to bring you more insight and healing support. You have the opportunity to recast the relationship and yourself as a part of it, as well as your attitude towards the relationship.

Know that there may be more insights that come to you while you integrate this experience. You may also experience spontaneous changes in the relationship because you have now done inner work in support of your healing.

Take some time now to sit with your experience. And when you are ready, you may gently transition back to waking consciousness and your daily life by breathing your way back. Each inhalation will awaken, enliven, and renew you as you return alert and refreshed when you are ready.

# EXPLORING the INTERLIFE

## Introduction to Exploring the Interlife

Exploring the interlife can bring understanding and healing to current-life family and relationship challenges, physical conditions, questions of life purpose, and a direct experience that we create our realities by the choices we make. Interestingly, one does not have to believe in past lives or life after life to benefit from the process of doing an interlife regression. Through extensive research from thousands of interlife regressions, past-life and interlife researchers, Joel Whitten, Andy Tomlinson, and Michael Newton, hypothesize that the soul survives physical death, that the soul has memory of a dimension of consciousness before and after incarnating, and that the soul can remember, often spontaneously, being in a non-physical dimension before incarnating. Does the interlife process help, heal, and empower us in the here and now? After facilitating thousands of group and individual sessions, I've witnessed that past-life therapy and interlife work often supports healing and transformation when no other therapeutic modality has helped.

In the hypnotherapy processes you will focus on soul agreements related to your current-life relationships. You will also explore your life work, skills, challenges, lessons, and current-life issues.

You will explore two aspects of interlife work. The first hypnosis process is an extension of the interlife work that you have done previously through past-life regression. (To prepare for this process you may use either of my two Past-Life Regression scripts. One explores a past-life relationship and the other script explores how a past life relates to a current-life question, concern or issue.) Choose a past life that you have previously explored through hypnotic regression in order to expand your understanding of the stages in the interlife realm and to experience how that past life is impacting your current life. Through the second hypnosis process, you will explore the interlife experiences prior to your current incarnation and explore the choices you made that are influencing and impacting your present life.

## Introduction to Interlife After Death Hypnosis

In this hypnotherapy process you will explore the interlife phases that relate to the life review of a past life. You will explore the past-life purpose, the relationship contracts, the connection you have with your soul group, your soul group's purpose, and any unfinished lessons that are affecting you in your current life. This interlife process will inform and empower you in the here and now of your present life and offer you a direct experience of the continuity of consciousness that goes beyond physical death.

## Exploring the Interlife after Death.

For this interlife hypnosis process, choose a past life that you have already discovered through a past-life regression. It will be most effective if you work with a lifetime that directly affects your current-life relationships, beliefs, challenges, or life concerns.

When you have a past life in mind, get comfortable in a place where you are free to relax. When you are ready, close your eyes. Take a few deep breaths. Allow yourself to be present right here, right now. With each breath your body becomes more still and comfortable. . . . With each breath your mind becomes quiet and focused. … With each breath, your consciousness expands. Your higher Self is with you throughout this process as your inner guide and inner knowing that is always directing you towards the highest good and healing. Your higher Self takes you to the level of consciousness and hypnosis that will be most productive for this interlife work.

Now bring the past life, with which you will be working, into awareness. Step into the lifetime and body as you remember it. Recall the events that are most significant in this past life. And recall the people who play the most important roles. Remember the feelings, the perspectives, and the beliefs that color this lifetime. Be aware of what it is like to be you.

Now move to the event of your death in this past life. How old are you when you die? What is the cause of your death? With whom, if anyone, are you with when you pass? Where are you? What are your last thoughts and emotions? What is it like to take your last breath? What happens after you die? What are you aware of now? Where do you go?

Move beyond the death experience, through the portal, into the realm of the light of the interlife. You experience a feeling of lightness and freedom as you are beyond the events of your death and leaving that lifetime. Who, if anyone, welcomes you? How do they respond to you? In what ways do they assist you in making this transition? In what ways do they assist you in detaching from your physical incarnation and in reconnecting to your greater totality as a soul? Notice your surroundings as you are together after just moving into the interlife. What are you aware of around you? Experience this dimension fully. How is it different from being incarnated in a physical body? In the interlife, how do you experience what you used to know as time? Experience your surroundings. Know, through all of your levels of awareness, what this dimension is like.

In support of your acclimating to this dimension, you are guided to a place of rest where you experience energy healing. This phase supports your energy body and consciousness in releasing any of the difficulties of your most recent incarnation. Your energy body is showered with cleansing energy that supports a delayering of any residual emotions or negativity. You shed the layers of traumas and difficulties of being in a physical body. You transition into the lighter and freer state of the interlife. Your cleansing is assisted by healers or guides who provide loving support. What do you experience? How is the clearing taking place?

The next stage is that of a life review of your past life. You access the events you experienced and the choices you made. During this stage you have access to the records of your soul's journey. Review your life and your life lessons with the assistance of spirit helpers who are non-judgmental and supportive. You understand your mistakes and experience the effects of your kindness and love towards others. What are the lessons of that lifetime? What are the important agreements you made with other souls? What is the nature of cause and effect? What is the purpose of that life? How is your soul progressing?

A team of guides and guardians assist you now in knowing what was successfully completed in that life and what still needs to be accomplished and learned that will move with you into future incarnations.

After the life review, you reconnect with your soul group. These are souls with whom you have had many incarnations. You experience them as a soul family… as a part of yourself. Your soul group has particular tasks to fulfill while incarnated. In life you know these beings as soul mates. Between incarnations you commune with your soul group and it is with them that you plan your future lives. As souls complete tasks and grow, they will move on to new soul groups that have more advanced lessons and tasks. What was your soul group's task to fulfill? What was your role in fulfilling your soul group's task? Which souls in your soul group played roles in your past life? Who were the people and what roles did they play? And what roles did you play for their soul growth?

In this dimension beyond time and space, what is your focus? In what ways do you express your consciousness and energy? What is it like to be free of a body and the limitations of the physical plane? With whom do you commune? In what do you engage? Describe the interlife environment? Take time to experience the full range of possibilities in the interlife. Allow all levels of your inner sensing and knowing to access this state.

Feeling complete for now, know that you may return to this state of awareness by repeating this process of exploring the interlife after other incarnations. You bring this experience back with you, fully remembering and integrating it into wakeful consciousness. Breathe your way back as I count you back from five to one. Open your eyes on the count of one, or when you are ready. Five, beginning to reorient to external reality … four, feeling your body … three, more than half way back … two, beginning to open your eyes … one, back in the room, refreshed and alert.

## Introduction to Exploring the Interlife Before Birth

This hypnotherapy process will regress you to the interlife before you incarnated into your present life to look at all the particulars of your present life: your parents and siblings, your strengths and weaknesses, your romantic and marriage partners, your life purpose and lessons, your physical body and intelligence. You will experience a knowing of why you are *you* and how you participated in choosing and creating the template for your present life.

## Exploring the Interlife Before Birth

This hypnotherapy process will pick up the interlife work where the last process ended. The focus of this process is the interlife preparation to incarnate into your current life. You will be guided through the planning stages and focus on the agreements you made for your present incarnation. Your experience may not follow all the stages of this process. Trust your own experience and use the following as a map of the interlife, allowing your own wisdom and awareness to explore the territory as it unfolds for you.

For this interlife hypnotherapy process choose a chair or sofa that has good back and neck support and sit with your legs and arms uncrossed in an open and receptive body posture.

When your body is sitting comfortably, take a deep breath. As you slowly exhale, it is time for you to let go of your thoughts and the activities of your daily life as you focus on being right here and right now. Continue to focus on your breath … breathing in relaxation, and letting go with each exhalation. … breathing slowly and deeply for a few more breaths. As you settle into yourself and focus more and more within, your body begins to relax and your mind clears. Relaxation flows down and through your body like water, clearing and washing away any tension or discomfort. You become more and more still and relaxed in your body, mind, and spirit. In support of your interlife work, you invite the infinite and wise aspect of your consciousness, your higher Self, to be with you as your inner guide. It is through the expanded and all-knowing awareness of your higher Self that you perceive and access the information that will give you understanding and insight into your present-life purpose. Your higher Self is loving, supportive, allowing, and accepting. It supports you and guides you in an inner way throughout this process.

Imagine that you are standing in front of the closet in your bedroom. As you push all your clothes aside, you discover that on the back wall of your closet is a small doorway or portal. The opening is illuminated with light. It is your entry point into the dimension of consciousness that is the interlife.

With your higher Self as your guide, you prepare to move into and through the portal. You take with you all the questions you have about your present life such as, "What are the purposes of your relationships? What are the lessons you came to learn? What are the agreements you made for your soul evolution? What are the agreements you made for your life purpose? And what are the agreements for your skills and work? What will be the significance of specific important present-life events?

Your higher Self takes you to the level of consciousness that is most productive in exploring your questions in the interlife realm. Step closer to the portal. You are standing in a beam of light that comes through the opening. The light is warm and loving. It penetrates through your physical body and touches every cell of your being. As I count from one to five, you begin to feel lighter and a growing sense of spaciousness. Your spiritual, non-physical body, steps out of your physical body through the portal and into the spiritual dimension of the interlife. Your spiritual body is energy; it can manifest into any form you desire through your thoughts. One. Two. Three. Four. Five. You are in a dimension beyond time and space. You are energy and consciousness. You perceive this realm of the interlife with your knowing, sensing, and spiritual seeing. In this state you are all knowing and aware. What do you perceive? What do you experience in this state of being? How do you feel?

When the pull of evolution moves you forward to the next phase of growth and learning, and when it is for your highest good to reincarnate, you meet with a group of highly evolved souls or elders. These wise ones have even greater knowing and insight than spirit guides. They are loving and non-judgmental. You are with these wise ones now. How do you experience them? These elders take you through a review of your past lives to help you get clarity on choosing a focus for your next incarnation. They support you in a reflective review of planning and choosing your options. Review your past lives now. A pattern or focus for your next incarnation emerges out of these life reviews. How do these elders and wise ones assist you in choosing what you will have as a focus and goal of your next incarnation? Who will you be in your next incarnation? Now review the contracts you make that will govern the template of your next lifetime. You will give and receive lessons in these learning and sharing contracts. What are your contracts?

As you review these aspects of your next incarnation, you understand how they will support your goals and lessons. Explore now the conditions of your birth.

Who do you choose as your mother? What does she have to offer you? What do you offer her? Who do you choose as your father? What does he, in particular, have to offer you? What do you offer him? Now review the contracts with your siblings, or your lack of siblings. In what ways do you fulfill the needs of the next incarnation for each other? Explore your culture, your environment, your stature, your physical body's strengths and weaknesses, your intelligence, your natural abilities, your challenges, etc. What do you discover?

Look also at your relationship with money and the materials aspects of life, your important friends, your partners or marriages, and your children. What life events will be presented to you as an opportunity to work through your lessons?

As you review these aspects of your next incarnation, notice how these choices relate to past-life lessons, relationships, and experiences. How do these choices support the karmic lessons and the evolution of your soul?

After knowing the template for your incarnation, before you are reborn into a new body, you are taken to a special area in the interlife to prepare for your incarnation. In this phase, you are shown the various potentials your next life offers you. You are also programmed with the necessary data that will allow you to recognize significant others and those in your soul group, who you will encounter and with whom you share mutual learning in your next life journey. What advice do your guides offer you before you incarnate?

Now go to the moment of your conception. What is the spiritual energy surrounding your conception and how does this spiritual force give life to your physical creation and to the journey ahead? What color(s) is your soul vibration as you incarnate? And when is it that you join the fetus? What do you experience? Usually the process of amnesia now begins and memories of the interlife now erase although sometimes people remember the interlife into early childhood. At what point do you begin to forget? What else comes to you about your incarnation that is important to know at this time?

Clearly remembering all that has come to you in this interlife process, you begin to come back to wakeful consciousness. You bring awareness and insights to your present life purposes and lessons. You know more clearly what you need to know about the purposes and opportunities of your life, here and now. This interlife process and the information of which you are now aware brings you insights into your spiritual nature and an expanded understanding and acceptance of your present-life circumstance with potential for transforming your world view.

I count you back now from five to one. Five. Beginning to feel your body. Four. Becoming more alert. Three. Breathing in energy as you become more enlivened and awake ... moving back through the portal through your closet and into this room. Two. More present in the room where your body sits now. And one. Eyes open and back in the here and now, fully awake and alert.

As you adjust to being back to wakeful consciousness, it may be helpful to take some time to journal or draw a few details and insights from your inter-life experience.

# EXPLORING FUTURE-LIFE HYPNOSIS

## Introduction to Future-Life Hypnosis

Quantum physicists hold that time, as we experience it on this physical plane, is an illusion and that there is only an eternal now. Yet, from the perspective of our daily consciousness, we are living completely entranced in the perceptions of the past and the anticipation of our future. Many of us are so haunted by the past or driven by fears of the future, that we are unable to be present in the now. We suffer because we believe we are unable to change the past and are anxious about being on an uncertain and driven path to the future.

By accessing quantum consciousness in hypnosis, we can be present and realize that Eckhart Tolle is accurate in saying that the power is in the now.

Present and past-life decisions, perceptions, and traumas that are affecting us in the now can be healed through regression hypnosis. In addition, present and future lessons, karmas, and difficulties may be resolved in the now through progression hypnosis.

Angeles Arrien, Ph.D., cultural anthropologist, states that "choice collapses time." By accessing the quantum field and your eternal, wise, and knowing higher Self, you can bend the perception of time as we experience it in our daily consciousness and bring peace and healing in the now. This script focuses on hypnotically guiding you to a potential future self so that you may have the teaching, experiences, and wisdom from this future experience *now*. By accessing the future "now," you can choose to act with more clarity and wisdom *now*. It is by acting in the now that you can live in more peace, fulfillment, and wholeness.

This script book offers you two future-life progression processes that are open-ended enough for repeated use in order to explore any future-life connections to your current-life questions, concerns, and issues. Know that doing a progression is a skill. The more you use these scripts and the more future selves you explore, the easier and more productive your sessions will become.

## Introduction to the Future-Life Progression in your Current Life

This progression will move you to a potential future self in your present life. For this hypnotherapy process, focus on a question that you would like to explore that is a current concern or curiosity. For instance, you can explore what might evolve if you quit your job and go into business for yourself. Perhaps you would like to explore where you are living and what your life is like after retirement. Or you can explore a future soul mate or a love relationship you would like to manifest. If you are faced with a choice in your life, you can compare the possible outcomes of your choices. You can progress to both a future self, which reflects the potential of one option and then progress to a future self that reflects the effects of the other option. It is very important to realize that your future progressions are based on your current-life track and perceptions. Work with the content of your progressions the way you would work with a dream. Bring back the lessons, messages, and meanings from your progressions so that you benefit from them now in your life. If the future looks challenging, reflect on knowing what you can choose and do in your life now to influence that potential future.

## Present-Life Progression

Take time to get comfortable and close your eyes. Begin to become aware of your breathing. You may notice the air of your in-breath is cool and the air that you exhale is warm. Each cycle of breathing begins to balance and harmonize your body, mind, and spirit. Breath is life … and as you breathe, you let go and relax into the flow of life, more and more. Feel and see the balancing taking place as you are present in this moment, right here and right now. It is in the now of this moment that you open to your own inner knowing, insight, and answers. It is in this moment that you move to the state of consciousness, which will most serve you in exploring your potential future self. This journey will guide you to this future self, which will teach and empower you in the now.

Imagine that you stand at the bottom of a hill. A beautifully landscaped hillside is above you. You see a series of terraced gardens. Each one is designed for specific effects and planted by color. It is late afternoon as you begin to ascend slowly up the garden path.

While you walk, notice the sensation of your footsteps on the soft, sandy path, feel a light breeze on your face and arms. The sun is shining and you are at peace. You enter the first terrace. On a small wooden sign you read that this terrace is planted with the intention of providing revitalization and physical vitality. You explore this terrace and discover a beautifully tended rose garden fully in bloom. There are hundreds of blossoms of deep red, coral, pink, and white. Their fragrance is intoxicating. You feel a stirring deep within. The sign reads, "Roses have long inspired poets and lovers. Rose has the property of cell rejuvenation and can soothe and heal the skin. It also clears your lungs." You experience the effects of breathing in the red-rose fragrance by noticing you breathe easily and fully. Your body is relaxed and vital. Your mind is clear and focused.

Continuing slowly up the path, the next terrace is an orchard of lemon trees surrounded by daffodils. Yellow from the fruit and flowers dominates this landscape. You pick a juicy ripe lemon and smell the rind. The yellow fragrance is distinctively clean, sharp, and tangy. The sign in this terrace reads, "Lemon stimulates the immune system and supports digestion. The aroma of lemon stimulates the mind and calms the emotions." As you walk through this garden you feel calm, focused, and present.

Enjoying the journey through the terraces you wonder what garden will be ahead. Around the next bend you smell a sweet perfume of flowers and discover the next terrace is delineated by blossoms of purple and violet. As you get closer to the flowers, the enchanting fragrance becomes more aromatic. You are among flowering bushes of lilacs. The sign in this garden states, "Lilac is used for emotional and spiritual benefits. Lilac drives away any worries and supports you in being balanced and whole." You stroll through the purple and violet clouds of fragrance and feel whole. While you walk up the path towards the next terrace, you notice that the sky is darkening and there is a growing stillness in the air. Dusk is approaching.

The next terrace is glowing white in the twilight. You smell a complex, warm and heavenly aroma that you recognize as night-blooming jasmine. Jasmine vines line the pathway. Standing on the path ahead of you is a smiling presence greeting you. This presence is loving, all-knowing, empowering, and wise. It is your higher Self and your guide for the next part of your journey. As you meet, you telepathically communicate to your higher Self what it is that you wish to explore for this journey. Your higher Self will take you forward in time to discover your future self. Your higher Self focuses on your intention for this progression, takes your hand, and invites you to walk through a portal, a jasmine covered trellis, into the future of your present life. Your higher Self will show you what is for your highest good and healing. You are guided to the future time and event that is most directly connected to your focus of this progression. You move through the portal now on the count of three. One. Two. Three.

You are standing in the body of your future self. Become aware of your feet. What do you experience? Allow your awareness to move up your body. Notice your hands. How are you dressed? How does it feel to be you at this time? How old are you? Become aware of your surroundings. Where are you? What are you doing here? How do you feel about being here right now? How familiar is this place to you? Who is with you, if anyone? If you are with others, who are they in relationship to you? How do you feel towards these people? How do you perceive they feel towards you? What is your focus in this moment? With what activity are you engaged? Explore the sequence of events around this present experience. Notice what you feel. What do you hear around you? What are your internal thoughts and self talk? What do you see? How do you respond to what is happening? How do you perceive how others respond if others are present?

Moving forward in time beyond this experience, you reflect on its effect. What is the significance of this experience for you? What is the effect on your physical being? How does this experience affect your beliefs or perspectives? What is your emotional and mental state as a consequence of this experience?

With your higher Self's guidance, you understand more aspects of this life event that bring you insight and wisdom. What is the purpose of this future event for your soul growth and evolution? How does this future event and your responses to it complete or create karma or lessons?

Now your present self joins your future self. Your higher Self supports this meeting by facilitating communications between you both. What does your future self want your present self to know? What advice would your future self offer you? What warnings? What gifts? What would your future self recommend that you do differently now to potentially change the future? And since choice collapses time, what wisdom and knowing from your future can you live now? Ask your higher Self if there is anything more that you need to know or do as a result of this progression. Receive the wisdom that comes.

Thank your higher Self and future self for this journey beyond time and know that you can use this hypnosis process again to explore any other issue of the present with which you choose to work. You remember this experience after coming out of trance. It will be helpful to write down the details and insights to ground the experience and to support its integration into your conscious daily life.

Your higher Self accompanies all parts of you back to the present time and place, as you move back through the trellis portal and begin the decent down the hill, revisiting each of the levels of the garden: the jasmine, the lilac, the lemon, and the rose. By the time you reach the rose terrace, you are ready to return to the physical dimension of your present life fully balanced, renewed, and filled with inspiration and understanding that empowers you right here, right now. When you are ready, come back into the room and open your eyes.

## Introduction to Future-Incarnation Progression

Where are we headed as humans? What will the future be for our Mother Earth? Who will you be in your future lives and how will you grow and evolve in Spirit?

Future-life progression will offer you a tool to explore these questions and any other ones that titillate your curiosity about what the potential future may bring. If time is an illusion and only a construct of the physical plane, then future lives may be happening simultaneously with our present life. Creating lines of communication between our present, future, and past-life aspects of consciousness can be incredibly empowering and informing about who we are and what the purpose of our existence and life journeys may mean. For this progression have a focus or question in mind that you would like to explore through a potential future incarnation.

## Future-Incarnation Progression

Prepare for this progression by having a question or focus you would like to explore. Sit comfortably with your back supported and your arms and legs in an open and receptive position. Invoke your higher Self to be with you as your inner guide and protector throughout this process and ask that this progression uncover information, insights, and healing in relation to your focus for your highest good.

When you are ready, close your eyes and take a few deep breaths. While you breathe, know that conscious breathing is one of the most effective ways to support your de-stressing and becoming present in the now. Notice how your breathing supports your becoming inwardly quiet and still. You breathe in relaxation and breathe out any stress.

Scan your body and become aware of any places where you hold tension or discomfort. As you breathe in, imagine the air of your breath moves to those areas and that the muscles soften and release any tension or holding. Like sand through your fingers, the tension moves down your body and out the bottoms of your feet.

Go now to a favorite place in nature where you have an elevated and expansive vista of the surrounding area. You may want to be on a cliff or hilltop, or high on a mountain peak, or even in a tall tree. You are sitting and relaxing safely as you take in the view. You feel fresh, cool air on your face and arms. You are calm and relaxed. You are free to be yourself and you feel safe in your world.

As you gaze upwards, you see a fluffy light-filled cloud. It is changing shape as the air currents move through it and around it. More and more light is shining through the cloud as it dissipates. Noticing that you feel warmer, you realize that there is a beam of light shining through the cloud directly on you. The light attracts you. It is loving and healing. The light comforts and relaxes you. You feel lighter and lighter and notice a sensation of lifting up and out of your body towards that light. You become the light. You are free of your physical body and are moving beyond time and space. Your higher Self is directing your consciousness to a future incarnation in a life that will be useful to explore as it relates to your present-life issues and inquiry for this progression. As I count from one to ten, you are directed into this future life and self. In a future body, time, and place by the count of ten. Moving as this beam of light … One. Two. Three … your higher Self directing you. Four. Five. Six … to a future body, time, and place. Seven. Eight. Nine … stepping into the body. Ten.

You are standing in a body or form in a future life. Begin exploring it by becoming aware of your feet. What are they like? Are they covered or bare? If they are covered, what are you wearing on your feet? If you don't have feet, what is your form like? If you are seeing a form, step into it and experience being the form. Become aware of your size and shape. How does it feel to be in this form? Are you male or female? How old are you? What is your vitality and life force like? What is the color of your skin? How are you dressed? Allow your awareness to move outward into your environment. Are you indoors or outside? What is in your surroundings? Notice if there are any structures, what they are and from what are they made. What are the purposes of the surrounding structures? If you are in nature, what is the terrain like? Notice the ecology of this place. What is the name of this place? Where in the world is this place? What year is it? How does the air smell? What is the temperature and the time of day? What are you doing in this place and what is your purpose for being here now? Are you alone or are others present with you? If other are present, what seems to be their purposes for being here? Who are these people? How familiar are they to you? If you know these people, what is your connection or relationship? How do you feel towards them and what do you experience they feel towards you?

Now, as I count to three, go to the dwelling where you live in this future life. One. Two. Three. What is your dwelling like? Describe the structure? What is it made of? With whom, if anyone do you live? Who are they in relationship to you? Go to the room where you sleep. Take in your surroundings and see personal belongings that are important to you. Do you sleep alone or do you have a partner or family with whom you sleep? What is your bed made out of? When you awaken each day, what is your typical routine? Where do you go and what do you do? With whom do you interact? In what activities do you engage? How do you feel about your daily life and routine? What is your family like? Your mother? Your father? Your siblings, if any? Your partner? Your children? What is your role in the family? What are the family relationships like for you now? With whom in your family do you have the most significant relationship? What makes it so significant?

In your lifetime what had happened that has impacted your personal life? What has challenged you? What gifts has life provided for you? How have you gone through the process of learning and being educated? How have you or will you be trained for work or for contributing to others? As you have lived, what are the politics of your society? What is the method of exchange for goods and services? How is racial, sexual, and ethnic diversity held in your culture? What is the source of energy that you use in your daily life? What is your spiritual orientation or belief system? How do you engage in the spiritual aspects of life? What has been invented during your lifetime? What is the technology with which you interface in your daily life? What is the common mode of travel? What medical discoveries have taken place in your lifetime? How are people healed when ill? How does your culture deal with death and dying and what are your beliefs about death? What is the ecological condition of your environment? What are the problems that you and your culture face?

Now, be in the presence of a significant person in your life. You may go either forward or backward in the future life to meet with this person as I count to three. One. Two. Three. Who is with you? What does this person look like? How do you feel towards this person and how do you perceive this person feels towards you? What role do you play in each other's lives? What is significant about this relationship for you? How does this person impact your life positively? What are the challenges this relationship creates for you? As you move through your daily life, what emotional state do you mostly experience? And what is the focus of most of your waking thoughts? What is satisfying about your life? What are the areas of dissatisfaction or concern in your life?

Go now to the event of your death in this future life, as I count to three. One. Two. Three. What is the cause of your death? How old are you? Who, if anyone, is with you as you pass? What are your thoughts and feelings at the moment of death? What do you experience at death? What happens next?

Go to the state or dimension between lives. What do you experience? From this state of awareness you have access to soul knowledge and expanded understanding. What was the purpose of the life you just finished? What lessons did you learn? What did you complete in that life … and what is incomplete for you?

Calling in the awareness of your current incarnation, your current-life and your future-life selves can dialogue and share insight and learning. What does your future self want to say to your current-life self? And what does your present-life self wish to say to your future self? Who in your future life do you recognize as someone you know from your present life? What do you know about your future-life relationship that will help you in your relationship in your present incarnation?

What messages does your future self have for you about your relationship in your present life? What lessons learned or unlearned in your future life can you apply to your present life now? Does your future self have any advice for you about what you need or can do now to learn those same lessons in your present life? What is the state of the world or your world in your future life? What values, discoveries, and wisdom from the future can inform your present life now?

In this place between lives, you receive healing and balancing of both your present and future lives, knowing that in this state all lives are concurrently happening in the now.

Ask your higher Self if there is anything more that would be helpful for you to explore or know before completing this process for now. When you return from this hypnotic journey, take some time to adjust to your wakeful state before engaging in activity. You may wish to write or draw parts of your progression so you can refer to them later in order to support the integration of this experience.

When you are ready to return, bring yourself back into the room, returning refreshed and alert, back in the room, in your present life, here and now.

# SPIRIT RELEASEMENT

## Introduction to Hypnosis for Spirit Releasement

Throughout the history of human spiritual traditions there has been a belief in a nonphysical existence that parallels the physical universe. People considered this physical world to be filled with spirits. According to Ireland-Frey, the Assyrian cuneiform texts from about two thousand five hundred BCE are the first known written accounts of ceremonies to the tribal gods and direct confrontation of spirits through prayer rituals used to heal people of negative spirit influence. In the North American indigenous shamanic traditions there is still a belief that mental and physical sickness is caused by either the possession of spirits or the soul loss of one's own spirit.

The shaman and healers of the indigenous cultures perform rituals and healing ceremonies to cast out the spirits so that the ill person can become balanced and heal. When he has found the possessing spirit, the shaman falls into a trance and tells how the spirit is affecting the patient and the patient's family. When he gets the force under control, the person is healed and the family is free from its influence. The captured spirit is either put into a spirit bundle of cedar bark and the medicine man shoots an arrow through the bundle, or he destroys the spirit by putting it in a rock that has been heated and then breaking the rock by pouring water on it.

As a psychotherapist, I have been applying a modern version of spirit extractions with my clients for over two decades. I have been trained in a more clinical approach, which uses the non-ordinary state of hypnosis. In the hypnotic state the client becomes her own shaman, which empowers the client in her own healing. The process is called Spirit Releasement Therapy. Through doing this work I have found that disembodied spirits attach to humans for many reasons. The spirit may not realize he is dead, or he may have some spiritual codependence issue that remains after death and he may not be able to let go and move on. Or the entity may have an addiction that keeps him bound to the physical plane to satisfy his addictive needs. In all of these cases, the spirit is waylaid and the host is drained of energy in ways which inhibit her life force and free will.

There are many symptoms of spirit attachment. Some symptoms are low energy, hearing voices, physical symptoms that seem to have no physical cause, compulsions, and mood swings. When a client presents any of the mentioned symptoms, I will do an extensive interview to find out the history of the symptoms and I will especially ask if there were any deaths or any energetic openings in the client's life about the time the symptoms began. Energetic openings could be: an accident, use of drugs or alcohol, surgery, extreme emotional states, loss of consciousness, or out-of-control psychic experiences. These types of experiences cause a disruption in the energy system, which weakens our protection, making us more vulnerable to an entity attaching itself to our energy system.

The main ingredients in clinical spirit releasement are empowerment and *love*. It is through our larger collective connection in spirit, whether we are in physical form or not, that the healing takes place. Today, in the therapy offices of clinically-trained hypnotherapists and licensed psychotherapists, healing rituals take place that come from the lineage of the shamanic traditions of indigenous peoples from thousands of years ago. These therapeutic "technologies" are rooted in a basic belief and premise of most spiritual traditions: we are spiritual in essence and we are able, through our spiritual practices, to realize our spiritual nature and divine source. Spirit releasement is the work of a modern-day shaman to restore spirit and reconnect it to its divine source.

In the spirit-releasement process that follows, you will have the opportunity to do an energy scan to determine if there may be an energy overlay or disruption of a spirit attachment, and you will be guided through a loving and empowering process to free you from any attaching entities and for supporting any entity that may be present in moving on to the next spiritual dimension. About ninety-five percent of releasement sessions follow a specific protocol and a fairly predictable client response. If, for any reason, you are not able to follow this process or the process does not work for you, please consult a spirit-releasement practitioner for a personal session where the particulars of your experience and needs can be addressed.

For your safety, if you are dissociative or if you have a history of mental-health problems, do not practice this spirit-releasement process on your own. Instead, consult a licensed spirit-releasement practitioner to be evaluated for the appropriateness of a hands-on private spirit-releasement session.

## Body and Energy Scan

For this pre-spirit releasement exercise, you will need some paper and a pen. Ask the client to report what he or she experiences when doing the body scan and write down what is reported.

Sit comfortably where you have privacy and will not be interrupted. Take a deep breath and close your eyes. Silently call in the support of whatever spiritual forces or deities in which you believe or with whom you work. Ask that you are supported and protected and that the highest good comes for all concerned. Now, invoke your higher Self as your inner guide and protector. Know that your higher Self will be with you throughout this process and that you can trust your experiences as they will be guided from within.

Through the eyes, sensing, and knowing of your higher Self you begin to scan your physical and energetic body, beginning with your feet and moving up, through, and all around, the auric field around your body. As you scan, notice any areas where you perceive darkness, blocking, stuckness, density, stickiness, smokiness, or fogginess … any area where the energy is distinctly thicker from the other areas of your body or your energetic field. Make a mental note of each area that has any darkness or energetic overlay; any area that is distinctly different from the rest. Take your time. Note any area that is, in any way, suspicious or of concern. Go up, around, and through your whole body until you finish at the top of your head.

## Spirit-Releasement Hypnosis

The following spirit-releasement script is a basic, and rather generic, spirit releasement. If the client is nonresponsive to this process, it may be because there is no entity present or because the client needs support by an experienced spirit-releasement therapist, who can work with more complex and anomalous attachments.

In this spirit-releasement process you will refer to the client by name when in trance to differentiate whether you are speaking to the entity or the client. The blank underlined spaces in the script delineate when to use the client's name.

Review your paper with the list of the body areas that you scanned. Choose one area where you perceived darkness, density or blocked energy to begin the work. As you sit comfortably in a private place, close your eyes. Call upon your higher Self and the higher Self of anyone else that may be present with you in spirit form and ask for the highest good for all concerned to come from this work. Call upon the forces of Light and deities of Light that work in the services of attached spirits and those who need protection and support in their releasement. Call upon any particular spiritual beings or deities with whom you work. In support of your further intention of healing for all, invoke the following star of light and vortex of energy:

*We are the Soul*
*We are the Light Divine*

*We are Love*
*We are Will*
*We are Fixed Design.*

*In the wisdom of the Soul, place a soul star six inches above your head as a representation of your higher Self. In the wisdom of the Soul, place a vortex of protective energy around your physical and energy body that begins six inches above you and goes into the earth thirty feet below. This vortex serves as a protective field around you and as it vortexes into the earth you are grounded, and focused throughout this process. We offer this spirit releasement for the highest good of all concerned.*

With the intentions and protection in place, focus on the stuck or dark area with which you have chosen to work. Using all your senses, what do you perceive there? Know that this darkness can be related to several causes: an injury, a trauma, blocked energy, or an attachment. Your role in this process is to trust your perceptions and to go with what comes. This process is offered for the healing of whatever this energy is expressing.

Imagine that you have astral or psychic hands and that those invisible hands are held over the area of the darkness, whether on or around your body. As your psychic hands lay over this area, they are transmitting pure light and love from your soul star through your physical and energy body by use of your psychic hands into the dark area. As this light penetrates, the darkness and the density begins to soften and dissipate, becoming more amorphous, like a cloud. As it softens and dissipates, together we (I, as the hypnotherapist, guiding you, the client, to inwardly) speak to the darkness now:

Whatever or whomever you are, we honor you and send you healing and light. This light is in honor of your evolution and transformation.

How old was _____ (client's name) when you first came to her/him?

What was the opening for you to be here?

Who or what are you?

Where were you before you came to_____?

What is your last memory?

Why did you come to _____?

How have you been affecting _____ (client's name) all this time?

As you ask these questions and get inner responses or impressions, if you have an experience that there is no separate consciousness there, trust that impression and simply keep sending energy through your hands to the affected area, with the intention of breaking up the energy and allowing it to leave your body through your out-breaths. The energy that leaves your body or energy field will be vortexed into the earth, clearing your body and energy field.

If, however, you have an impression that there is a consciousness there and a being without a body is with you, proceed with the releasement process.

We now speak to the entity:

Remember and describe your last memory before you came to be here with _____. What happened to you? What happened to your body? Where is your body now?

When you no longer have your body, it means you are dead. Did you know that you are dead? Go back to the moment of your death and notice around you that there is a warmth and Light. The Light was there for you at death. And the Light is here for you now. Look or feel around you and tell me what you see or feel.

We call upon a guide of Light for you or someone who you loved and trusted, now in spirit, to be here for you now. As you look or feel into the light, who has come for you? What do you feel? What message does this being have for you? We place a soul star above and a vortex around both you and this guide, as well. Reach out and touch this spirit guide's hand. What does it feel like?

You have been here interfering with _____'s body and energy. Now that _____ knows you are here, we ask you to join the guide who is here for you and move on to progression. The guide can tell you about the Light and who and what awaits you there. We ask for healing from whatever kept you attached to this dimension after your death. We turn you over to your higher Self so that you remember you have a divine purpose to fulfill and that you cannot fulfill that purpose staying here now. Do you have any messages before you go?

Say to the entity: Gather up your energy and take the hand of the guide. We bless you into the light as you move on to progression. Go in love and peace. Receive the healing and love that awaits you.

You observe what happens to the energy now as the process continues. When your client reports the experience that the energy is gone or has dissipated as much as it can at this time, you complete the process with this sealing meditation.

In the center of your belly, imagine a sun that radiates light throughout your whole body. As the light glows and fills your body, it moves into the auric field outside your body creating a protection around you. This light moves into the area that previously held the darkness and fills that space completely with light. You are reclaiming this space as your own, allowing your energy to take up residence in this area, completely.

Over the next few hours, days, and weeks, periodically repeat this sealing meditation so that your energy field is fortified and protected in an on-going way. When you think about the entity that has just released, know that it is in the Light, safe, and healing.

When you are ready, you can open your eyes and return to the room.

## Important Guidelines for Post-Releasement

To integrate your experience and to support your body and energy system in balancing after the releasement process, you can do the following:

- Drink lots of water.

- Eat grounding foods: protein, whole grains, and meat if you are not a vegetarian.

- Continue to do the sealing meditation on your own, as needed.

- Continue to use your psychic healing hands and send light to places in your body that want or need support.

- Get a massage or some energy work: Reiki and Emotional Freedom Technique can be very supportive.

- Give yourself some time to integrate the experience before you work on any other dark areas that you perceived.

If you experienced that the entity did not leave, you can tell it that it can no longer influence or harm you because it is wrapped in the vortex of Light. Ask its guide or loved one from the Light to assist it in moving on and healing whatever is stopping it from letting go. Also consider that maybe you are holding onto the entity and ask for your guides to help you in healing whatever is causing you to hold on to it. Remember that the basis of this healing is *love* and empowerment. At least now you are aware that there is an interference and you have some tools and resources to work with it.

Sometimes, in the spirit releasement process, there are anomalies that occur that need support by a spirit-releasement therapist who knows the territory and has the techniques and tools to assist the resolutions and releasements when the attachments are more complex in nature. If you are not getting resolutions from using this self-guided process, seek the support of a skilled and experienced spirit-releasement therapist. We offer on site and SKYPE sessions through HCH Institute or you can do a search on the web for a trained spirit-releasement therapist in your area. Also, HCH offers training in spirit-releasement therapy through the Hypnotherapy Certification program, as well as advanced training in spirit-releasement therapy. Good books for self-study are *The Unquiet Dead* by Edith Fiore, Ph.D., *Spirit Releasement Therapy* by William Baldwin, Ph.D., *Freeing the Captives* by Louise Ireland-Frey, M.D., and *Remarkable Healings* by psychiatrist, Shakuntala Modi, M.D. These books will give you a comprehensive understanding of the therapeutic process, a discussion of cases with their therapeutic outcomes, and an outline of the benefits of spirit-releasement therapy.

# TALKING with the DEAD

## Introduction to Talking with the Dead

One of the most difficult human experiences is dealing with the mortality of our loved ones and the finality of our own lives. If the existence of a soul and its survival of bodily death could be proven without a shadow of doubt, our lives as humans would drastically change. We would face death with more acceptance, peace, and equanimity because we would know that the loved ones who are dead are not gone; they have just gone ahead.

In the field of parapsychology there have been many experiments and attempts to prove that our consciousness survives physical death; that is, our soul continues to exist. In 1907 an MD in Massachusetts named MacDougall engaged in an experiment to prove that the soul survives bodily death by weighing the soul at death. Ian Stevenson, a highly credentialed and respected psychiatrist, used strict scientific protocol and spent decades collecting thousands of reports of children, who spontaneously recalled specific verifiable details of recent past lives.

In the 1990's world renown researcher of near-death experiences, psychiatrist Raymond Moody, researched an ancient practice the Greek oracles used to consult with the spirits of the deceased. Based on his research, Moody developed his own psychomanteum, a small, mirrored room which creates a modern version of scrying similar to crystal gazing, that he used in a therapeutic process to help grieving people connect with their deceased loved ones. People who have used the psychomanteum as a way to bridge the dimensions of consciousness between life and death believe it can work to assist communications between the living and the dead.

Dr. Gary Schwartz is engaged in experiments at the University of Arizona, working with mediums to research after-life communications with subjects' deceased loved ones. In addition, quantum physicists are coming to the understanding that consciousness, which is energy, exists independently of matter. Because consciousness is who we are as spiritual beings living in a timeless reality, at death consciousness continues to exist.

People often report having contact with their deceased loved ones. These spontaneous contacts happen through any of the senses: hearing their voice and receiving a message, seeing them as apparitions or in what appears to be a solid form, or even feeling their presence. Sometimes people even experience contact with their deceased loved ones through the sense of smell.

The following hypnotic process is often a potent experience for you if you are grieving the loss of a loved one. Using the talking-with-the-dead hypnosis process will support you in becoming your own medium so that communication can take place with your departed loved one. As you engage in this process, a wide variety of experiences is possible. You may believe you are imagining being with the dead, or you may have a transformational experience because your contact seems as real as life. If we are all energy and there is no time or space, then technically you should be able to telepathically, clairvoyantly, or clairsentiently connect and communicate with the energy of your loved one.

Whatever your experience of doing this hypnotic process, you will have a chance to express yourself to your loved one in the quantum state of hypnotic consciousness. You will have to decide for yourself if you actually make contact with the dead, or create a therapeutic meeting that you imagine in your heart and mind in support of working through your grief. In either case, this process is intended to support your grieving and to create an opening for those who have not yet had a spontaneous meeting with the dead.

This process will invoke your higher Self and the higher Self of any souls with whom you communicate. It is common in doing this process that the person with whom you want to contact does not show up, but you connect with someone else. You may have a conscious intention or goal in mind and discover that the higher Self has a different intention. You will ask for the highest good for all concerned so that you are safe and protected in doing this work and you can trust your experience as being what you most need for your healing.

In this process the communicating may not be through sound; it may be through telepathy, through images, through sensation, emotions, smells, or knowing. Be open to receive the experience in whatever forms it comes.

To prepare for your hypnosis process, set an intention. With whom do you want to meet and what do you want to say? What do you want to know from your loved one? Have some paper and a pen, colored pencils, crayons, or felt pens available to use directly after the talking-with-the-dead process.

## Hypnosis for Talking with the Dead

Find a place where you can sit comfortably and adjust your body so that your back is supported and your arms and legs are uncrossed. When you are ready, close your eyes. Take a deep breath. As you exhale, you begin to settle comfortably into your sofa or chair. For protection and the highest good of all concerned, we call upon your higher Self and the higher Self of any deceased person with whom you make contact. We ask for protection from your guides of Light and from any spiritual forces or deities with which you work and trust.

Go now to a special place, a gathering place where you can meet your loved one. This place may be known to you through your actual daily experiences or it can be a place you create in your mind and heart. This sacred ground is where you will enter the portal between worlds. This place is a protected, beautiful, and peaceful place. You are safe. Your higher Self is with you as a support, protector, and guide throughout this process. You ask your higher Self to assist you in making contact with your departed loved one.

Your awareness is drawn to an opening or portal that you discover in this special place. It may be a doorway, a space between boulders, a hollow in a tree, an opening to a cave, or a hole in the ground. Move towards this opening, and silently call to your loved one. Send a prayer to him or her to meet with you.

As I count from one to three, move through the portal and stand in the realm of Spirit with your loved one. One. Two. Three. You are standing in the interlife, the place where spirits go after death. Using all your senses, you become aware of your surroundings and the presence of your loved one. What do you experience? How is this presence known to you? Notice what you feel emotionally and energetically? What do you see? What do you smell? What do you want to say to your loved one? What is the response? Receive what comes. Do you hear words, feel thoughts, or see pictures? How do you perceive your loved one? As you commune with each other, ask whatever questions you have. Share whatever messages you wish to relay. Receive the responses as they come to you in whatever form they take.

Your higher Selves are present guiding this meeting and your communications. Continue the communications now. Allow your communications to flow. Share your deepest feelings, thoughts, and experiences.

When you feel complete, thank your higher Selves for this meeting. Say goodbye to your loved one for now. Move back through the portal. Once again you are in your special, sacred place. Sit awhile and reflect upon what you wish to bring back with you from this experience. What is the essence of your communications and meeting with your loved one in the realm of Spirit?

You return to the room now, noticing your body is sitting in the sofa or chair. Breathing in full breaths of air refreshes and renews you as I count you out of hypnosis from five to one. Five. Becoming more alert with each in-breath. Four. Moving your body. Three. More than half-way back. Two. Eyes opening. One. Back in the room alert and refreshed.

To support the integration of your communications, it is helpful to do some journaling or drawing about your experience.

# 7. HYPNOSIS for CHILDREN

*T*hese hypnosis scripts for children are written as bedtime stories. They are filled with metaphors for teaching and healing with lots of positive embedded suggestions. They may be adapted to be used as hypnotic stories in sessions, as well. And remember to use EFT with kids. They usually respond very quickly to EFT. I recommend teaching EFT to the whole family of your children clients so that everyone can use it for self care and for support and reinforcement for the client at home.

## HYPNOSIS for SLEEP

### Introduction to Hypnosis for Restful Sleep and Sweet Dreams

This sleep hypnosis is a bedtime story that introduces the child to animal helpers or guides. It includes many positive images and suggestions to enhance feelings of comfort, safety, and well-being so that he or she can fall asleep easily, sleep deeply, and have healing and empowering dreams.

### Sweet Dreams Sleep Hypnosis

You have had a full day and now it is time for rest. It's time to relax and to let go of all the busyness of your day. While you settle into your cozy bed, you can listen to this special story that will help you sleep well and have wonderful dreams. You can close your eyes and experience this story in an inner way, letting your imagination come alive with colors, sounds, smells, movement, and feelings. In this story you go on an adventure and discover many wonderful things.

Your backpack holds all you need on this journey: water, your favorite snacks, and some of your special belongings. Now that you are ready, go outside to play in your familiar safe surroundings.

It is late afternoon. The air smells clean and fresh. You see many familiar things around you. Look at the plants and smell the flowers. You sit under a tree and watch a ladybug crawl on a blade of grass. Lie back and watch the clouds through the leaves enjoying the sun and shadows on your face and arms. You begin to feel sleepy and close your eyes. You enjoy the comfort and safety in these familiar surroundings. You are safe and relaxed and daydreaming wonderful feelings, thoughts, and visions.

In your vision, you walk on a path through a field. The grass is tall and wild flowers of many colors are everywhere. Butterflies playfully flutter around you. Feel excitement as you explore this new place and an adventure unfolds. Off to the side of the path you see the grass moving and the wagging of a tail. A dog is sniffing and exploring, too. You welcome the dog and it joins you with a happy smile and a friendly nudge. You are meeting a new friend. The dog leads the way down the path as you throw a stick ahead and play fetch. You wind through the field and up a hill. At the top, you and your wagging companion rest, share a snack, and take in the view. What a beautiful place. See the path below you. Feel the fresh air on your face and hear the wind

*Spiritual Hypnotherapy Scripts for Body, Mind, and Spirit*

127

through the trees. After resting well, you begin the decent down the path moving towards the trees. You walk slowly taking in all the details of the surroundings, enjoying every step, every sight and sound along the way.

As you enter a forest, you feel layers of soft leaves under your feet. Birds greet you with their sweet and friendly songs. This forest is home for many animals and as you walk, you meet more new friends. A woodpecker, an owl, a bunny, and a chattering squirrel join you and show you the way through the forest. You are not alone. You have many helpers and friends who guide you to a place of comfort and peace. As you walk together, you explore. What do you discover? What happens next?

Nearing the middle of the forest, you are surprised to discover a hidden pond. The calm water glistens in the late afternoon sun. Dragonflies flutter over the water, catching the light on their green and blue wings. Sensing your arrival, frogs welcome you and your friends to their home and special place. This place is a place of wonder. Look into the water and see pollywogs swimming around the reeds and pussy willows. The light of the setting sun reflects on the fluffy purple and orange clouds. Hear the rustling of the willow trees blowing in the afternoon breeze. This place is special and wonderful.

Sit on the water's edge, taking in the beauty of the surroundings. Take off your shoes and socks and dangle your toes in the water. It is warm and relaxing to be here in this peaceful place. You enjoy another snack and drink some water. You know that you are safe. Your animal friends are with you. If you have any concerns, the wise owl advises and supports you. If you want a hug, the bunny snuggles with you. If you are sleepy and want to rest, the dog protects you. You are free to be yourself. Your needs are met. You are happy and safe.

Looking across the pond into the trees, you see a little tree house that is almost hidden in the leaves and branches of a big oak tree. Inviting your animal friends to explore it, you walk together on the bank of the pond and notice all the creatures that live in the water. A turtle is resting on a floating log, a school of fish swim under the water lily pads and a mother duck waddles by with her ducklings close behind.

When you get to the oak tree, you notice a wooden ladder leading up to the tree house. Inviting the bunny into your backpack and taking care, you climb the ladder with your animal friends close behind. You discover many fun and interesting things waiting for you. There is a little bed, a chair, some storybooks, and a trunk filled with toys and treasures. A sign on the wall reads, "Children - This Place is for You." Because you are an adventurer and willing to explore, you can make yourself at home here. Other children who have found their way to Hidden Pond left the toys in the box. Children leave a special part of themselves here for the other visitors to play with knowing that their treasure will still be here when they return. Please leave one of your special things here for others to enjoy and to have for yourself when you return. You look into your backpack, put the bunny comfortably on a pillow on the bed and find a special toy or treasure to put in the trunk. What do you choose to share and safely leave for your next time here?

This is a place of happiness, freedom, and joy. Know that you can take the path, through the fields, up the hill into the forest to the pond and return here to the tree house and your treasure anytime you like. This place is a special place just for you and it is as close as closing your eyes and daydreaming or sleep dreaming your way here again. Feeling full in your heart, tired in your body, and calm in your mind, you are ready for sleep. Get comfortable in the bed, snuggle with the bunny and close your eyes. Know that the dog watches over you, providing safety. The owl is ready to guide you into wonderful sweet dreams and you are ready to rest.

Feeling all the joy of being here right now … resting well. You can sleep now. Sleep, safe and sound, through the night, in your safe place, sleeping well. Sweet dreams.

When you awaken in the morning, you are rested and renewed, looking forward to the beginning of a new day, with the ongoing help of your new inner friends … with more adventures ahead and many, many more comfortable nights of wonderful rest and sweet dreams.

# HYPNOSIS FOR SELF ESTEEM, COMMUNICATIONS, AND HEALING TRAUMA

## Izzie the Cricket

This story is a special meditation about a cricket named Izzie. When you are ready to listen to this bedtime story, get cozy and snug in your bed and close your eyes. This story will help you to have a wonderful sleep and healing dreams; dreams where you create an experience for yourself in which you feel free, safe, and whole.

A wise part of you knows exactly what you need in this meditation. If you like, this wise part of you can be with you to share with you in this healing meditation and to protect you and guide you through the story.

In this healing meditation Izzie is our cricket friend. You can imagine the sound of Izzie's voice as he sings.

Izzie is like every little cricket. He eats, sleeps, plays, and goes to school to learn about what all crickets need to know to have a happy, productive, and good life. One day Izzie is playing with his friends: Jeremiah Rabbit, Benny the Cat, Suzi Raccoon and Rusty the Fox. They are playing like all friends do when suddenly fussing and grumbling began between the friends. They were having harsh words and a fight breaks out. Jeremiah Rabbit is so angry that he begins yelling at Izzie. It isn't long before the other friends begin yelling at him too. Izzie is confused. He is the smallest of the friends but also the smartest. He realizes that anything that happened could have been talked about and worked out among friends. But the yelling continues. It is a loud scary ruckus to his little ears. Izzie is scared. Since he is so small he can't outrun his friends so he crawls into this cricket box and closes the door. He would show them. He thinks he is safe all quiet in the dark. After he disappears, the animals quiet down. They can no longer see Izzie and he is so quiet they forget all about the argument. When the ruckus finally calms down, they go on playing without him and they miss Izzie's laughter, playful ways, and his special songs.

Izzie stays in his box and doesn't even come home for dinner. His mom is so worried she calls his wise grandfather to ask for some help. She is sad when she doesn't hear Izzie's sweet song at dinner and she really misses him and wonders what happened.

The wise grandfather finds Izzie in his box on the playground. He is cold, hungry, and feeling very alone. Grandfather takes Izzie home immediately. Slowly Izzie comes out of the box with encouragement but he still feels upset after the incident with his friends and he doesn't really want to talk about it … so he just goes to bed after a light supper of leftovers. Izzie is exhausted. He falls into a deep sleep. He has difficult dreams which are his attempt to work through his hard day. The next morning Izzie doesn't sing either. He is still feeling confused and sad and he doesn't know how to tell his mom about what had happened. Izzie goes back into his box. It is just easier to stay in the dark and be quiet. He stays quiet day after day for a long, long time, feeling alone and sad. But sometimes when no one is around, he opens his box and comes out and sings to himself. Because he has been so quiet for so long, he doesn't even recognize his voice. It sounded different to him. What Izzie did not know is that crickets' voices change as crickets get older and Izzie's voice is more mature now. Because Izzie has been so quiet for so long, he doesn't realize that his voice has changed. He hasn't sung enough to himself to know his own new voice.

Well, Izzie's friends have grown, too. They have forgotten about all the childish fights and interactions that once took place. They also have forgotten the lovely sound of Izzie's songs. They really want to play with Izzie again but they didn't know how to communicate. They got frustrated and sad when Izzie went into the silence of his box. They don't understand why Izzie won't come out and sing with them.. And Izzie doesn't really understand either. By now Izzie really wants to play and sing with them but he has just forgotten how easy and natural it is to open up and just let the song and words flow.

Once again, wise grandfather comes to the rescue. He says, "Let's help Izzie. Let's get to the bottom of this mystery of why Izzie will no longer sing and why he is so sad." The grandfather said, "You really want to sing. You just forgot how easy it is because you have been in your quiet, dark box too long. You now remember how natural it is to open up and let it out. How wonderful it is to be understood and heard. We are here to help you remember how, when you were little, when you had a thought or a feeling, you could just let it out, as easily and naturally as breathing or blinking your eyes. Those thoughts and feelings flow out as sounds, as words, as songs, and as meanings that express who you are, what you like, dislike, and how you feel.

Izzie's mom and grandfather take Izzie to a very special and safe place where Izzie is given lots of love and understanding. And Izzie's mom is always close by.

Izzie is given a very special healing meditation. In this place the healers used sound to heal Izzie: the sound of rain stick. Whenever Izzie hears the sound of the rain stick, all the old fears, hurts, sadness, and confusion wash away. The door is open and Izzie is free to come out to sing again. You can feel now how Izzie feels … as you imagine hearing the rain stick. Feel all the old fears, hurt, sadness, and confusion wash away. Feel how natural and easy it is to let your words, your thoughts, and feelings flow out like the rain stick. You feel like the rain stick. Your sounds flow easily and naturally like water. You don't even need to think about it. It is effortless and natural and joyful.

Well, Izzie responds so well to the healing place, this rain stick, and healing meditation that the very next day … when he awakens, Izzie begins to sing. It feels so good to have his voice back and to hear the natural flow of his song. The next day he sings with his sister. She is so excited that she dances and plays with Izzie like she never has before. She feels she has a brother to play with now. The next day Izzie sings with his parents. His mother is so happy that she cries tears of joy and love. She is so happy to have all of Izzie back as a part of her family. She says, "Every time you hear a rain stick the healing continues. You let go of more and more sadness and fear. You feel stronger and stronger and more and more whole. You have something to say about your feelings, too."

Well, Izzie got more and more confident that he had a song to sing and something to say so he began singing with his friends and teachers at school. Izzie thought, "This is so easy and it feels so good to have a voice, and thoughts, and feelings, and to be heard. There is so much to sing about! There is so much to express." And your voice is the perfect instrument to communicate all that you are and all who you are. The more you use your voice the more comfortable with it you become. It begins to sound familiar, like the voice of an old friend.

The wise grandfather said, "Yes Izzie. You can sing and sing and sing, You are free and happy and confident to let your voice sing out and be heard. You are free to express yourself."

All Izzie's friends, family, and teachers are so happy for Izzie. The grandfather is happy for Izzie, too. But Izzie is the happiest of all.

Now you may want to let this story settle into your mind and heart while you have a wonderful night's sleep … with lots of rest and wonderful dreams. You can wonder what you will say about them when you wake up fresh and renewed in the morning. Night, night. Sweet dreams.

# HYPNOSIS for CONTROLLING BODILY FUNCTIONS

## Hypnosis for Bed Wetting and Potty Training

It is the end of your day. I invite you to get all cozy in your bed as you listen to my voice and get really relaxed. You can adjust your pillow and body so you are comfortable. Get ready to let go of all your thoughts and the busyness of your day. Your body looks forward to this time. It has been active and busy for a whole day and it wants this time to relax, to renew, and recharge.

Remember that if you choose, you can close your eyes, allowing your imagination to see pictures and to feel sensations and feelings in an inner way, like you do in daydreams and night dreams.

Just like in your dreams, you can imagine the pictures that go with the story I tell you. You can learn from the story whatever will help you in your life. You can remember what is most helpful to you and let go of the rest. Know that listening to this story over and over is very comforting to you because you learn more and more each time you listen. You look forward to listening to this story and getting help for yourself each night. You know that you get a more relaxed sleep and are more confident about yourself in the day ahead.

Now that you are comfortable in your bed, you can really begin to listen to your body. Your body talks to you constantly, not with words, but with sensations. Listen to your body now. Perhaps it wants to take a deep breath or move your body position so you can be even more comfortable and still. As you lie in your safe and warm bed, pay attention to what your body tells you now. You remember how your body tells you it is too warm or it is thirsty. You remember when your body tells you when you are hungry or tired. You know how your body tells you when it is full after a big meal or when it wants to sleep and rest. Take a moment to listen to your body now. What does your body say in this moment? What does your body feel? Notice any place that there is any tension or discomfort. Breathe relaxation into those places. Your body is telling you with sensations that it wants to relax. Notice how you can respond to your body and that your body appreciates your focus and care. Your body likes to be heard and receive your response. It rewards you with good feelings and appreciation of your focus and care.

When you listen to your body and you know what your body wants, you can treat your body well. Your body appreciates it when you listen to it and you give it what it needs and wants. You may have had the experience in the past that your body communicates to you when it wants or needs something. When you listen and respond by giving your body what it needs and wants, your body is happy and it works well in appreciation of your listening and responding with respect and love. If you don't listen to your body, your body gets upset. Sometimes it has to scream at you to get your attention. Have you ever noticed that your body eventually gets what it wants? When you listen to and respond to your body, especially when it wants something, it can really relax knowing that you will take care of your body. You feed your body when it is hungry. You rest your body when it is tired. In a relaxed and easy way you eliminate any concern your body has that in the past you did not listen to your body. You eliminate all fear that your body will feel hurt or unheard because you listen to your body and you respond to your body's needs easily and comfortably. It is as easy as taking a deep breath. You can relax and let go. It is as easy as relaxing into a favorite and fun activity.

You remember when you were a little boy (girl) and you wanted to learn to ride a bike. At first it seemed scary. You thought, "I might hurt myself if I ride a bike." But your natural curiosity and interest in growing up supports you in trying something new and wonderful. You give yourself the opportunity to learn a new way of growing up and building natural skills and confidence in doing what every kid learns to do.

So you hop on the bike. But when you were a little boy (girl), your body at first doesn't know how to respond. But your body will learn and tell you what it needs. You just have to listen.

The first time you ride a bike there is a lot to learn. You feel a need to hold on tight at first. Sometimes at first kids learn to ride standing up on the pedals. Then, with experience, you learn how to relax and feel more in control. The more relaxed you become, the more in control you are. All bike riders know that to be in control you learn to trust and relax.

When you ride your bike, your body talks to you. Your body and mind talk together. And you recognize when it is time to wait and when it is time to go. You learn how to relax and go with the flow, enjoying the ride. You learn to trust that *you* can do it. You relax more and more as your confidence grows. Before you know it, you are riding your bike. You are comfortable and find it as easy to go as easy sitting down, without even having to think about it.

Now as an older child, your body has learned the joy and easy of bike riding. Now, as an older child who is growing up, you feel so much more trusting and in control because you learned to listen to your body. You feel what you body says and your respond to it trusting yourself and your body. Your body knows what to do and it does it naturally and easily.

While you go into a wonderful deep and restful sleep, you are hearing these words and you receive the messages into the deepest part of yourself. You know how to use these words and ideas in ways that support you in the here and now in learning to trust yourself and your ability to listen, to feel, and to respond to your body. You begin to feel better and better about yourself and your body. Your body becomes your friend because you make friends with your body. You learn how to talk with each other in feelings and sensations that you understand and to which you naturally respond. It is as easy as taking a deep breath. It is as easy as riding a bike. You know how to sit down, relax, and let go at appropriate times … times when your body is ready to go … not before … not later … at just the right time.

Let's pretend that we can listen in on the communication between your mind and your body even though they don't talk very loud.

Let's say that your intestine or bladder fills up and send a message to your brain and says, "Hello brain. This is your intestine or your bladder speaking. I am full. And the brain sends a message back, something like, "Well, we are busy now," or "We are outside playing now," or "We are in class now. So keep the gate closed and keep the poop or urine inside because it wouldn't be good to open up the gate now." Then the intestine or bladder sends a message back to the brain, "Well that's fine for you to say. I really have to go. I am really full." And the brain says, "Well, keep the gate closed and I will send a message to the mouth and the tongue to ask where the bathroom is and if I can be excused. And then I will send a message to the ears to hear the answer and then a message to the legs to walk to the bathroom and to the hands to close the door. Then, I'll send a message to you to open the gate and to eliminate in the toilet where it belongs and then close the gate again." And that's the way it really happens, isn't it? Even though they don't talk aloud.

The brain is the boss of the body. The brain takes care of you even when you are asleep. It may be dreaming, keeping your heart beating, your lungs breathing and telling you to kick the covers off if you are too hot, or to turn your pillow over. Sometimes the brain and the body get into the bad habit of not listening to each other and they need some reminders and some training just like you trained yourself when you were younger to ride a bike. And now that intestine and bladder and that brain know how to listen and what to do without even needing to talk about it out loud. In this relaxing imagining you have learned how to give them instructions to talk with each other whether in the night or day so that you can wake up each morning in a comfortable dry, clean bed, and you come home from school feeling fresh and clean every day.

Now you know that your mind and body are getting along very well. They are becoming good friends. They cooperate with each other. Your body is being heard. It knows that you can respond appropriately now. So you can just go to sheep. Have some wonderful dreams and look forward to a new day of ease and comfort. Night, night. Sweet dreams. Rest easy. All is well.

# 8. EMOTIONAL FREEDOM TECHNIQUE

*I*f you haven't heard about Emotional Freedom Technique (EFT) or you would like an introduction to what it is and how it works, I suggest that you go to the HCH Institute YouTube channel and watch the *Introduction to EFT and How to Use EFT* videos, which are excerpts of my EFT trainings at HCH.

These videos teach about the benefits and effects of this simple, fast, and highly effective energy therapy technique that can be used for all negative emotions, physical pain, limiting or negative beliefs, and addictive cravings. EFT is safe. Anyone can use EFT, even children and you can use EFT anytime on yourself.

According to Gary Craig, the creator of EFT, new EFT practitioners can achieve 50% or better effectiveness. More experienced and skilled practitioners usually have upwards of 85% effectiveness. It is very probable that EFT will be an effective tool for you to use personally and with clients, especially if you practice using it! Combining EFT with hypnotherapy is highly effective and will support healing and transformation that is, at times, miraculous.

EFT is a form of energy therapy similar to acupuncture but instead of using needles, you will be lightly tapping on your meridians, or your body's energy ley lines, to align your body's energy system so that you create a state of balance and well-being.

EFT is based on the premise that all negative emotions and physical pain are the result of a disruption in your the energy system. For example, if you have been a smoker, not smoking creates a major craving and emotional distress when the physical body and the emotional self do not get the nicotine it is used to getting. The smoker feels anxious, edgy, or compelled to find the time and way to smoke. Smoking, then, quells the craving or anxiety for a time at least. Then the cycle starts all over again.

EFT will break that cycle. When you think about smoking or when you have any physical or emotional distress over not smoking, you can use EFT, instead of smoking, to quell the physical sensations or the emotional states that get triggered. You will be able to choose to breathe air instead of smoke rather effortlessly while you actually balance out your energy system and move towards a state of ease, comfort, and relaxation.

The following script is open enough so that you can teach and use EFT for any presenting issue. To help you get started using EFT, following the script will be examples of set-up phrases for a variety of focuses in hypnotherapy.

Note: In early 2014, Gary Craig revised the EFT procedure to be streamlined and simplified. This script reflects these changes. The scripts on Holly's hypnotherapy CDs and the HCH YouTube videos on EFT reflect the original version of EFT which is just as effective as this new version, but longer to use.

*Spiritual Hypnotherapy Scripts for Body, Mind, and Spirit*

# EFT Tapping Points

1. Karate Point
2. Top of Head
3. Inside Eyebrow
4. Side Eye
5. Under Eye
6. Under Nose
7. Under Mouth
8. Collarbone
9. Under Arm
10. Nine Gamut

## Learning EFT

The basic Recipe for EFT is in four stages:

1. Measuring the SUDS (intensity)

2. The Set-up Phrase

The Sequence of Tapping with the reminder phrase

4. Re-measure SUDS

1. Choose a focus for your own healing while you learn EFT. A physical discomfort (such as craving a cigarette) is a good focus with which to begin because you can determine that EFT is working while you learn. Sit comfortably. Tune into your discomfort. Determine on a scale from zero to ten, ten being the most intense and zero being nothing at all, what level of discomfort or distress you experience right now. (This scale, called the SUDS level, stands for The Subjective Units of Disturbance Scale.) Remember this number as your beginning SUDS level for your physical discomfort. You will know EFT is working because the number will go down after a round or more of EFT.

2. The set-up phrase:

State the set-up phrase aloud. You will fill in the blank with whatever issue on which you want to focus for the EFT session. The phrase is: "Even though I have this _____, I deeply and completely accept myself." Using your pointer and middle finger on your dominate hand you will tap the karate-chop point on your sub-dominate hand. This point is in the middle of the fleshy area on the outside of your palm between your pinky finger and the wrist. See the enclosed diagram.

While you continuously tap on the karate-chop meridian, say the set up statement, "Even though I_____, I deeply and completely accept myself." Say it aloud one time while you tap.

3. The tapping procedure:

Have the diagram of the meridians handy to refer to while you learn the tapping points. For each meridian you will tap lightly about seven times.

Using those same two fingers on your dominate hand, tap with a moderate speed and intensity of pressure on the top of your head. (See the diagram.) While you tap, say aloud one time, "This _____," filling in the blank with a word or short phrase that represents the focus for your EFT session. Example: " This cigarette craving", or "This shoulder pain," or "This stiff neck."

Now, in the same way, tap on the side of your eye. Say aloud, "This_____." Now tap under your eye, say the short statement aloud. Now tap under your nose again repeating, "This _____."

Now tap under your mouth between your lower lip and your chin. Say your short phrase after each sequence of tapping.

Now tap on your collarbone towards the middle on either side at the base of your neck. See the diagram. Now tap under your arm, about four inches below your armpit.

Take a deep breath and tune into your discomfort.

4. What number represents the intensity of your discomfort now? The number will usually be lower. Keep this SUDS number in mind.

You have just completed a full round of EFT.

Keep repeating this sequence until your SUDS is at a zero or a tolerable level so that you are free to go about your business without discomfort. While you tap, you will most likely notice that the issue changes from your focus to another aspect of the issue. For instance, wanting to smoke could turn to anxiety, to sadness, or to feeling rebellious. Pay attention to your feelings, sensations, and state of being. If the focus of your experience shifts, simply go with the new aspect. You can stop in the middle of the tapping sequence and start again with the new set up such as, "Even though I feel like I want to rebel and smoke anyway, I deeply and completely accept myself," or "Even though I feel angry," or "Even though I feel sad that I am giving up my friend, cigarettes", etc. Be honest with yourself and audacious. Go with whatever aspects come up. Following the aspects is the art of EFT and will push your success rate up the percentage scale.

Instead of using a basic set up like, "I want to smoke," you can state more elaborate phrases that capture more of the subtleties of your experience, such as, " Even though I am angry at myself for smoking all these years, I still deeply and completely accept myself." Another example would be, "Even though I resent that I can't smoke anymore ..." or "Even though I am worried that I will start smoking again, ..." Be honest with your feelings and concerns and tap on those issues.

The EFT process will naturally bring to the surface the deeper issues underneath smoking. Keep tapping and clearing the feelings and issues as they emerge.

How long of a tapping session is effective? Tap until you are able to feel comfortable or until the level is at a zero. Periodically, during the day, when you can take the time, tap on any related issues that are emerging around your stresses and daily routine. It is really important to tap out any triggers that in the past would have caused you to feel distress.

You can successfully use EFT on addictive cravings, phobias, chronic physical pain, anxiety, grief, guilt, low energy, and negative thoughts and beliefs. You can apply EFT to anything and everything. For more training and support on using EFT, contact HCH about our classes and low-fee clinic. You can also download the EFT manual for free on the HCH Institute website downloads page: www.HypnotherapyTraining.com, and go to the HCH YouTube channel to view our training videos about EFT.

And remember to keep tapping. EFT will help you only if you use it.

Sample EFT Set-up Phrases (no change from here)

## Sample EFT Set-up Phrases

Set-up phrases are an important part of EFT and the following sample phrases will model many examples. Here are some basic phrases you can use to get started. Of course, use only the ones that resonate with your experience.

Phrases may be generalized as global statements and move towards very specific aspects of the problem.

"Even though I _____, I deeply and completely accept myself"(or "*want* to accept myself," if you don't yet accept yourself).

- **For Weight, Emotional Eating, and Body Issues:**

  I feel deprived …

  I feel abandoned and hurt …

  I feel lonely and bored …

  I feel anxious and eating stops these feelings …

  I feel empty …

  I am angry …

  I feel fear …

  I feel responsible and guilty for _____...

  I use eating to stop the pain …

  I am embarrassed about my body …

  I am out of control around food and eating …

  I think about food all the time …

  I live to eat …

  I am afraid I will act out sexually if I am trim and attractive …

I punish myself with food …

I am obsessed with potato chips …

I overeat when alone …

I can't resist snacking before dinner …

I want something sweet after dinner each night …

I use food for entertainment … (or for a reward)

It is too late for me to change …

I always gain weight after I diet …

I don't deserve to be thin …

I feel hopeless about my overweight problem …

I feel anxious with small portions …

I have overeaten since I was traumatized …

- **Sample Set-up Phrases for Exercise:**

    I am too lazy to exercise …

    I don't have the time to exercise …

    I hate to exercise …

    I am too tired to exercise …

    My body hurts …

    Exercise is boring …

    I would rather _____ than exercise …

    I get distracted and forget to exercise …

- **Sample Set-up Phrases for Physical Issues and Pain:**

  I hurt all over …

  I have relentless back pain …

  I am exhausted from feeling pain for so long …

  I feel hopeless that the pain will ever stop …

  I blame _____ for my pain …

  I worry that I will never heal …

  I feel _____emotion with this pain …

  I am angry with myself for being careless to have this accident …

  I wonder what my life will be like if I heal …

  I worry that the pain will go away before my court date for the accident …

  This (these) _____ Fill in the blank with the symptom, for instance:

  high blood pressure ...

  high blood sugar …

  chronic migraine …

  menstrual cramps …

  night sweats …

  hot flash …

  sore knee …

  premature ejaculation …

- **Set-up Phrases for Anxiety and Fears:**

  I worry all the time …

  I am filled with anxiety and fear …

  I am terrified of _____ …

  My life is limited by all my fears …

  I fear death …

  I am anxious and tied up in knots …

  I feel unsafe …

  I don't trust _____…

  My heart races when I _____…

  I am afraid to go out in public …

  I am afraid to _____…

  I am afraid of _____ever since _____…

  I am afraid of having this surgery …

- **Set-up Phrases for Learning, Memory and Test Taking:**

  I have difficulty remembering …

  I can't focus for long …

  Memorizing is hard for me …

  I hate taking tests …

  I blank out when I take tests …

  I take too long to take tests …

  I am insecure about committing to answers on tests …

  I space out in class …

  I seem unable to remember _____…

  I forget what I went into the garage to find …

  I have difficulty following directions …

  My short term memory is weak …

  I get distracted and don't pay attention …

- **Set-up Phrases for Emotional Distress:**

  I get angry when _____...

  I have an emotional melt down when_____...

  I have such deep grief over _____...

  I will never forgive _____ for _____...

  I feel resentment towards _____ for _____...

  I feel such deep sadness …

  I am jealous about _____...

  I feel destructive rage …

  I feel alone and abandoned …

  I feel empty inside …

- **Set-up Phrases for Limiting or Negative Beliefs:**

  I am not lovable …

  No one likes me …

  I can't _____...

  I never _____...

  I will never find love …

  I don't deserve it …

  It will never work out …

  I can't have my needs met …

  I will never have enough _____...

**Note:** The SUDS level reflects how strong or true the belief seems. After tapping the belief to a zero, then tap in a positive alternate belief that is the opposite by continuously tapping the nine gamut point until the new belief is a ten.

- **Set-up Phrases for Addictive Cravings and Habits:**

  I want to smoke …

  I crave sugar …

  I have an urge to bite my nails …

  I want to drink …

  I play computer games into the wee hours of the morning and avoid _____…

  I shop to entertain myself …

  I _____ because I am so anxious (or bored) …

- **Set-up Phrases for Trauma or PTSD:**

  This _____ triggers my memory …

  I am on edge when _____…

  I was abused …

  I witnessed _____…

  I can't tolerate _____…

# 9. BECOMING the ULTIMATE HYPNOTHERAPIST

## HYPNOSIS for SUCCESS in your HYPNOTHERAPY PRACTICE

Now that you are a certified hypnotherapist, your focus becomes cultivating the art of being a business person and a healer. This artistry will come from regularly using your new skills to deepen your confidence and trust in yourself, your healing tools, and your clients' abilities to engage in the work of healing themselves. The other aspect of cultivating the art of being a hypnotherapist is working with self-hypnosis and EFT to transform any of your own blocks and to reinforce, integrate, and fully embody what you learned while in training. I created these Ultimate Hypnotherapist scripts to support you in becoming the best hypnotherapist you can be. The four processes include:

- a manifesting prayer following the procedure for a Science of Mind treatment in which you work with your own goals and affirmations

- a learning enhancement hypnotherapy process using the metaphor of a crystal cave

- a hypnotic skill rehearsal

- a cosmic marketing hypnosis process to magnetize clients.

I offer these tools to you with love and empowerment knowing that you will pass on the love and empowerment to those whom you support in your practice.

### Guidelines for Manifesting

We human beings are constantly manifesting. The power to manifest is already a part of you. It is your Being. We manifest through our higher Self or the part of us that is our individual expression of the Divine. Our thoughts, words, and actions are our tools. We manifest in our lives that upon which we focus. Most people manifest passively and unconsciously; they are unaware of how their unconscious thoughts and words manifest outcomes in their lives. It is very important for us, who want to be conscious manifestors, to become exquisitely aware of what we focus upon, consciously and unconsciously, and how to directly engage our thoughts, words, and actions so that we create our heart's desires. These simple steps will help you become more conscious and more directly involved in manifesting your goals and dreams. The following are general guidelines woven into a hypnotic skill rehearsal for becoming an active and conscious manifestor in your life.

*Spiritual Hypnotherapy Scripts for Body, Mind, and Spirit*

1. Choose a goal to manifest.

Make sure that your goal is your own; that it is congruent to your own heart-felt desires and in true alignment with whom you are as a person. You, and only you, can decide if your goal is truly important and of value. Write your goal or goals down.

2. Check the use of language of your goals.

Ensure that your goal is moving toward what you desire, not toward what you do not want. Get specific about the details of what you want. Make a list of those details to map out the specifics.

3. Write suggestions that focus on manifesting your goal.

Be positive. Use present tense. Affirm that your goals are coming to you at just the right time and for the highest good of all. Give the statement some "juice" or emotion.

While working on your affirmation, you may become aware of negative self-talk, limiting beliefs, or unconscious attitudes that need clearing.

Use the manifesting process as an opportunity to flush out any blocks or unconscious beliefs, using your tools for transformation. Muscle testing can be used to check for psychological reversal. Inner work with EFT or hypnotherapy may be needed to clear any blocks.

Next, say your affirmation aloud and feel how it resonates in your body. Make sure that it feels right and important to you, especially in your heart chakra. If it does not feel right, keep working on the specifics until it completely resonates and makes your heart smile.

Now you will use hypnosis to activate the quantum field to direct your thoughts into form. Have your written affirmation close by so you can review it if necessary while doing the manifesting hypnosis process.

## Hypnosis for Intentional Manifesting

When you are comfortable and ready to go into hypnosis, simply take a deep breath and close your eyes. With each breath your consciousness expands and you become more receptive and aware. As you deepen, you access a state of calm and creative receptivity. … Conscious manifesting is a tool of a spiritual master. Know that you are a spiritual master in training!

1. Repeat your Affirmations.

Using the voice of your inner hypnotherapist, slowly state your affirmation now. Repeat it several times and feel with emotion the clarity of your intention.

As you feel your intentions and emotions while you say your affirmation, what color or colors are the essence of your goal? When thinking your affirmation, you imagine a big ball of energy that is the vibrational intention and the color of your goal.

2. Broadcast it.

By focusing on this color in your solar plexus, the color expands through your body, into your auric fields, and out into the Universe. The vibration of your thoughts and words are broadcasting into the Universe and attracting to you opportunities and exactly what you need. Surrender this ball of energy of your affirmations and intentions to the Universe. Imagine swirls of the color of your affirmation rippling out through the Universe. Know that what *IS* at this moment is perfect and right.

3.  Feel it in your Body.

Now step into the embodiment of being your future self. You are the person who has already manifested the goal. Awaken all your inner senses and experience what you feel, see, hear, sense, think, and, if appropriate, taste and smell. Associate in the experience as fully as possible. You live these goals. Look at yourself and then out at the world through the eyes of success. Feel what it is like as you embody the attitude, thoughts, and perceptions of this success. Fill in the details. You vividly experience being and living this success.

4.  Know it as Reality.

There is no time in spirit. It does, however, take time for goals to manifest in physical-plane reality. Know that your goals will manifest in the time and way it is best for you. The law of Cause and Effect is in action. "Ask and you shall receive. Seek and you shall find. Knock and it shall be opened unto you." In your daily life, you support your goals by acting as if you already have what you want. Validate even the smallest steps.

5.  Reinforce it.

Every day do something in alignment with the reality of living your goal. The Universe gives you daily signs that lead you on the path of manifesting. You are alert to the opportunities that show up. You explore the opportunities that attract your attention. You respond to the cosmic "leads" that appear. Daily, you engage in your life as a part of the manifesting process. You are open and receptive to opportunities coming in surprising ways.

6.  Give Thanks.

Hold gratitude in your heart for the abundance of the Universe and the knowing that you are manifesting opportunities and exactly what you need as your goal becomes clearer and closer. Celebrate and enjoy the process, feeling gratitude for and anticipation of the unfolding, being joyous that you are on this creative path. When you are ready, you bring yourself back into the room feeling refreshed and wide awake.

## Manifesting Prayer

Use this guided Science of Mind spiritual process with your written affirmations to manifest your goals. Have your affirmations available to read.

Center yourself and close your eyes.

The Divine is. Whatever you call it: God, Great Spirit, The One, Infinite Intelligence, Holy Spirit, Total Love; it is always the same. It is ever present, timeless, and changeless. It is pure love, joy, and total peace. It is completely powerful to heal you and this situation in your life.

The Infinite and you are one. In this oneness, you are infinite intelligence, unconditional love, deep peace, harmony, and joy. In your *true* Self, you are what God is and God is expressing through you right now as the complete solutions and manifestation of your present goals.

Now read your affirmations and goals aloud.

In total gratitude for the order and beauty of your life and for the perfect working of the spiritual laws which respond to your thoughts and words, you are confident and joyous that your highest good is already manifesting through you, as you.

Filled with gratitude, you release this manifestation process to the Universal Law. You know it was done before you even asked. You hold the highest good for yourself and all involved and declare it to be so. And so it is!

## Cosmic Marketing for a Successful Hypnotherapy Practice

Sit comfortably, close your eyes and take some time to clear your thoughts, to be present in this moment, and settle into your body. With each breath, you expand … moving toward your center. With each breath, you deepen and let go. Your higher Self is present, guiding and supporting you through this hypnotic process. You desire a career that is fulfilling, one that brings independence, one that supports living in alignment with your authentic self, one that supports the manifesting of your material needs, and your own evolution along with the empowerment, healing, and transformation of others. You remember the initial excitement and motivations that moved you to become a hypnotherapist. Access the visions, feelings, and emotions behind these motivations now.

With your current, specific goals in mind, focus on the qualities of the clients you want to manifest into your practice. What are their interests and focuses for their hypnotherapy? How can you serve them in doing the work? What feelings do you experience when you think about these clients? How do you experience having rapport with them and feeling towards them?

Go to a time when you are interacting with a client.

Feel the positive feelings, the mutual empowerment, and love between you. Feel this love in your heart and imagine that it circulates in a growing spiral originating from your heart chakra. It spirals until it is as large as your body. And it continues to expand to fill the room. It grows larger expanding beyond your work space out into the community. You call upon your spirit guides to support its movement and connection with clients who want to do the work.

Through your loving intentions, and this spiraling energy, you are sending out a call from your heart to all of the souls who can be assisted through your work. You offer support for their highest good. Magnetize this thought in this spiraling energy. Imagine the spiral is the color of the rainbow, the seven colors of the chakras. Each color represents the vibration of the type of healing each client needs. The red flows to those who need support with issues of health, safety, and survival. The orange connects with those clients who need support with their creativity, procreativity, and their abilities to share intimacy. The yellow spirals out to those who need healing of their sense of personal empowerment and the capacity to empower others. The green moves directly to the hearts of people who are in need of heart-opening or healing from emotional wounds of the past so they can give and receive love. The flow and vibration of blue moves to the throat chakra of those who want and need authentic communication and empowered, creative personal expression in their lives. The purple flows to the third eye of those who are ready to open up intuitively and to work with their greater knowing. And all of the colors are vibrating with the luminescence of the white light which activates the soul energy above their bodies, drawing these people towards your loving support and care. This energy that reaches them communicates how you will make a difference for them and how the work contributes to their empowerment and well-being. Imagine just how their healing unfolds. You call to the people who value and honor the work. You call to those who are in need of support and who are ready to do the work.

Feel and see yourself drawing these clients to you. They come at the right time for their, and your, highest good. You are most magnetic when you focus on how you assist them. As you continue to circulate this spiral of energy, you ask your higher Self to let go of any unconscious blocks, fears, or neediness. You surrender to manifesting whomever and whatever can best be served by your work. Continue to energize and expand the spiraling of energy from your heart. You thank, in advance, your clients, their guides, and higher Selves for the gifts of working with them. The spiral continues to expand through the county, state, continent, and through the world.

Imagine that as people learn about you and connect with you, they are like stars lighting up. See hundreds and then thousands of stars lighting up around you. Imagine lines of this spiraling light move between you and all the people whom you can serve. How does it feel to reach ten new people a week? Twenty people a week? A hundred people a month? Thousands of people a year? The spiral continues to touch more and more people who recognize that they choose to work with you.

Observe the healings and transformations that your clients make in their lives. Feel the gratitude and joy of doing this work and the abundance it brings you on all levels. Thank your guides and higher Self and the guides and higher Selves of all your present and future clients for the opportunity to be a part of their healing journey. With a sense of joyous well-being, you look forward to the connections you make in person and by phone that bring these clients your way. With a full and trusting heart, you return to the room when you are ready, feeling calm, refreshed, and renewed.

# LEARNING ENHANCEMENTS for HYPNOTHERAPISTS

The following script is specifically for hypnotherapists to facilitate learning enhancement. The specifics in this script can be changed to support learning enhancement for any field of study.

**Crystal Cave Learning Enhancement**

This hypnotherapy process supports reinforcing and accessing all that you know about hypnotherapy to build self-trust and confidence in being a hypnotherapist.

Sit in a comfortable position and close your eyes. Through your many experiences of hypnosis, your body and mind are conditioned to relax while you take in deep breaths and exhale fully. Notice how your body responds. Enjoy a growing sense of ease and comfort as you breathe in and let go. Over the months of hypnotherapy training while learning about being a client, facilitating sessions, and using the vocabulary and techniques of doing the work of hypnotherapy, your unconscious has also been actively engaged as a student. While you experience the class activities and lectures, read about hypnotherapy, practice self-hypnosis and facilitate sessions with others, all that you have seen, heard, and felt is encoded within your mind. Working with metaphor, imagine your mind is a spacious cave.

As you approach this cave and its entryway, you are fascinated to explore its innermost realms. You enter through a portal-like opening. It is quiet and dark. As your eyes grow accustomed to the darkness, you move farther into the cave and notice the glow of a small fire in the center of a large domed area. You are astonished to discover that you are standing under a rainbow of light as the firelight illuminates thousands of crystals that line the walls and ceiling of the cave. While enjoying the magnificent colors or reflected light, you also are aware of the sensation of energy flowing through and around you. You feel heightened and alive. Your mind is clear and focused. Your body is vital yet calm.

Wanting to take in this experience more completely, you sit by the fire to relax. You notice the glimmering of a large golden pot sitting against the wall at the base of this crystal rainbow. Could this be the pot of gold that so many have sought? You are in a state of awe with the energy and beauty of this magical place. Resting in this state of wonder, you become aware of a familiar wise and loving presence. Your higher Self has joined you. Your higher Self says, "By coming to this very special place, you have discovered a resource that will support you in many ways. This cave holds all of your knowledge and all of your potential for manifesting a wealth of wisdom, skill, and success in your work. Accompany me as I show you how this is so."

Higher Self walks you to the edge of one end of the rainbow that glows with red. "All the crystals in the band of red light are imbued with all you need to know about surviving and thriving in business. Red holds all you learned about marketing, generating clients, bookkeeping, office rental, and managing your files and paperwork. Red grounds you in the material realm of being a hypnotherapist. As you continue to grow and learn in the area of business, as well as in organizing and managing your practice, this information is stored in the red illuminated crystals." Your higher Self shows you that all you need to do to access this practical information is to reach into the red band of light, touch the crystals and activate the knowing. "Having direct access to this wealth of practical wisdom is very assuring and grounding. The red crystals hold the techniques you know to support clients who have anxiety, physical pain, phobias, insecurities and health issues: Stored here is the lowering the pain threshold technique, trauma work with EFT, bi-lateral stimulation, the re-wind technique, and manifesting processes for fulfilling goals and dreams."

Next your higher Self guides your hand to the crystals in the band of orange light. Higher Self explains, "The crystals in the orange ribbon of rainbow light hold all you learned and will learn about self-care, staying balanced, and having healthy and appropriate boundaries with your clients. Orange crystals hold the learning about ethics and legal issues. Touching the orange crystals accesses all it takes to build and maintain rapport with your client: genuine empathy, eye contact, mirroring body posture and being congruent in your words and behaviors. Here are the techniques you use with clients who have issues with blame, guilt, sexuality, desire, self-image, creativity or personal values: the shame technique, power animal journeying, shadow work, psychosynthesis to work with sub-personalities and reframing for habits and addictions."

Next you move to the yellow band of crystals. Higher Self says, "These crystals contain all you know about empowerment and being empowered. Yellow holds the skill of open-ended questions, positive use of language, following the client's process while being flexible in allowing the process to unfold for the good of the client. Here is the wisdom of putting the client first and keeping the focus on the client while in session. In the yellow crystals are the techniques that can help clients with self-esteem, self-mastery, trauma, abuse, fear of rejection, oversensitivity to criticism, or indecisiveness. Techniques include inner critic, energetic protection, soul retrieval, co-dependency work and the Affect, Somatic, Linguistic Bridge technique for healing trauma."

Next, higher Self places your hand on the green band of crystals. You immediately feel the energy of love as you touch the green. "These crystals are encoded with your ability to be compassionate and caring for your clients. In green, you access the heart and meaning of doing this work. Here are the techniques that support clients in opening up to healing and love and those that heal the emotional wounds of the past. In the green band of crystals are the tools for the healing of fear, hate, jealousy, envy, and feeling entitled. Green holds the capacity to balance the giving and receiving of love between you and your client and between the client and the client's higher Self. Techniques related to these crystals are inner smile, EFT, inner child, inner family, parts work, and work on life purpose."

Next your higher Self guides you to the blue ribbon of light illuminating the crystals below it. Higher Self says, "All of your language skills as a hypnotherapist are related to this area. Pacing and leading, using non-directive suggestions, open-ended questions, empowering the client's free will. Encoded in the blue crystals are the tools for empowering will and choice making, and creative and authentic expression. Working with self-expression and helping clients with authentic communications are the focuses related to these crystals. Techniques for skill rehearsal, learning enhancement, and sandplay are related to the blue crystals."

And finally your higher Self takes you to the beginning of the ribbon of purple in the rainbow. "These crystals relate to the intuitive knowing and guidance you receive while facilitating sessions. These crystals connect you with the wisdom of your higher Self and your spiritual knowing. These crystals are vibrating with your soul energy and purpose for doing this work as a hypnotherapist and healer. These crystals invoke the quantum field in your sessions. The techniques related to these crystals are the higher Self communications, the Inner healer, and the connection to past lives, guides, dream work, talking with the dead, and spirit releasement."

Finally higher Self says, "All the colors of the rainbow are illuminated with sparkling white light. All the experience, wisdom, and information stored in this cave flows from the divine source of this light."

As you follow the ribbons of the rainbow to its end, you stand by the pot of gold. You reach into the pot and feel a warm sensation like liquid sunlight. Your hand absorbs this golden light and travels up into your arm and fills the rest of your body. You now embody the wealth of information you have learned as a hypnotherapist.

You always have access to detailed knowledge and all of your hypnotherapy tools in this special crystal cave. As you continue to learn, new information will be added in just the perfect place to the color bands of crystals. You may return to this crystal cave anytime to reinforce and expand your knowledge and embodiment of the wealth of all it holds. You look forward to feeling the depth of knowledge and practical wisdom that is yours as you slowly move through the cave, out of trance, and back into your world.

## Ultimate Hypnotherapist Skill Rehearsal

Using this hypnotherapy process will build confidence, reinforce your skills, and support your evolution in the art of being a hypnotherapist. Each time you use this skill rehearsal, the positive effects exponentially support your embodiment of excellence.

Get comfortable as you take this precious time to engage in your evolution as a hypnotherapist. Close your eyes. Recall your many experiences of trance and begin moving into the familiar receptive state of mind, body, and spirit where you access your higher Self and your deepest place of knowing and creating. Using the metaphor of a yardstick or any other technique that works well for you, begin the process of deepening this expanded, safe, and fertile state of trance. Your higher Self moves you to the level that will be most effective and productive for you.

Feeling relaxed and focused, imagine beginning a new day as a highly successful hypnotherapist. While in your office, you move through your morning routine, preparing for a day of working with clients. You are excited to embrace this day. You look forward to meeting with your clients and anticipate that they benefit from your time together. As you review your schedule for the day, you note your scheduled appointments, when you take breaks, time for phone calls, bookkeeping, business planning and networking. How long is your workday? What do you feel as you embrace this day?

What do you most look forward to experiencing today? What is the biggest challenge or opportunity of your day?

Look around your office and appreciate your workspace. The colors, décor, and *Feng Shui* of the room are inviting and peaceful. Your furniture is comfortable and situated so that communications are enhanced. This is a healing place. You benefit from the energy and comfort of working here. Your clients often comment on how simply being in this space with you is healing. Your workspace is protected, safe, and inviting.

Your client arrives. You greet each other and sit in your usual places. In the interview you build rapport while listening attentively and matching the client's tone and tempo of voice and representational systems. You assist the client to clarify the goals and the focus for today's session. You take time to educate the client about the technique you mutually decide to use and with fluidity and ease you answer any questions the client asks. As you facilitate the session, you have direct access to all you know about the art of hypnotherapy.

Using your client's favorite induction and deepening techniques, you guide your client into trance. Your client responds. … You notice slower and deeper breathing, body stillness, and changes in the client's use of language and voice. You empower your client with open-ended questions as you move the session toward the focus for the day. You are sensitive to the subtleties of the client's responses. You allow the process to unfold, trusting the client's wisdom, following the client's cues. The client accesses inner guidance, insight, and clarity. The client reaches the goal for the day. In the last ten minutes or so of the session, you direct the session towards closure. Once your client is out of trance, you dialogue about the session and suggest on-going self care with EFT and self hypnosis. Your client schedules the next appointment and leaves your office, expressing gratitude for your skills and support. As you reflect on the session, you feel deep appreciation for the opportunity to share your skills and to experience the grace of your client's healing. This session, along with many others, supports your evolution as a hypnotherapist. Create an anchor for yourself now that you can activate, at will, to reinforce this skill rehearsal and your thoughts, feelings, and embodiment of being the ultimate hypnotherapist you can be. Every time you use this anchor you more and more deeply reinforce your confidence and skills. You experience on-going growth, refinement, and mastery of your skills while living the life of a successful hypnotherapist.

Now bringing back all the benefits of this ultimate hypnotherapist hypnosis, you come back to the room refreshed and renewed.

# ABOUT the AUTHOR

Dr. Holmes-Meredith's teaching and therapy practice is grounded in four decades of teaching, psychotherapy, hypnotherapy and metaphysics. She teaches with an engaging experstise, ease and competence that builds professional skill and confidence in her students. Holly integrates a psychospiritual perspective in her teaching, models client empowerment and practices hypnotherapy as an art. In the last fifteen years she began studying and adding hands on healing and energy therapies to her work including Reiki and EFT.

Holly trains hypnotherapists at HCH Institute and works with private clients using a transpersonal approach. She specializes in regression therapy, pain management, working with phobias, anxiety, and spiritual issues.

This book is the result of her journey as a client, student, teacher and practitioner of transpersonal hypnotherapy.

# REFERENCE LIST

Alexander, K. (1994). *Defining the higher self: a theoretical model and techniques*. Rosebridge Graduate School of Integrative Psychology.

Atwater, P.M.H. (1996). *Goddess runes*. New York, NY: Avon Books.

Ball, P. (2004). *The essence of tao*. Edison, NJ: Chartwell Books.

Cade, M. & Coxhead, N. (1979). *The awakened mind: biofeedback and the development of higher states of awareness*. New York, NY: Dell Publishers.

Freedman, T. (2000). *Hypnotically facilitated past-life reports: a comprehensive overview of research*. Canastota, NY: Post-Doctorate Research.

Harman, W. (1991). *A re-examination of the metaphysical foundations of modern science*. Sausalito, CA: Institute of Noetic Sciences.

Hastings, A. (1991). *With the tongues of men and angels*. San Francisco, CA: Holt, Rinehart & Winston.

Ireland-Freye, Louise, (1999). *Freeing the captives*. Charlottesville, VA, Hamptom Roads Publishing Company, Inc.

LaBerge, S. & Rheingold, H. (1991). *Exploring the world of lucid dreaming*. New York, NY: Ballatine Publishing Group.

Lao Tzu. (1972). *Tao te ching* (G. Feng & J. English, Trans.). New York, NY: Random House Publishing.

Lao Tzu. (1919). *Tao te ching* (D. Goddard, Trans. *Laotzu's tao and wu wei*). New York, NY: Brentano's Publishers.

Lao Tzu. (1904). *Tao te ching* (W. Gorn-Old, Trans.). Retrieved from http://web.archive.org.

Lao Tzu. (1997). *Tao te ching* (U. Le Guin, Trans.). Boston, MA: Shambala Publications.

Lao Tzu. (1916). *Tao te ching* (I. Mears, Trans.). Retrieved from http://web.archive.org.

Lao Tzu. (1905). *Tao te ching* (C. Medhurst, Trans.). Retrieved from http://web.archive.org.

Lao Tzu. (1991). *Tao te ching* (S. Mitchell, Trans. 1st ed.). New York, NY: Harper Perennial.

Lao Tzu. (1913). *Tao te ching* (D. Suzuki & P. Carus, Trans.). Retrieved from http://web.archive.org.

Lao Tzu. (1904). *Tao te ching* (C. Ta-Kao, Trans.). Retrieved from http://web.archive.org.

Stöppler, M. *Sleep* (n.d.). Retrieved from http://www.medicinenet.com.

Toropov, B. & Hansen, C. (2004). *The complete idiot's guide to taoism*. Middleton, MA: Beach Brook Productions.

Two Disciples. (1981) *The rainbow bridge*. Escondito, CA: Triune Foundation Publications.

# RESOURCES

**HCH An Institute for Hypnotherapy and Psychospiritual Trainings**
3702 Mt. Diablo Blvd.
Lafayette, CA 94549
*HCH@HypnotherapyTraining.com*
*http://www.HypnotherapyTraining.com*
925 283-3941

The International Board for Regression Therapy (IBRT)
*www.IBRT.org*

Earth Association for Regression Therapy (EARTh)
http://www.EARTh-association.org

To purchase hypnotherapy and EFT CDs:
*http://www.cdbaby.com/Search/*
*SG9sbHkgSG9sbWVzLU1lcmVkaXRo/0*

Purchase downloads of Dr. Holmes-Meredith's Hypnotherapy CDs
*www.cdbaby.com/Search/*
*aG9sbHkgaG9sbWVzLU1lcmVkaXRo/0*
OR go to *htpp://www.cdbaby.com* and search for Holly Holmes-Meredith

To read Dr. Holmes-Meredith's articles:
*http://ezinearticles.com/?expert=Holly_Holmes-Meredith*

Watch Dr. Holmes-Meredith's teaching and hypnotherapy sessions on You Tube:
*http://www.youtube.com/user/hchinstitute*

Sample Dr. Holmes-Meredith's Hypnotherapy CDs
*http://www.HypnotherapyTraining.com/cfm.cds*

Emotional Freedom Technique:
*http://www.Emofree.com*
*http://www.EFTUniverse.com*

Peaceful Music for Hypnosis by Paul Michael Meredith:
*http://www.PeacefulMusic.com*
To sample and purchase Paul's peaceful music go to:
*http://www.cdbaby.com/Search/*
*cGF1bCBtaWNoYWVsIG1lcmVkaXRo/0*

Cover portrait of Dr. Holmes-Meredith by Karen Bates:
*http://www.KarenBatesphoto.com*

Printed in Great Britain
by Amazon